Welcome to Lost Lake, a peaceful North Country town. In Jerry Wilber's new book, you'll join the regulars for pie and coffee at Mom's Cafe over on Main Street, where The Professor lectures on the news of the day. You'll learn Uncle Jake's secrets for catching walleyes and muskies, and see how Ol' Gladys masters bluegills and crappies through the ice on Whatchamacallit Bay.

Best of all, you'll observe the changing seasons and the daily flow of life through Jerry's insightful, sensitive eyes. Along the way, you'll learn some things about being a better hunter, citizen, fly-fisher, camper, canoeist, cook, parent, spouse, friend.

Open this book to any day of the year and you'll see why … *of Woodsmoke and Quiet Places* deserves a special place in your home.

"Jerry's prose is at once soothing, humorous and evocative. When one of his passages transports me to Mom's Cafe over on Main Street, I not only feel I'm actually there, I can smell the coffee and hot apple pie."

CHUCK PETRIE, *Ducks Unlimited Magazine*

ABOUT THE AUTHOR

Readers across the Great Lakes region know Jerry Wilber for his warm, whimsical writings about nature and the outdoor world. Jerry, wife Karen and daughter Katie live on eighty wild acres near Lake Superior and the mighty Brule River. Jerry is the author of the popular *Wit and Wisdom of the Great Outdoors* and a contributor to *Harvest Moon: A Wisconsin Outdoor Anthology*. He has written more than 2,400 newspaper and magazine articles and 600 radio programs. His short stories have appeared in magazines throughout the United States and Canada. He is a hunter, fisherman, wilderness camper and professional fly tier.

ABOUT THE ILLUSTRATOR

Terry Maciej is a wildlife and nature artist whose work has been widely exhibited across the Midwest and Eastern states. He lives in Pengilly, Minn., and co-owns an art and frame shop in nearby Hibbing.

… of woodsmoke and quiet places

JERRY WILBER

illustrations by Terry Maciej

The Cabin Bookshelf

1234 Hickory Drive • Waukesha, WI 53186

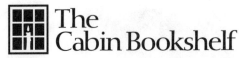

... of Woodsmoke and Quiet Places
by Jerry Wilber
Illustrated by Terry Maciej

The Cabin Bookshelf
1234 Hickory Drive
Waukesha, WI 53186

Publishers Cataloging in Publication
(Prepared by Quality Books, Inc.)

Wilber, Jerry.
Of woodsmoke and quiet places/by Jerry Wilber.
p. cm.
Preassigned LCCN: 97-65477
ISBN 0-9653381-1-8
1. Outdoor life I. Title
GV191.4.U6W55 1997 796.5'0973
QBI97-40434

Library of Congress Catalog Number: 97-65477

Once again,
for Karen and Katie —
who else is there?

acknowledgments

Though I am fiercely independent, I am, nonetheless, the product of more than luck and looks. I'm the product of those along the way who have loved or liked and tolerated and supported and encouraged and otherwise helped me. Without them, what would I do? Where would I be?

There's Karen and Katie, of course, my right arm and left-hander and the owners of my heart. There's my father and mother, Gene and Irma, and my brothers and sisters and nephews and nieces, and Marge Pascale.

There are the Amanns, Lorne and Rosalyn Persons, Gary and Kathy Phillips, Wally and Bernice Decker, Ted Garceau and Steve Zawacki and the Foley, Minn., High School class of 1970, Stan and Sara Skelton, Pat Abrahamzon, Mark Anderson, Steve Johnsen, the Kowaliks, Randy Hurst, Roy Sheppard, the Rowekamps, the Kaldors.

There's Ted Rulseh and Terry Maciej.

There's the memory of Joe Pascale, Jr., a fine, fine father-in-law, and the memories of Cal Foss, of Robert and Donavon Mackey, of Randy Anderson, of my brother Bill.

And there's Jim and Suzanne Weinandt.

Thanks.

introduction

So long as there are those who hike through bobwhite country or whip-poorwill country or firefly or huckleberry or wild rose country with packs on their backs; so long as there are those who follow trails that squirm over countrysides like fishing worms; so long as there are those who swim through Indian summer afternoons with strung-out lines of wild geese and butterflies, and join Mercury in the evening sky, and paddle canoes into silences ...

So long as there are those who explode touch-me-nots with a touch and smell the smells of gun oil and hunting clothes and pickling cucumbers and pressure-cooked string beans in the kitchen; so long as there are those whose hearts nearly break at the sight of mallards and pintails and wood ducks answering mysterious calls to go and go ...

So long as there are those who lie on their bellies to drink from springs and watch giant puffballs appear magically in the cool damp of woods, and those who hopscotch over dewy spider webs shining in the early morning light, and those who celebrate great orbs of red and orange leaves decorating sugar maple trees ...

So long as there are those who celebrate meadowlarks on fence posts setting the day upright with the blessedness of their songs; so long as there are those who carry shotguns into woods and cornfields and shoulder rods and reels and bows and arrows down narrow paths ...

So long as there are those who, no matter the luck, never come home empty-handed, for they bag buckets full of splendor, catch some breaths of life and snag trophy chunks of their birthright ...

So long as there are those who, though they carry the weight of eighty autumns on their shoulders or be but children, go out to where the wild is and come home, no matter the luck, with gamebags overflowing and creels fulfilled ...

In other words, so long as there are people like you, then we'll forever have woodsmoke of campfires with us, and quiet places that make our hearts glad, and books like this will not be useless.

MACIEJ

a brave new year

JANUARY 1

Happy New Year. Happy brand-spanking New Year. Happy New Year to this new year that's opening up before us like an aha, a whoop-de-doo, good-time maneuver. And Happy New Year to you who will sometime this year sleep out where loons call in the night, where there's a yip-yipping of old and winter-weary coyotes.

Happy New Year to you who sometime this year will hitch your hopes to gurgling trout streams, who'll take kids skiing and marshmallow roasting over campfires. Happy New Year to you who'll read a good book on the great out-of-doors, who'll feed the birds, who'll clean your shotgun on a regular basis, who'll exchange Christmas gifts of neckties and genuine leather handbags for the essential stuff of fishing tackle.

Happy New Year to you who'll ride canoes on rapidly rolling rivers, who'll hike into mazes of pine trees, who'll wander through summer nights and rainbows, who'll cast for falling stars, releasing those you don't need. Happy New Year to you who'll hear the miracle call of Canada geese and answer with reasonable accuracy, and to you who'll hunt for dreams of twelve-pointers (though dreams of less-pointers will do).

Happy New Year to you who will, in all the seasons, go as best as you can out to where the woodsmoke of hope keeps company with the quiet places of your soul, where you'll have no need to query lost-and-found for directions to the wild blue yonder, where you'll figure out how to put together disassembled moons. Happy New Year to you, old friends, and new ones, to whom we wish a life of great abundance down the trails of this new year, and down all the trails of your lifetime.

life in the fast lane

JANUARY 2

These are amazing days. We've come around the corner of another new year, and we're all holidayed out. Most of the Christmas trees have found themselves out in the cold by now, stuck up in snowbanks and redecorated with bird seed and suet balls and the leftovers of Aunt Fern's fruitcakes, poor birds.

After some discussion, we've decided that it's Mercury hanging low in the eastern sky just before sunrise where, in fact, the sun used to rise. Like birds that have to fly and fish that have to swim, campers are sorting out, cleaning up, replacing and repairing tents and stoves and sleeping bags in anticipation of upcoming and ice-free adventures. Hunters among us are reloading shells, for as surely as prayers are heard in heaven, there are hunting seasons coming on in the far-off fallish future. In the quiet corners of dens and basement laundry rooms, fishing flies are being tied — some neat and trim and fast, and others not so neat nor so trim and not very fast at all. The kids are taking us ice fishing and on bone-shaking toboggan rides. We've never learned how useless it is to argue with mountains, even small ones. On cross-country skis we're trying to keep up with Grandma in this single-daylight time of January.

And, one page at a time, like falling, fluffy snowflakes, we're reading books that take us away, out there into the great out-of-doors, while we're snuggled before fireplaces against long and melancholy nights. And, with visions of springtime in our heads, we're poring over growing piles of seed catalogs. At least that's how it is here at Lost Lake where I live, and I suppose that's about how it is where you live, too.

all bets are off

JANUARY 5

It's a mid-winter morning. Early. A moon has got itself tangled in the trees on the other side of Lost Lake. It's a pumped-up moon, a morning kiss. I watch it and wait for the coffee to boil and the fire to take, and I think of something that happened last August. It involved two of our college boys, home for the summer.

As was their custom, they were fishing on the banks of the river, which feeds into Lost Lake at Whatchamacallit Bay. Also, as was their custom, they tired quickly of the heat and the sport, shucked their clothes and went skinny-dipping. Those vast fields of pink and sweating flesh, as you can imagine, were very appealing to the hordes of nearby mosquitoes. The boys were neck-deep in the water, mosquitoes hovering over their heads. One of them, in the way of college boys, made a wager that he could get out of the water and stay out, exposed to the hungry bugs, longer than the other.

"Ohhh no you can't," said the other. It was agreed they could smoke cigars, in the way of college boys, as their only defense. Sitting on the bank, wincing as stings and bites were inflicted upon their bodies, they smoked with a fierce energy as the misery grew excessive. Both held out for a full minute when one, in the act of admitting defeat, accidentally touched the rear end of his companion with the glowing end of his stogie. The latter leaped into the river in agony, swearing he had been stabbed by the granddaddy of all mosquitoes.

It wasn't until the next day, when a healthy blister developed where a mosquito bite should have been, that the truth was exposed and a new winner declared.

rescue

The brute enchantment of January sometimes wears thin — sometimes, in fact, releases a stampede of misery, as it has today. So a bunch of us regulars have come off the lake and ski trails to hole up in Mom's Cafe over on Main Street, home of the original bottomless cup of coffee, though it was never planned that way. We're on our second or third refill when the needle on the juke box hops a groove, and one of the boys, a friend of one of our daughters here for the weekend, stumbles in with what looks like a case of frostbite.

JANUARY 6

Most of us are members of the volunteer fire department or have ten-year-old kids, so we're quick as a tic in emergencies. Mom gets to the boy first and announces that what appears to be frostbite isn't quite, but frostnip, which doesn't stop us. We lay him out on the counter and see that the blood circulation at the affected area has come to a dead standstill, and ice crystals are forming on the outer layer of his skin, which is numb because the nerves are whacked out of kilter by the intense cold. It's white and cardboardy stiff.

Whereas frostbite requires more drastic measures, frostnip usually responds to immediate warming, so three of us throw logs into the woodburner Mom uses as backup on cold days. A couple of others race to the glass showcase, declaring the candy bars therein emergency rations, and feed them to the kid to warm his insides up. A couple of others confiscate the apple pies as eminent domain for the first-aid crew, to keep our spirits up when the victim experiences some pain as his blood warms and his nerves thaw out. There's an element of human pride in doing good works, and there's more we want to do, but the kid appears to be recovering and Mom runs out of apple pie, so we let it go at that.

hard times

JANUARY 7

The sun is a dim, half-hearted circle of a suggestion low on the horizon, which is nothing new and doesn't bother me. I'm protected by a moat of double-paned picture windows. On the outside in the snow, bobcats are chasing down hassenpfeffer suppers, and great horned owls on broad and silent wings are sailing along as quiet as the cold. They'll be laying their eggs any day now. And Ursa Major, the Great Bear, the Big Dipper, is slowly making its way up in the northern sky, mostly under the camouflage cover of God-tossed clouds, and my Uncle Jake isn't feeling so hot.

Ever since Christmas, with everything looking so wind-swept and lonely, and the only sounds outside being the sighs of snow-heavy branches, he's been feeling a little bit like a let-down Ponce de Leon clanking through the lilies, so I snowshoe over there to cheer him up.

Jake has picture windows of his own and sees me coming across the lake. Before I get there, he's got the cribbage board out and the cards dealt. After a couple of games and a fortified cup of coffee, he tells me the story. As I said, he hadn't been feeling well, so he went to the doctor, who prescribed some pills, some "pick 'em up, old-age pills." Jake's an active outdoors type whose tackle box and fanny pack don't have room for pill bottles. So he found another way. He got a defunct ballpoint pen, separated it from its inner contents, and replaced the insides with what the doctor ordered. And now he's got his pills close by and handy, clipped to the pocket of his black-and-red-checkered shirt, and he gets them dished out one at a time.

About then a medium piece of January sunshine shoots out of the sky, so we get up and struggle out to our ice fishing shack to test the invention.

a true story

JANUARY 8

They say if a story gets told often enough, it becomes the truth, so you can accept the following as fact. I do. It was told to me late one night at the Elkhorn Tavern and Wildlife Museum by a newcomer to Lost Lake, J. John Johnson-Smith, who claims to be a descendent of the House of Usher, which includes the Queen of England on his mother's side. This, he says, vouches for his veracity.

According to J. John Johnson-Smith, back where he came from everybody's favorite activity was catfish fishing, as it is the world over. That's what he was doing one night. The fishing was good and the catching even better, until he ran out of bait.

The out-of-bait J. John Johnson-Smith heard an old bullfrog celebrating the moonlight on the other side of the bay. Knowing how much catfish like old bullfrogs, he sneaked three hundred yards through the muck to find this one. Just as he was about to pounce on it, a granddaddy garter snake slipped in and swallowed it whole. J. John Johnson-Smith needed that bullfrog, and he needed it bad, so he got hold of that snake, squeezed out the frog, put it in his bait box and took off for the fishing hole. About halfway there, he got to feeling guilty about swiping the snake's supper, so he backtracked, recaught the snake, pulled a half-pint whiskey bottle from his fanny pack and poured a double shot down the snake's throat as payment.

Having put his conscience to rest, J. John Johnson-Smith went back to fishing. Fifteen minutes and two catfish later, he felt a tugging down around his ankles, and there was that garter snake with a frog in its mouth, looking to make another trade.

As I say, it's a true story but, this being a free country, you may have to hear it a couple more times before you start to believe it.

fancy footwork

JANUARY 9

If you haven't been there, you don't have any idea that life for an outdoorsman isn't what you think it is. What appears calm and dull to you is filled with uncertainty and danger to us. Within every shadow, behind every bush, under every stone, around every bend of every curve in a creek, there lurks the possibility of an emergency, yet we don't complain because, under the camouflage coat of each of us, there beats the heart of a make-do kind of guy. Or gal. Never was that made so clear to me as yesterday at Mom's Cafe over on Main Street.

Several of us regulars were seated at our regular table when, Bang! Ralph lost a screw from his eyeglasses. Without so much as a blink, Mom whipped a twist tie off a loaf of stone-ground whole wheat bread, peeled the paper off the end of it, stuck the wire in where the screw should have been, and saved the day.

That got me to thinking. What would Ralph, who can't see two inches without his eyeglasses, have done if this had happened when he was perched up in his bowhunting tree stand, or in his canoe coming down the chute in the Raging Rapids of No Name River, or camped out, or sneaking through thick brush on the blood trail of a wounded cape buffalo, or the hundred other places outdoorsmen find themselves? In Ralph's case he might have calmly used a number twelve fishing hook, or a needle he keeps in his possibles pack. In the here and now, however, it was a twist tie, which can also be used as a makeshift guide on a fishing pole. Ralph was grateful, too, but Mom said all the thanks he needed was for Ralph to pay his bill. Naturally, Ralph opted for a hip-hip-hooray instead, and we joined in, lest paying your bill got to be something Mom expected from all of us.

desire under the elms

JANUARY 10

Winter is twisting and turning on the dead branches of January, and the winds of winter are sweeping slantwise from the sky, driving us inside to snuggle under buffalo robes of cotton and polyester. Somewhere outside there are foxes snacking on frozen berries, though they prefer the heartier stuff of meat and potatoes, minus the potatoes, and cottontails around the corner and over the snowbank prick up their ears at the very thought of it.

Then, off the south side of the house, we spot an icicle dripping drops, dripping a kind of voodoo magic, and a smell comes to us from somewhere. We get an itch in places we haven't scratched in a while, and our thoughts slip from under the blankets to the transient world of camping out. Ahhh, camping! And it hits us that we have not reserved a single campsite for the upcoming season of milk-and-honey plenty, so we get busy.

No two campers have quite the same requirements or expectations; not everybody wants the same thing from a campsite. Some want to set up temporary housekeeping alongside a sandy beach. Some want to boil morning coffee within ear and eyeshot of an icy trout stream. Some take comfort in numbers and want to commune with nature while communicating with camping-out neighbors where sounds of radios mingle with owls' hoots and loons' cries. Others, like me, must have the solitude of lonely outposts. Some want to fish for walleyes, some for catfish. Some want to take little kids along. and some grandma and grandpa.

So, with our hearts set on the horizon, we decide to do a little planning now. We'll do a little researching. We'll send out a couple of letters of inquiry, so we'll get just the campsites we want and need just when we want and need them the most.

it's as simple as that

JANUARY 11

Sundays are mine to do with as I wish. On Sundays I can hunt and fish and camp and canoe, but on Saturdays I have agreed to work in and around the house. On Saturdays, I haul ashes, seed and weed gardens, split wood, mow lawns, shovel snow, clean garages, and mend screen doors and bicycles. I don't mind.

Each fall, however, I must spend two Saturdays hunting deer, and the two before those in preparation. And I use up a couple of Saturdays for partridge hunting, not counting opening day, which is technically a Saturday. Here at Lost Lake, fishing season opens on a Saturday, too. It is a non-working, holy-like holiday of fishing obligation. The following six or seven Saturdays are holy-like holidays of somewhat lesser obligation, but fishable nonetheless. I hunt ducks only on Sundays, of course, except for the five Saturdays early in the season and the three late, which are justifiable exceptions.

To bowhunt in the traditional sense, I must sacrifice weddings, funerals, birthday parties and occasional Saturdays, but since Saturdays are my days to work in and around the house, I limit myself to a handful. I take four ten-day canoe trips annually. I can't do that without using up a pair of Saturdays per. And when the temperature gets above zero on a Saturday in January, and the snow stops falling, I think it's okay if I go rabbit hunting and ice fishing for northern pike and crappies, don't you?

Note that I do no duck hunting in Argentina, no bear hunting in Ontario, no sheep hunting in Tibet. Though I want to, I do not fly to Alaska for any reason whatsoever, since that would require the use of my day to work in and around the house, and because to everything there is a season, and a time to every purpose under the sun.

a dreamy vista

JANUARY 12

A fellow asks me how it feels to haul a ninety-seven-pound king salmon out of Alaska's Kenai River while I'm drift-fishing with my fourteen-year-old son in a sixteen-foot aluminum boat. I say fine. I don't have a fourteen-year-old son, I don't have a sixteen-foot aluminum boat, and I've never been to Alaska. To tell you the truth, I think he's got the wrong guy.

That was last week. Today, I'm sitting on a five-gallon pickle pail in my ice fishing shack, and I get to thinking how an ice fishing shack is more than a handful of cheap two-by-fours holding up a half-dozen sheets of half-inch plywood and a Plexiglass window. An ice fishing shack lets me fish when I really need to. It lets me cook up three or four venison sausages and wrap them in ketchuped, store-bought bread with one eye while I keep the other one on my jig stick. In ice fishing shacks, husbands and wives get reacquainted with no more distractions between them than a good-news-bearing bobber. In an ice fishing shack, fathers and sons and daughters, nose to nose and shoulder to shoulder, talk softly and find out they still love each other after all.

In ice fishing shacks, you can straighten out the health-care mess, solve the crime problem and ease the world's food shortage with a pickle pail full of panfish. Not a little fine missionary work has gone on in ice fishing shacks, and they've saved the sanity of many cabin-fevered men and women. They're a refuge against the cold winds of a purgatorial world and shelters against the elements of routine.

And in an ice fishing shack, you can dream of hauling a ninety-seven-pound king salmon out of Alaska's Kenai River as you're drift-fishing with your fourteen-year-old son in a sixteen-foot aluminum boat while you're sitting on a pickle pail, waiting on the whims of a six-ounce bluegill.

cold fury

JANUARY 13

I stop by Mom's Cafe over on Main Street for coffee. My second cousin Howie's there working on his income taxes; he is distraught. "You won't believe," he says, "all the money I've spent on life insurance in my life, banking on the chance I'd be lucky enough to die young. But it's not happening. If I live to a ripe old age, I've lost all that money. I'm done with it." I don't say anything. "Same thing with fire insurance," he says. "It's gone. If my house burns down tomorrow, I'll take it as a sign from God that it's time to move."

Then the door busts open, admitting a blast of cold air and a guy looking like the very devil. We don't know him. "Shut the door," says Mom, and pours him a cup of coffee that's been sitting there since the morning rush a long time ago. The first swallow causes the guy's eyeballs to bulge, but it takes a cup and a half of the stuff before he's ready to tell his story.

He says he was munching on a piece of toast in front of the picture window at the motel on the edge of town when he spots a little doe about done for. Hot on her heels are his pampered poodle and three other dogs. The poor deer, he says, plunged through the deep snow while the dogs skipped right along on top of it and, before his horrified eyes, closed in and playfully tore the doe apart.

"You darn fool," says Mom. "Don't you know all dogs, no matter their credentials or the low-bred status of their owners, chase deer given the chance and five minutes in the woods?" He throws the bum out. And then, not wanting something so terrible on our conscience, we slip out to check the status of our own kennels.

to each her own

JANUARY 14

Outside, the North Wind is chewing on a cookie moon and oak roots are dying to be useful. Inside, my neighbor Gladys is restoring to their original newness the cork handles of her old fishing poles. She rasps a little pile of sawdust off a wine cork and mixes it with a waterproof glue until it reaches the consistency of her chicken gravy — thick. With an old table knife, she forces the goop into the nicks and gouges, piling it a little high and letting it dry for a couple of days, which is not a long time in January. Then, with a very fine grade of sandpaper, she sands the humps smoothly gorgeous.

She also keeps half a dozen or so wine corks floating around in her tackle box to pincushion loose hooks also floating around in her tackle box.

What else Gladys does with wine corks is make poppers. First, she takes a razor blade to the cork and roughs out the general configurations of a tadpole or frog or some willy-nilly figment of her imagination. Then she shapes a concave scoop in the front with a drill and Dremel attachment. On the bottom, she cuts a lengthwise groove with a hacksaw blade, deep enough to accommodate a hook. She mixes epoxy from the model airplane section of a toy store, applies it to the shank of the hook, inserts the hook and fills the groove full and flush with the cork. After that, she uses coarse sandpaper to further shape the lure and goes on down to fine to smooth it out. Then she dips it in sealer and paints it with model paint — sometimes very fancy and sometimes quite plain. When it dries, she comes on over to my place, puts the popper on my fly-tying vise and ties on hackle for legs and tails.

And as to the obvious question of how Ol' Gladys comes by so many wine corks, well, that we figure is her business.

justice for all, etc.

JANUARY 15

Some people look up at the stars and see nothing but stars, but others look up to get a fix on reality. That's because the stars were once human beings, too. It's true.

A long time ago there was this grandfather who was a star. Like so many grandfathers, he was a heck of a fisherman. He was such a good fisherman that his family never went hungry, not even in winter. This full-bellied proposition came to a screeching pause, however, when the old man's favorite grandson and protector, Chinook, feeling his post-adolescent oats, took off to the other side of the mountain to see what there was to see.

It was then that Cold Wind, a real lazybones, came into the picture. He was so lazy he wouldn't even go fishing, though he and his family did go hungry, as you can imagine. It took him awhile, but he came up with a plan to steal fish from Chinook's grandfather, who caught them by the stringerful. So he did just that, day after day, week after week, bringing considerable hardship to Chinook's family.

At last, however, Chinook returned and got the skinny on Cold Wind and vowed to put an end to this travesty of fair play. He hid in his grandfather's smokehouse and waited for the thief to come crawling in, which he did. A melee ensued. They went round and round, socking each other left and right, until Chinook finally beat the stuffings out of Cold Wind, proving himself the stronger. He's still proving it, too, blowing in on a blast of warm air every once in awhile in January and pounding the dickens out of Cold Wind.

If you look just right some night at Orion up there in the January sky, you can see Chinook in his canoe, protecting grandfather's fish from the clan of Cold Wind. To those of us who look at stars with a purpose, it gives us hope.

between naps

JANUARY 16

Snow is piling up on trees, mail boxes, fence posts, telephone poles and slow-moving pedestrians. It's making snow mountains out of snow molehills, and the cold moon, a lonely old thing, is hurrying the sun to bed. These are the times that try men's souls and drive them to their tackle boxes. At least that's what they do to my Uncle Jake.

Finishing off the last of the holiday eggnog and the leftover fruitcake, Jake sighs and dumps everything out of his tackle boxes onto the dining room table, which is big enough to hold the entire family between football games on Thanksgiving Day. He's got a lot of stuff.

He weeds out much of that which did him no good at all during the previous season and divides it among a number of small containers, each labeled with the name of a kid — a grandchild, a neighbor — all of whom measure worldly wealth by the heft of tackle boxes. They will not outgrow this. Jake cleans and polishes the equipment that has proven itself worthy and is in good working order and returns it to its newly scrubbed chambers, each according to its size and function.

Any gear that needs mending goes into a larger receptacle to be lovingly restored on other nasty days and long winter nights when Aunt Clara joins the ladies at the bowling alley and there's nothing on TV. Rusty items he dunks overnight in a cup of water fortified with a couple of the hissing tablets he uses to soak his dentures. Beyond-repair tackle is deposited in a three-pound coffee can to be later transformed into decorations for the row of deer antlers in the woodshed, and for the little Christmas tree that annually adorns his reloading-flytying-bait-fixing table. When his shoulders sag under the weight of winter, this gives him a lift.

here's looking at you

JANUARY 17

My kid has a birthday every January. Today is her eleventh. There must be some mistake, I think, some mistake, for it's her fifth, or sixth, or seventh or eighth at most. But no, it's her eleventh. She is adamant about that, and I concede the impossible. On the guest list for today's party is a neighbor boy, a fine boy who cannot be eleven either, but just as certainly is. Being neighbors, they play together. She pushes mountains of sand with his toy trucks; he seems as willing to do duty in her playhouse. They ice-skate, shoot their bows and BB guns and go fishing.

Once I heard an older boy tease them about their relationship, and it got me to thinking about the day Katie comes to me with a for-real boyfriend. What the heck do I do then? First, I suppose, I'll try to smile. Then, I suppose, I'll try to tell her to go at this togetherness stuff with the same care as she'd face the sun on an early morning. I'll try to tell her to let it develop like the lingering songs of meadowlarks that kind of enter your soul and lift a piece of it to Heaven. I'll recommend she nourish it with falling rains, rising mists and sunbeams gleaming on wrinkles of open water, to let it grow gradually until she can smell it, and it smells like a wild rose (though I'll try not to overdo it). If it's for real, I'll try to tell her, go catch for this boy's supper a dozen whispering stars (that's the legal limit), a half-gallon of rainbows and a bunch of ripe tomorrows, and send him out to hunt up a full moon, if he can, and a red and yellow fire to warm the corners of her heart, just to check him out.

Speaking of hearts, I'll try to tell her that no matter what happens, mine will be with her always, and that if love doesn't make the world go round, it makes the ride worthwhile, though I didn't think that up myself. That's what I'll try to do, I suppose.

limited access

JANUARY 18

I am up to my entomology in outdoor catalogs when I get the message that, "Out they go."

"Not so fast," I say. "There might be something in there I need." It was time to whittle the stack down to a manageable size. It had been time to do so some time ago, but one of the things I love to do is look through my outdoor catalogs. Within those pages, I become the suave and debonair hunter with the polished, high-booted foot resting modestly on the belly of an elk I just got with an expensive new rifle shown in another catalog. My high-priced and costly hunting britches match and complement my high-priced and costly hunting jacket, all leathery and soft. I am never dirt poor when I page through the pages of chamois shirts and wool socks.

My catalogs take me to rugged mountain streams gleaming in the sun. I am the one locked on to the tail-dancing trout with the eight-foot, three-inch graphite two-and-a-half-ounce custom-made rod and the priceless reel. I am the one wearing the extravagant water-repellent, double-stitched, new and improved fishing vest with thirty-five bulging pockets. I am the one with the out-of-sight neoprene-coated waders and the laminated, maple-bowed, walnut-handled and cotton-corded landing net.

I'm aware that the ability to shoot straight means more to hunters than the pants they wear while they're doing it. I know that possessing a true sense of direction in thick thickets is of more value than shiny shotguns and new canoes. I know that. But I need to dream. I need to dream of cozy campsites and tightly pitched tents, of unpatched clothes, of socks that don't settle in bunches down in the corners of my boots, of rustless rifles, of binoculars with two lenses. It puts me at ease.

the light fantastique

JANUARY 19

My daughter was in the Nutcracker this year. That's a ballet, and I sat through a dress rehearsal and four performances. Somewhere between the snowflake scene and the finale of the second or third show, my mind drifted to other dance performances I have seen. I particularly recalled a disco type of dance performed by many outdoorsmen, but most recently by my Uncle Jake. This is a traditional movement done by those deep in the woods who stumble upon an underground hornet's nest. Jake's interpretation included a wild, circular waving of arms, a leap that took him airborne for ten or fifteen seconds followed by several little stomping steps between each of a long series of broad jumps.

Another favorite is a theatrical combination of bolero and hokey-pokey usually performed by trout fishermen wearing 36-inch-high hip boots wading icy 38-inch streams. There are variations to this routine, but most involve toe-dancing and a pantomime wherein the principal dancer appears to be climbing an unseen rope, accompanied by a crescendo of whoop whoop whoops, reaching a peak as the water rises to crotch level.

There is also a Highland fling performed by people meeting black bears picking blueberries in the same patch. This is especially appealing when the bear joins in. Other favorites include the mosquito fandance, the portage shuffle, the bunny hop, the rattlesnake stomp and the fox trot, but none is quite as heart-swelling as a tutued, mouse-eared little girl taking a curtain call while her old dad blows a gasket at the beauty of it.

not wishin', fishin'

JANUARY 20

Sometimes we hold onto poor excuses with the same grip with which we hold onto cherished possessions. For instance, here in the middle of winter, we're not catching many walleyes. In fact, we're not catching any walleyes, so we're subscribing to the long-held notion that walleyes don't bite here in the middle of winter.

We know better. All we have to do is look over at Ol' Gladys, who's dredging up so many nice fish. If we look over at her real close, we see she's concentrating her fishing over what's left of a good growth of underwater vegetation on a drop-off. She seems pretty definite about that. Further study reveals she's setting a tip-up at the top of the drop-off, one halfway down it or so, and one near the bottom. It appears that when a fish bites at one of the levels, that's where the fish are, and we casually stroll over there to fish at that depth, too, or close enough to it to catch them coming or going.

If we get closer, we find she has attached a two-foot, six-pound-test monofilament leader to twenty-pound braided line. If we get our nose right in there without being too obvious, we detect the smallish split shot pinched six inches above the hook and a three- to four-inch fathead minnow stuck to it just below its dorsal fin. With my head in the hole and my coat over my head, I observe she's fishing a short foot off the bottom, and she's giving her supper plenty of time to play around before she sets the hook. So if you want to play an active role in dispelling the myth that walleyes don't bite in the middle of winter, you'd better get out here and do what good Ol' Gladys and I are doing.

hip-hip-hooray

JANUARY 21

The man in the moon leaned over the ledge and gazed wistfully down on us last week during the regular meeting of Lost Lake's Fish and Game Club. My Uncle Jake was addressing the assembled members and guests. The gist of his presentation was the theretofore not completely understood fact that anyone who indulges in the ancient and honorable sport of fishing can manufacture a whole lot of his or her own tackle at the substantial savings of forty to fifty percent!

As you can imagine, a gasp of disbelief rippled through the couple dozen of us in attendance, and everybody jumped up and gave Jake a standing ovation. Then, before the chairman could ask if there was any old business, they beat him to the refreshment table.

Not only will this be a tremendous money saving opportunity for us here at Lost Lake, where everybody fishes, but building our own tackle can provide other benefits as well. My cousin Matilda, for instance, who tripped over a chair on her way to the coffee pot, can, while making her own tackle, develop the eye-hand coordination of which she is devoid. And Ben, with the newly acquired tic, can replace the basket weaving his doctor ordered (there's no money in it) with tackle making. And so on and so forth.

I myself will experience the pure joy and singular satisfaction of catching fish with stuff I have created. Though it concerned me somewhat about where to place the blame on those days when I come up fishless, I remembered that some goals are so worthwhile it's a glorious thing even to fail at them — and made a mad dash for the brownies before they were gone.

apparent discrepancies

JANUARY 22

If ten pheasant hunters gather around a single bird fairly shot, no two of them see it quite the same. When the pheasant goes slack in the air and cold in his hand, one hunter sees the clatter of a plate and fork and knife and the bird entering his body to become a part of him, of his skin, his eyes and heart. Another sees this pheasant as a ray of sunshine and a crag of a rock where he stands close enough to the great warm heart of God to feel its beat. On the face of a third is written the look of a lover. That is sufficient.

A fourth hunter eyes the fading bird and sees a dream, a vision of a blind old river timelessly clutching at the shore and letting go. He smells the river in the pheasant. He smells the filmy trees at the river's edge and on the beach there. He doesn't understand it; he doesn't have to. A fifth sees a great avalanche of thunder thrilling him through to his toes. He draws in his breath deep as an outgoing tide, and, since he is no poet, he lets it go at that. A sixth sees a snorting, overblown trophy. He is new at this. Let him sleep on it for a little while. Let him grow. A seventh sees the twisted magic of Aladdin's lamp and blesses his luck. An eighth sees it as a drop of dew around which all the heavens revolve. A ninth sees a surging bewilderment wild and wide where the breakers in his soul struggle left and right for meaning. I think that one is me. A tenth squints his eyes like a fox and looks away.

Where have I gone with this, I wonder? It was supposed to be about the economics of hunting, about dollars and cents, about nickels and dimes, about cash registers and receipts, but it's so hard to speak of that and pheasants at the same time.

consumed with a vision

JANUARY 23

A fast-food establishment opened this morning south of town. It's a franchise offering curbside service. It didn't take long for the word to get out. Before sunup, there was a line of customers you wouldn't believe. I don't know who was there first — a couple of crows, I think.

The special of the day was roadkill deer, but it varies. Sometimes it's skunk or muskrat or squirrel. Sometimes it's a doe that got old and froze. Sometimes it's a baby bird that fell from its nest or failed a trial flight. Occasionally it's a pheasant wounded by a hunter or a raccoon that's starved to death and laid itself down for the last time. It's hard to say. Sometimes it's a muskie washed ashore.

The diners included the feathered and the furred, the big and the small, the two-legged, four-legged and no-legged. They were, in other words, magpies, jays, ravens, crows, coyotes, chickadees, skunks, opossums, bears, the whole weasel family, bobcats, wolves, some hawks, eagles, bone-hungry porcupines, insects of all kinds — thousands of them — and worms, possibly at the top of the food chain, depending on your point of view.

Maybe we've seen too many funky vultures circling too many wasted pilgrims crossing too many Death Valley deserts in too many old movies, but we don't always look kindly on these scavengers. We aren't so crazy about a pair of beady-eyed characters playing ping-pong with a grouse's gizzard. Their sins, however, are not so numerous. Thanks to these cleaner-uppers, nothing in the wild is wasted. Nothing smells too bad for too long, proving again that there's room here in the glow of the moon for all of us, great and small.

chumps

JANUARY 24

When you live in a place like Lost Lake and you get to town — say to Mom's Cafe or to the Post Office over on Main Street — you're already halfway out of it. Actually, Main Street is the only street we've got, except for two that meander here and there and don't go anywhere. We're a small town. About everybody here knows everybody else, and we basically trust one another, which can be a fault that gets out of hand.

Take my Uncle Jake. It requires considerable effort these days to get a smile out of him. He's suffering from an over-application of that trusting business, or an under-application of good sense, though we don't mention that to him because he feels so bad already.

A couple of weeks ago, the fish quit biting on Lost Lake, so Uncle Jake and his second cousin Eugene made a reluctant departure from here on a scouting mission to a lake with a better reputation than it deserves, a couple or three hundred miles south. After a hard day on the ice, they stopped at a roadside establishment. It was then they demonstrated the lack of the vigilance their hometown had weaned out of them and lost their ice fishing gear, auger and everything. Somebody stole it. Jake is on a fixed income. He worked hard for, saved religiously for and took much pride in that stuff, and now it's gone, lost to thieves masquerading as fishermen.

He says to tell you to save yourself the heartache he's experiencing by recording the serial numbers of and engraving your name and address upon all your hunting and fishing gear, to lock it up when you can, and not to leave it unattended in the back of your pickup truck. He says the world is a strange ball of goo sometimes, and the theft of outdoor sporting equipment is a big, bad, sad business, so be careful.

slightly mad

JANUARY 25

The storm was whistling in from the north; the wind was blowing long and strong; snow was piling up. We had ice for whiskers and snow for beards. We had frost in our hearts and sleet in our souls, and it was okay until our grit was dashed by the arrival of eight sleek seed catalogs. Then we became lizards, mindlessly basking in the tropical luxury of spring. We ooohed over early carrots dug young and sweet. We aaahed over rutabagas singing with life. We relished tomatoes oozing with goodness and melons unmarred by the climatic quirks of purple zone three. Visions of hot, sensuous cucumbers and white clouds of cauliflowers danced in our heads. We heard off-stage crickets picking banjos on heat-tolerant cabbages.

We turned the pages to rushes of radiant roses as big as your fist and begonias and flowers we've never even heard of. The gardens of our mid-winter imaginations grew lush and faultless. We felt the sun shining on the pages of our doldrums and the earth responding with alphabetic assurance: asparagus, brussels sprouts, chard, daisies, eggplants (no eggplants), fuchsia, horseradish, ivy, kohlrabi, loganberries, mushrooms, nasturtiums, okra, parsnips, radishes, spinach (no spinach), sweet peas, turnips, watermelons, yucca (what's yucca?) and zinnias. Shirtless, we dug and ditched, weeded and watered. We heard frogs singing green songs and soldier bees buzzing apple blossoms. We went fifteen rounds with those catalogs, and all of it — drought, bug and blossom-end rot resistant, sturdy, tall and tender.

Then, in the midst of this golden moment, ripe with confidence, crisp, vigorous, sweet and firm, the fire wept to be fed, the wind crawled in under the door and blew out the candles on my little girl's birthday cake, and we stared blankly out the window.

armageddon

JANUARY 26

The sun almost came out for a little while yesterday, and my blood began to stir, but then it didn't, and once again lethargy triumphed, so I took to the couch for a nap, and I had this awful dream.

In my dream, I see a roomful of little kids, six or seven of them. My own is in there, too. These kids are playing games. They're giggling and laughing. They're having a ball. And then I see one of them is fooling around with a gun. A real gun. In my dream, I yell at him to stop it. I yell at the kids, especially mine, to clear out, but they don't hear me. I try to run to them, but you know how it is to run in a dream.

Finally, I make a small contribution to gravity and fall off the couch. I am glad to do it, but though wide awake now, I can't shake off the grim reality of that dream.

If you own a gun, and you have children in the house, ever, even on a temporary, visiting basis, and your gun is not locked up or well out of the reach of those kids, you are putting them on the path to martyrdom. Hiding the gun is not the answer. Kids easily find what's hidden. Disassemble it. Make it inoperable. Buy a trigger guard that blocks the trigger and can be removed only with a key. Put the gun in a safe. Anything. Keeping it loaded in the house is out of the question. If you have it for defense, you can load it quickly enough if you have to.

I don't know how that dream came out, but I know there could be no greater nightmare than losing my child and no more painful hell than bringing on that loss through my own brutal carelessness.

cheers

JANUARY 27

My Uncle Jake hikes across the lake to the Post Office for the morning paper, reads it and makes a beeline for the Elkhorn Tavern and Wildlife Museum, though it's a little early for him. He slams the paper down, orders a shorty and starts his engine.

"Somewhere around 80 percent of all tweety birds," he says, "will not live to be a year old. For rabbits, the number is even higher, and for every six thousand eggs a lady bass lays, one might live to a catchable size. Everything out there gets eaten by something else, and there's nothing inhuman about it. Robins don't hate the worms they dine on. Owls have no ill feelings for the baby rabbits of their dinners, nor do wolves for the fawns they feed their pups. It's the doggone natural order of things."

"But it says here," he says, waving the paper, "that we human beings don't fit into this natural order. It says when we kill an animal, fish, bug or bird, it constitutes the same felony as the killing of a little kid does. That's baloney! We're created to be dependent on other living things the same as robins, owls and wolves, though we usually pay someone to do the killing for us, sparing us the blood and guts of it."

"Heck," he says, "I respect the integrity of people who don't eat meat, or wear leather, or catch mice or squash bugs, but it says here," he says, waving the paper again, "that they're gonna fight to the death to keep the rest of us from doing those things, too." With that, he storms out.

All alone, I get to thinking about what Weninock the Yakima said: "My strength ... my blood is from the fish. The fish and animals are the essence of my life. It is not wrong for us to get this food. I raise my heart to the creator for this food that has come." And I drink to that.

something cooking

JANUARY 28

As cautiously as a heron wading in bourbon, I maneuver the slippery path to Mom's Cafe over on Main Street, where I smell something funny. This isn't uncommon at Mom's; nevertheless, it's hard to concentrate on a cup of coffee with that kind of distraction floating around, especially since I am also thinking of ordering a wedge of cherry pie. So I ask Mom straight out if he's cooking something back in the kitchen that's a long time dead without the benefit of refrigeration.

"No," he says, "I am baking my hunting boots."

"Oh," I say, not fully convinced of his sobriety. "Is this a new recipe?"

He clears up the mystery of this particularly peculiar pungency. He tells me that after hunting season last fall, he took off his boots, tossed them into a corner and abandoned them there, as they had become a casualty of the natural elements and old age and took on water from twelve feet. Only now does he decide to do something about it. For years, he tells me, he had worked a commercial goo into them with only marginal results. Then, while baking a batch of sugar cookies, he hit upon a thought. He cleaned the boots. He coated them (the tongue too) with a mixture of mink oil and silicone. With an old toothbrush, he worked the stuff into the seams. Then he put them in an aged aluminum pan and popped them into the oven set real low. In about half an hour, he says, he'll take them out, confident in their recaptured ability to keep his feet dry.

I ask him why he didn't get himself a new pair instead of going through all that monkey business, and he says he was going to, but then he'd have to charge a nickel more for a cup of coffee to pay for them. It never ceases to amaze me how you can sometimes find the milk of human kindness in the unlikeliest of places. Still, I skip the cherry pie.

an unscheduled eclipse

JANUARY 29

A guy I know hit a deer. He had himself twenty thousand dollars of hard-earned wampum wrapped up in that combination of cold steel, safety glass and bucket seats that he called his dream machine. He had himself eighteen gallons of super premium no-lead no-knock gasoline. When he wound it up and turned it loose, he was a regular king of the jungle. Then, yesterday, he hit a deer. He rounded a curve and a one-hundred-twelve-pound doe stepped in front of him.

He could have swerved right, which would have plunged him into the ditch and slammed him into another deer standing there, four-footed and resilient, and then into a culvert. He would have rolled over and over and over under the hot and cold waverings of the moon in the time it takes to sneeze. He could have, but he didn't.

He could have veered left in a great stir of noise and lights into an oncoming people-packed van. He could have braked hard, hard in keen neglect, and the eighteen-wheeler hot on his trail would have flatly written his epitaph. He could have locked the brakes and lost control of that cold steel, safety glass and eighteen gallons of super premium no-lead no-knock gasoline and got himself transmuted to the four wild elements. He could have, but he didn't.

He could have tapped the brakes to slow down, to warn the truck behind him. He could have tapped the horn and flicked his lights to alert the deer and the oncoming van, so he did. Then, with no safe deerless path lying before him, he hit the deer, as little of it as possible. Just before impact, he let up on the brakes, raising the front end of his vehicle, so the animal went somewhat under it, which kept him alive and the damage to the dream machine less than it might have been, because that's the law of the jungle.

random acts of kindness

JANUARY 30

Ol' Gladys' ice auger is on the fritz again, so she calls me up to go northern fishing with her. It's close to noontime and, by golly, we're going fishing, which is something I can live with over and over again. Right away, we arrange ourselves along a weedy drop-off that starts around eight feet deep and drops to twenty. We string our holes in a line that begins at the shallow end and concludes at the deep.

Some people claim that the brains of ice fishing persons are as numb as their feet, but Gladys and I and a million other tipper-uppers are onto the fact that some of the finest and biggest northern fishing of all time takes place in January. The ice cover gives the fish a sense of security. They feel comfortable cruising weedbeds for nourishment. Then, too, the spawning urge hits northerns early, and the need to feed is heavy upon them.

Gladys and I tie number two single hooks to four-foot leaders of twenty-pound monofilament attached to a much heavier Dacron line. Then we hook costly eight-inch shiners just ahead of their dorsal fins and add a split shot to keep them put and wiggling like silvery beacons in the darkened world of hungry northerns — about a foot off the bottom or just above the weeds.

In the middle of our first peanut butter and jelly sandwich, a flag springs into action, and so does Gladys. She kneels over the hole and carefully turns the tip-up so the line on the spool directly faces the running fish. In a minute, it stops. Says I to Gladys, "I think we're onto something here." Then the line takes off again, and she whoops, sets the hook and, hand-over-hand, brings in the line, arms swinging like a windmill in a hurricane. "Oooh, yes," she puffs, "I think you're right." I get a kick out of that, because she hardly ever compliments me.

dwindling peace of mind

JANUARY 31

On that part of the southwest quarter of the southwest quarter (SW 1/4 of SW 1/4) of section 16 of township so-and-so, north of range 12, lying northerly of a crooked line lying parallel to several thousand feet north of the south line of said southwest quarter of southwest quarter (SW 1/4 of SW 1/4), or thereabouts, is a trout stream hidden beneath the brittle flanks of January. As my life depends upon trout streams, I get out there every chance I get.

How cold it is outside, though, and an avalanche of snow and cold has slid off the roof, blocked the door and dammed me up, separating me from my trout stream. Lucky for me, though, I'm a dreamer, and without so much as a glance in the mirror, I leave my stubborn skin and follow a trail of metaphors on a beam of late January sunshine, like a bird migrating, like a clock about to chime, like a ball hit sharply to shortstop.

Inch by treacherous inch, I negotiate the cradled dangers of February. Weightlessly, I orbit the scuffed and muddy month of March. I pirouette around rocks in my path and disappear too swift for detection. I sneak up and down isles of cedar trees like ushers in scary movies. Suddenly, I hear the black waters of my stream. Ah, there's nothing quite as pretty. It's like meeting my mother for the first time.

I stay there, too, for the longest time, until mottled clouds and leaking stars and gushing moons get out of control and come crashing, piece by piece, through my roof and, stocking-footed, I make my way down the carpeted hallway to get a mop.

MACIEJ

excu-u-u-u-se me

FEBRUARY 1

The telephone rings. It's February returning my call. I answer carefully and proceed cautiously. February is nothing to fool with, and I know it, yet I do what I have to. I ask February why it's withholding the toast and strawberry jam days of spring. I ask when in the world the merry purply clouds are going to escort these cold winds off into the distant past. I ask the whereabouts of dancing dandelion magic. I inquire after the songs and verses and green, green melodies doing the booga-loo down flower-lighted lanes. I get carried away. "Let it roll, February," I say. "Let it roooLLLL!"

At the other end there's silence for thirty, thirty-five seconds, and then, in a voice that wraps around me like the choke hold of a serpent, February growls, "You weak-livered, yellow-bellied son-of-a-gun, don't you know I've got a world to run?" February says this in a pitch somewhat higher than absolutely necessary, I think. But that's not all.

"I've got a world to turn!" February says. "I've got a wind to blow. I've got snow to fall and water to run and laundry and floors to scrub. My pipes are frozen; my seas need salt. I've got shadows to cast, voids to fill, sunsets to reset. I've got earthquakes on my mind and floods and tumultuous tides. I've got rainbows to build, at today's prices, and music lessons. I've got Homo sapiens coming out my ears, and lamentations worldwide, and you want me to drop all that for a little sugarplummed ecstasy and honeyed dreams of green? Now, get outa here."

Which I do. But I learn two things about February. Number one is it has no sense of humor. And number two is, once you get it going, you can't shut it up.

born in a barn?

FEBRUARY 2

I don't know if it was cabin fever or not, but there was this cold February day when a bunch of us gathered at Mom's Cafe over on Main Street to prolong the process of our decay. The sun was shining just enough to thaw itself out, but not us, no. Suddenly the door opened, and there appeared in the shimmering light a young man who spoke in a loud voice.

"Monofilament line gets surprisingly dirty," he said. "To clean it, pull the line off the reel and lay it in a circle upon your living room floor. Wet a small rag, hold it around the line in front of the reel and wind it back on, pulling it through the damp cloth. A couple of drops of anise oil on the rag will give the line a pleasantly wormy scent. And do not submerge the reel in water to clean it. Periodically, take your reel apart, remove the old grease and lubricate it lightly. Adding new oil and grease to old will create problems for you like you wouldn't believe."

"To continue with a new thought," he said, his voice ringing with passion, "spray your broadheads with dark-colored flat paint to keep them from shining into the eyes of deer and alerting them to your hiding place. Apply a thin coat of Vaseline to the painted heads so they do not rust.

Furthermore, charcoal briquettes, when placed in paper-fiber egg cartons, will keep your pack clean and will light like anything on the trail without lighter fluid. When preparing a shore lunch, set the egg carton on fire, with the briquettes in it, of course. By the time you have filleted the walleye you have caught, the coals will be done enough to grill it."

Then he was gone. The raw air in the cafe was fairly tingling with what we had experienced, and from that point on the lad's reputation for holding the door open longer than anybody else at fifteen degrees below zero spread throughout the land and stayed there.

time well spent

FEBRUARY 3

You are fishing and fishing and fishing. You are filling a hole in the day with fishing, and the mean and stingy, ho-hum, don't-catch-nuthin' luck you are having seems like a cruel joke. It's not the first time, either. You sit there fishing, gasping for your fair share of sunshine, or you stand there in a trout stream, suffering the symptoms of an incipient nervous breakdown, or you cast or drift or troll, retrieving time after time after time nothing but limp and empty lines.

Unable to shake the clammy hold of misfortune, you question your manhood or your womanhood. You ask yourself, with more than a hint of wistfulness, where you've gone wrong, and you contemplate the possibility that, where the savage business of fishing is concerned, you're nothing but a bone-headed bumbler. While that option does exist, it's also possible this rank miscarriage of justice is but a temporary malady that time will heal. Don't feel so bad. We're all more or less in the same boat.

When we hit the water, same as you, recklessly bent on an afternoon of fishing, the law of averages states positively that we will spend an average of eight-tenths of an hour to catch and land each crappie, perch and bluegill that we catch and land. Likewise, we will have to put in 2.6 hours per brook, brown and rainbow trout; 5.3 hours per smallmouth bass; 6.0 hours per largemouth; 8.1 hours per walleye; 8.6 hours per northern; and a hundred hours for each muskie of legal size and status.

So, you see, you may have set your standards too high and should consider doing what we do when we have to, which is misrepresent the gospel truth. This is particularly effective when the nearest witness is 10.5 hours off in another direction.

on top of the world

FEBRUARY 4

I watched all day, and I watched all night. I watched until my eyes froze open, and I saw it, the whole deal, the entire shebang — February — from the first to the twenty-eighth or ninth. I saw the tracks of wolves on the move. I saw quarter-pound baby bears being born to mothers dreaming of beetle sandwiches and blueberry pies.

I saw red-nosed kids toboggan-sliding around the corner of January and landing smack-dab in the middle of life. I saw older folks, more experienced, on showshoes and skis, wading and crunching over slippery fields and snow-filled forests. I saw chickadees at bird feeders. I saw foxes snacking on frozen berries. I saw rabbits, just over the ridge, pricking up their ears and checking their back trails.

I saw drifting owls silently dropping from the night, plunging talons into white-footed mice who'd been hunting last suppers of seeds and bark. I saw an hour more of daylight than I saw on that shortest of December days. I saw squirrels digging two-and-a-half feet under the snow for caches of acorns buried last fall. I saw tiny springtails yo-yoing on that same snow, like pepper on fried egg whites. I saw ruffed grouse on web-footed snowshoes supper shopping for popple buds, and pheasants feeding on sumac berries. I saw, just where you'd expect it to be, wintergreen. I saw the empty ribs of a deer stripped and naked. I saw unmistakable signs of fuzzy catkins — the beginning of life for them — on pussy willow branches.

I saw a red-tailed hawk. I did. I did. I did! I saw people studying seed catalogs and sorting fishing tackle, planning for a spring out there somewhere on the hazy horizon of tomorrow. I saw all that and more, much more, here at Lost Lake where I live, and if I were to come over there where you live, I'd probably see about the same thing.

not by bread alone

FEBRUARY 5

Dogs track up kitchen floors. They shed on sofas and rarely make beds or do dishes, but you tell your dog a joke forty-seven times, and on the forty-eighth he'll laugh his tail off like it was news to him. You spend the day with people and events lined up to hack off pieces of your hide, yet when you pull up in the driveway, your dog's glad to see you, even if you're only half there — so glad, in fact, that you can't tell if the dog's wagging the tail or the tail's wagging the dog. Who else thinks you're so cool? Who else gives you his undivided attention even when the only news you've got is bad?

When your dog asks, "How you doin'?" he really wants to know. Who else wouldn't think of mentioning down at the Elkhorn Tavern and Wildlife Museum the number of easy coming-in shots you missed? Who doesn't give a rip if you omit a day of shaving? Miss a week of showers, and dogs shake your hand, and say, "Hey, what's that new cologne?"

You don't have to have meetings with dogs. They never require flattery, though they're pretty much impressed with whatever you do. "Way to go, Pal!" they say, even if it isn't. Dogs are rarely insulting.

"Come to supper," you tell a dog, and he comes.

"How do I look?" you ask a dog, and he'll say you're the cat's meow and a regular movie star even if you're not.

Dogs are understanding, too. "I lost my job," you tell your dog, and he'll grin and say, "What the heck," and "Let's go fishing."

out of sorts

FEBRUARY 6

It's this world we live in. It's kitty kick the door down and heaven help the person who bruises easy and mends slow.

Take one-and-one-half pounds venison, cube it and dredge it in one-quarter cup flour and a tablespoon of salt.

A guy stops by to borrow my chainsaw. "You have cut yourself shaving," he says. "No," I say, "the dog has walked over my face with snowshoes on, though we have very little snow." I owe him the use of my chainsaw, but not the particulars of my life.

Add one-quarter cup olive oil to a deep skillet and brown the meat in it with three-fourths cup onion and one-fourth cup green pepper, both chopped.

The truth is, winter's nearly over, and where did it go? Since the pond froze in December, I have skated on it maybe five times and hunted rabbits twice.

Add two-and-a-half cups tomatoes and one teaspoon paprika.

Sometimes I look at myself in the mirror and wonder what's the use. Three times before Christmas, maybe four, I went fishing, and only half that since. Better a skeleton's life than this.

What the hell, if you like paprika, add more. If you're not so crazy about it, do as you like.

Speaking of snowshoes, I had mine on twice, though it wasn't necessary either time. I didn't go skiing six times.

Cover and cook over low heat until the venison is tender. About an hour.

I didn't even shoot this deer. I should throw it to the dogs. I feel like a runner edging off first when the catcher signals it's time to go home.

Add a half cup celery and a cup carrots, cook another forty-five minutes. This makes a nice goulash.

I sent a letter to myself. It came back address unknown.

Serve with fresh-baked bread, a tossed salad, low-fat dressing and a hearty burgundy. If that's not right, it's close enough.

how to hunt turkeys

FEBRUARY 7

A lemony light from the early-morning east is horizontally projected across the bleary fog of February. It enters your house through your kitchen window, it drifts over your breakfast table spread with oatmeal and strawberry jam, and your thoughts spin to thoughts of turkey hunting. Mine do.

More specifically, my thoughts turn to the 18,756 turkey hunting tips contained in my closetful of turkey hunting books, turkey hunting essays and turkey hunting tapes for turkey hunters. Being aware of my obligations to you, I'll list them in the here and now, not necessarily in order of importance.

#1. Learn everything you can about the sport of turkey hunting from turkey hunting books, turkey hunting essays and turkey hunting tapes for turkey hunters, though …

#2. You can't beat experience.

#3. Do not hunt where there are no turkeys. Scout the area before the season.

#4. Learn to call. If you are a beginner, don't try to get fancy. Stick basically to the basics.

#5. Devise a game plan and stick to it if possible.

#6. Listen to the advice of experienced hunters and follow their example.

#7. Pay close attention to details of clothing. Camouflage your underwear.

#8. Different weather conditions call for different tactics. A still, crisp morning requires setting up in one place and yelping fairly softly. A blustery wind requires louder calling and periodic movement.

#9. Don't be discouraged by a false note you …

… but then the lemony light slips back into February, and you sit with your back to the window, and memories hang on you like a too-large coat, and your thoughts droop to thoughts of old oatmeal and strawberry jam gone bad. Mine do.

it doesn't take much

FEBRUARY 8

Is it right? This continuous sticking of zippers? I walked around half a day the other day with my zipper half undone, shattering the frail decor of my confidence.

The care of zippers is of utmost importance. You should keep your zippers clean, using an old toothbrush to get gunk out of them. You should lubricate your zippers frequently. Again with an old toothbrush, lightly oil them with mink oil or Vaseline. Include the fabric strip to which zipper teeth are attached. Don't fold your zippers at sharp angles. This may unset the teeth and strain the border material and stitches.

Never force a sticky zipper with perhaps a pair of pliers. Don't overload one by closing it against abnormal resistance — chewing gum, mud or cloth stuck in where it should not be. Keep your zippered gun cases, camera cases, sleeping bags and tents dry if you can lest, like me the other day, you walk around half a day with a zipper undone. Dampness raises havoc with zippers.

Have you ever given up on a good gun case, a fine camera case, or a perfectly wonderful tent because its zipper gave out? Have you given up on a beautiful hunting coat because the zipper quit? Have you given up on a sleeping bag because its zipper gave you trouble? Then isn't it time then you tripled the lives of your zippered outdoor gear by following the basic tenets of good zipper management, so you can live fruitfully and harmoniously without the fear of your life being reduced to a hill of beans? Isn't it time you found yourself cozily zippered within your zippers while the heavens roar, and you become happier than you dreamed possible?

long ago and far away

FEBRUARY 9

For a minute, we stood stiffly at the front door of my house, the soldier and I. We hadn't seen each other since one beery night at the end of the summer after our high school graduation, when we swore an eternal oath to friendship. For us, there would be fishing trips forever, and duck hunts and rapids as wild and free as we thought ourselves to be. The next morning, he boarded a bus for a faraway bootcamp, and I for the halls of ivy.

And now, now at last, we were getting tangled up in the handshaking and the howyadoings. Into the house we trooped, talking of old times, laughing at ourselves as eight-year-olds bravely embarking on our first overnighter campout until darkness transformed bushes into bears and whispering winds into ghosts. And how we came of age trading in cane poles and braided line for magnificent Zebco 202s and miraculous monofilament. How it was I who dived into freezing water to scoop his first steelhead to shore with my bare hands. How he tracked my first arrow-killed deer. How he shot my decoys by mistake, and how I dropped his ice chisel to the bottom of the lake. How we argued over angleworms and dry flies, over Chevies and Fords, and over a pretty cheerleader who liked someone else entirely.

My mother bandaged his skinned knees; his pulled a sliver from the bare bottom of a little boy who had slid down an unplaned two-by-six. We could not remember fast enough. One cup of coffee, two, three, and he was gone again.

I spent the next days routinely at work and home and the places in between. I wrote and lectured. I mowed the lawn and played ball with the kids. I laughed and frowned and ate and slept, but for a week, more or less, my heart was with the blue-eyed, brown-haired boy who was no more.

in good time

FEBRUARY 10

Over in the next township, somebody found the forequarters of a deer with bullet holes in it. They had been separated from the hindquarters. The hindquarters, of course, were not there. We don't think too highly of poachers here at Lost Lake, don't like them at all. In fact, we'd like to hang a few, but the incident got me to thinking. Who among us has ever considered the proposition that poachers should be pitied? Sympathized with? Understood?

When you, for instance, go into the woods or up to the mountains with your rifle, you enter sacred territory. You know that, and you carry yourself accordingly. You become a part of them — the woods and the mountains — one with them, a part of their very souls, and a rainbow to you is a rainbow is a rainbow. You become a wind spirit of coming and going. There is an anxious, eager ache in your Adam's apple.

But, and we have no basis for self-righteousness here and mean no disrespect, when a poor poacher goes into the woods or mountains, he smells only blood, and the hunt is only a blood ritual. When he leaves the woods and the mountains, he smells of blood.

When you take your fishing pole to a river or wade a lake with your boat, there are hidden fires burning in your heart, hidden moonbeams laughing in your heart, and heaven rides on your shoulders. But when a poacher invades a river or plows a lake with his boat, his heart is not in the right place, and the water to him is only his killing ground.

When you take your gun onto the prairies, you go honorably and return with honor. But a poacher, because he's forgotten what it's like to be an eager kid coming into a first set of antlers, goes as a liar, a cheat and a thief and returns having sinned against the universe. So you see then, do you not, that a poacher is to be pitied first, and then hanged.

getting focused

FEBRUARY 11

You say cheese, and it comes out pffft. A picture is supposed to be worth a thousand words, but most of the time and for most of us, it isn't. Especially it isn't for us outdoor types who want to capture the results of a mighty good fishing day or the antlers of a very decent buck on film. We want the camera to be a witness to the truth, and the finished photograph to be a trophy, a monument to our knowledge of the great outdoors and our incredible good luck. What we get, however, is a mug shot — sunglasses that make us look criminal and hats and caps that hide our faces in dark shadows. The light is harsh. The background is cluttered and distracting. Rather than looking like the outstanding outdoorsperson that is us, we appear stiff and goofy, and the fight has gone out of the fish and glory from the rack.

To capture the drama and excitement of those golden moments, we should shoot our photos in the coming up of the sun or the going down, when the warm color tones are heavenly-glowing. We should be creative. We should shoot the boat being launched or a close-up of a rod-bending big one coming in. We should shoot beauties sizzling in the frying pan. We should shoot high. Shoot low. We should take off the sunglasses and slide the hat to the back of our head. We should look at the walleye, at the turkey, the deer, the pheasant, and not googly-eyed at the camera. Rather than a stringer of dead fish, we should shoot one dandy on a bed of ferns. From our tree stand we should shoot the chickadee that sits on our bow. We should shoot an oak leaf or a wee pasque flower. Then, when we want to get wild, we can dig out the picture album and get into a country state of mind.

hurry up and wait

FEBRUARY 12

I appreciate just about every kind of bird there is, including vultures, but right about now, I like mergansers best, and I'll tell you why. February is chipping away at the great weight of winter. The slippery ripples of days are getting longer at both ends. The winds, once cold and standoffish, are sighing through the trees of loneliness and calling, "C'mon over." Creeks granted a little elbow room are calling, "C'mon in." And an under-the-weather sun, feeling somewhat stronger, is calling, "C'mon up," and, "Don't be a stranger." Those calls may be whispers, and you might have to strain to hear them, but mergansers don't have to. They're among the first to RSVP, the first to pack their bags and get a ticket back. That's why I like them so much.

Of all the anxious waterfowl to come north in the spring, it's mergansers who are so eager they sometimes get ahead of a slow-poke thaw and are forced to retreat, to wait for spring to catch up. In the air, mergansers are low and in-a-hurry flyers, following every twist and turn of a river in follow-the-leader formation. On the water they float long and low, especially the larger males. Sometimes they're mistaken for loons. Like wood ducks, they nest in hollow trees, on broken-off stumps or in the cracks of rocky shoreline cliffs. When she feels they're ready, a mother merganser nudges her youngsters from the high nest of their birthplace, and the little ones drop and bounce like balls of cotton and head, helter-skelter, for water. In the fall, they hang around until the last minute, until things have frozen over, and then skedaddle in a quick hurry.

But that's getting ahead of things. Right now, we're keeping our eyes on the alert and our hopes up waiting for mergansers to open the gates of the springtime migration and the welcoming floods that follow.

an elegant evening

FEBRUARY 13

Nothing grows faster than a fish from the time it bites until the time it gets away. Take my Uncle Jake. Once he lost a fish so big he dislocated both arms in describing it. It was truly something to witness. First, his voice dipped down deep with the telling, and then it swooped up again like a cantankerous crow's.

Actually, Jake is notorious here at Lost Lake for his fishing savoir-faire, which is why he's my favorite uncle, and why I stopped over there a week ago last night. He was hunched over the coffee table in front of the fireplace, rearranging his fishing tackle. "Making the good better and the best perfect," he said. Jake has no modesty and needs none.

On sheets of last Sunday's society page, he had laid out gold and silver lures. With bright red fingernail polish, he was adding large red eyes to them, and painting thin red lines down spinner blades. He said red markings like that can excite sluggish fish, like northern pike, into striking, and if they don't, he can take the stuff off with nail polish remover. I thought that was fantastic and told him so.

Then, after a couple of beers, he threw a log on the fire and showed me how to turn ordinary spinners and spoons into sonic lures by drilling holes into their rear-end sections — one-eighth inch in smaller lures and one-fourth in larger. This creates little turbulences and bubbles and buzzes that alert fish to their availability.

I don't know where my uncle comes up with this stuff. It's a Zen thing with him, I think. I wanted more, but my aunt came in and chased me away. She says that after a couple of beers we get goofy. She's temperance, which is, I think, a Zen thing with her.

look before you leap

FEBRUARY 14

If some young guy came up to me and said he was in love, I'd look him in the eye and say he was nuts. I'd say, "Stop the presses, hold the phone, and you're nuts."

"You don't know the first thing about love," I'd say, "until you look at this person you're referring to, and you see eagles in flight and feel what it's like to drift over snowbanks of stardust."

That might sound like I'm overdoing it, but love's a serious business. I'd say, "You're not in love unless and until you feel like a wolf all alone on a winter night with the moon flung on your back, and you want to howl. Until when you see snowflakes falling, you're seeing frosting on the cake of childhood and sunshine all over the place." That's what I'd say.

I'd say, "You're not in love, not at all, until you've walked among stars through the infinite fields of heaven with the object of your affection. Until you've climbed mountains together and snagged whirl-dancing clouds and rested before red and yellow fires beneath the North Star and Orion. Until you've been sung to sleep by loons." That's what I'd say.

I'd call him a dope and say, "You're not in love until you two have been paddling as one through ten-thousand raindrops and wandering tribes of butterflies. Until you've been one with trout-chasing rivers of good times and one with hoot owls flying high, and one with Mariah the Wind."

"You're not in love," I'd say, "until you've seen the moon rise from the water. Until you've seen the moon dancing over pine trees. Until you've seen the moon mend broken hearts. Until you've seen all the wonders of the moon."

He might interrupt me here to ask how I know so much about love, and I'd say, "Why, I've been there, boy, and I'm there right now, and Valentine's Day's got nothing to do with it."

a stiff upper lip

FEBRUARY 15

It's a smallish thing, and gone to seed, but under my graduation picture in the high school yearbook they wrote: "I am the master of my fate, the captain of my soul." It was pretty accurate, too, when I was seventeen-and-a-half. Now, I sit at my desk with a cheese sandwich, a stale beer and a lamp that doesn't quite take the room from the dark. Outside, two dogs, mine and one far away, answer bark for bark.

I try to think of the sun rising and setting every day without financial aid or material gain, and how rain falls without anybody having to turn on the faucet. I try to remember how breathing doesn't cost me a nickel. It's what I do when problems pile up.

I think how we're all babes in the woods at one thing or another, and how lucky I am there are no cures for partridge fever. I think of giant men and women I've known, and a few giant kids. I think of the miracle of trees leafing out in spring when you figure they'd forgotten how, and then the miracle of October when they turn such colors you've never dreamed of. I think how every year I'm surprised at that, though I know better.

When life gets me down, I turn my thoughts to eagles and rainbows, and how the more you try to describe them, the less you do. I think of rivers and what wonders rivers are, and stretches of prairies, and how you can roll up pieces of birch bark and carry on conversations with moose. I think of trails made by Indians and buffalo, some of which were lit with the same moon that shines tonight in its cool, easy way. I think of camping out on one of those pine-covered benches above a lake, and the everlasting smell of sage. I think of a whole family of mountain goats I saw one time sunning themselves on a mountain. I think of the times I've visited Aurora Borealis.

When I'm alone and down and out and feeling blue, that's what I think about, if I can, though of course you can't make a thrilling story out of things like that.

what the doctor ordered

FEBRUARY 16

I had a long talk with Georgie. He's married to my second cousin Matilda. I told him, "Sometimes a person takes to drink because he sees himself a failure and then fails all the more because he drinks. It's one of the quagmires brought on by the complexities of modern living."

His indignation rose higher than a Mississippi flood, since he hasn't touched a drop in two years. I told him not to read any symbolism into that, and what I meant was the hullabaloo of today's world is a morass of stress and strain that leaves us with feelings of helplessness that can be alleviated and counterbalanced by a week or two of camping out in the great outdoors. That as campers shelter and provide for themselves they become empowered. That they develop pride and self-reliance. That this is especially so if they have mastered the simple art of making bannock, once and still an essential element of life.

To make bannock in camp, I told him, you need to mix up at home in a plastic bag two cups of flour, half a teaspoon each of salt and sugar (if sugar appeals to you), and one tablespoon of baking powder. At camp, you mix in enough cold water to make a thickish dough, and then you have to make a decision. You can flatten the dough into a well-oiled frying pan and cook it over a fire. Be careful. It cooks quickly — ten minutes to a side. Flip it often. Serve it hot for breakfast, slathered with butter and jam. Or you can roll it out on the bottom of your overturned canoe into a two-foot rope and wind it through and around the forks of a couple of sticks held together as one, like a pretzel. Roast it over a fire to golden brown.

"And there you have it," I told him, and there you have it too — a particularly convenient cure in the great outdoors for whatever curious aberrations beset you.

writer's cramps

FEBRUARY 17

Everyone's a writer these days, even Mom from Mom's Cafe over on Main Street. His is a book on cooking in the great outdoors. He asked me to read the rough draft, and I said, "Okay," and he said, "Don't you dare copy any of my ideas," and I said, "You got it." He knows me pretty well.

In his book, he says to put a handful of marbles in your double boiler, so when the water boils down they'll make a racket loud enough to hear even if you're splitting firewood. And if you want to separate frozen bacon slices, to roll up the package diagonally before you open it. And if you get yourself an old goose and want to eliminate its wild taste, to stuff the cavity with cut-up raw potatoes and toss them out when it's done. And if you're roasting hot dogs for a crowd of kids, to take a hay fork, hold it over the fire to disinfect it, and then stick the hot dogs on. He says you can roast a lot of hot dogs like that.

And he says one way to give meat on the barbecue a good flavor is to toss garlic cloves on the coals. And if you've been out awhile and aren't sure which eggs are still good, he says to put them in a bowl of cold water. Those that sink are fine. Use the ones that bob up on one end pretty soon, and stand clear of those that float. And if you can't remember which eggs are boiled, he says to give them a spin. Cooked ones will, raw ones won't.

And he says if your marshmallows are hard as rocks to put them in a plastic bag and dip it in hot water. And if your garlic won't peel, to smack it with a rock. And an excellent marinade for deer and moose meat is a good Italian dressing. The usual stuff. To help out at the cafe while he's writing the book, Mom brought in a nephew from Chicago named Sal Manella. That makes me nervous.

acts of god

FEBRUARY 18

Some people say there is no God, but there is. He's a saxophone player, and He plays to give intellectual and emotional support to the silent rumblings deep in the bowels of February. You've heard Him. He kisses the air, tooka tooka tooka, with that saxophone in a rambling incantation to fundamentalist trees, stiff and frozen to the earth, but reaching for the stars and glory days of what's ahead.

He goes twee tweet tweet to snow forts running out of time and rows of snowball ammunition in need of explanations. He goes waaa waaaaa wa to great horned owls nesting or nested and egg laying, and to mudpuppies doing mudpuppy things in the river, and to skunk cabbages poking their smelly heads out from the cover of darkness. He goes cha cha cha to goldfinches taking on the dandelion-yellow colors of their Easter outfits. He goes chuga chuga chooo choo to practical-joking groundhogs and putta putputput to ravens getting ravenously into the courtship thing.

He pours out the lonesome in His soul, going dum dada dum dada do for sunsets and sunbeams bouncing off the lake. Sitting all alone in a corner, He goes sh sh sh and wah wah wah back and forth in the night. He keeps time to the tick-tocking drips of icicles sliding off the roof, and to woodpeckers beating heads against telephone poles in the name of love. He sweet sweet Sweet Georgia Browns until He lands splat in the remains of a February snowbank, plumb wore out.

You can feel the season changing and, like a dancer waiting in the wings for the music to begin again, you listen for the whispering leaves to come clattering, chattering, rattling, but all you get is God, working over a saxophone, going ditty ditty doom baaaa, which is okay if that's the way it is, though you wish He'd say it with bluebirds, meadowlarks and rosebuds instead.

it's in the dictionary

FEBRUARY 19

The tent was pitched. The sweet smell of pine filled the air. Supper was cooking over a slow fire. The first stars appeared in the twilight, doing loops around the dead moons of Jupiter. This was a while ago. We pulled up a couple of logs to sit on, and a fellow stopped by and said hello, and we said hello right back and "What's cooking?"

"Life," he said, and plopped down on a rock close by. "I want to know the meaning of life." So I told him.

"Life," I said, "is towering mountains and tossing oceans when the tide is out. Life is spring in the air, ordering new liners for your boots and chocolate ice cream bars and nibbling fish, definitely nibbling fish. And life is getting a birthday card that reads 'hooked on you,' and a breeze coming to the aid of a wilting day. Life is dawn slipping in like a canoe entering a great lake after an easy portage, and reading Henry David Thoreau and Sigurd Olson and Gordon MacQuarrie. And life is the splattering trumpet sounds of pheasants' calls and loons' cries day and night, and a line of pine trees stammering politely up against the horizon, and the small capitulation of raindrops."

"But life is more than that," I told him. "Life is an outcropping of peace around a campfire like this one, a touch of red left under a bridge after a rainbow peters out. Life is being led by the nose by an elk's tracks in the snow or a moose's through mud. Life is the fruitfulness of legends and glaciers at the end of their ropes, and thundering surf. Life is sitting in the shade with a giggling child, well protected from street noises."

"I didn't know that," the fellow said with the look of a religious fanatic. "And is life," he asked, "fields of wildflowers and songbirds and enormous sunsets?"

"It is," I said.

"Thanks a lot," he said. And he was gone.

i can eat crow, but i don't hanker after it

FEBRUARY 20

Though it happened a little over a year ago, it was an experience I'll not soon forget. "Come on over," I said to Harold over the telephone a few days before the onset of trout season, "and we'll check out our stuff."

Checking out your stuff a few days before trout season is a very good thing to do. You don't want trout season to come and not be ready. "Okey dokey," he said, and hung up, and to get a head start, I pulled everything out of the closet, the last item of which was my chest waders. One of the best ways to ruin your day is to wade into a wet trout stream in March with your waders on and have the cold water rise on the inside as fast as it does outside. Wowee! That is walking on the wild side.

At the thought of that, a light bulb went on inside my head, and I went into the bathroom, put the waders on, climbed into the tub and filled it, not too hot and not too cold. If nothing leaked in five minutes, everything would be fine and dandy, or so I thought. To tell you the truth, I felt a little silly sitting there like that, especially when Harold walked in. You should have seen the look on his face. "What in hell you doin'?" he said in a voice that took more air in than it let out. "What in hell's it look like?" I said. Two seconds later, he was back with the camera.

The reason I'm holding the rubber ducky is that I picked it up to throw at Harold, and the little boats just fell in by accident. He put the pictures up in the Post Office, at Mom's Cafe over on Main Street, and at the Elkhorn Tavern and Wildlife Museum. They're still there. I feel bad about it, too, but not as bad as I'd have felt with leaky waders in the frigid waters of opening day of trout season. Anyhow, yesterday I had the lights off in the bathroom, just in case, and the door locked.

gone but not forgotten

FEBRUARY 21

I lost a friend last week, a close friend. His departure was recorded by two nurses and verified by a doctor. His wife was busy at the time, but when notified, sighed a sigh of relief. His child didn't give it much thought, but a sister with whom he shared his childhood anxiously waited in the hospital cafeteria. When informed, she ordered a Danish and was comforted that the end, long overdue, had come at last, and that he didn't suffer much.

The news of his passing traveled quickly. "No one," some thought, "could live as he lived and expect it to last forever." Others whispered to themselves, "Good luck, old fellow, you'll need it." The proprietor of the Elkhorn Tavern and Wildlife Museum shed a tear, did some calculating and laid off two bartenders. Managers of several outdoor sporting goods stores ordered their wives to cease philanthropic activities and their children to give up sportscar dreams. His boss replaced a calendar print of a black bear from behind his desk with the picture of the company president that had originally occupied the space. I myself offered to give his shotguns and hunting rifles a good home. Others offered to take his dogs. His wife's mother rushed to her daughter's side to help her weather the ordeal. His child continued to give it no thought at all.

Yes, this bon vivant, this young man of the great out-of-doors, is gone. Gone is he who at a minute's notice dropped an ax or rake or pen or book, picked up a whim and dashed off with it. No more will he be there to rise with the full moon to chase the North Star and Orion. Last week, you see, he became a papa. A pop. A dad. A father. As his child entered the world, he put away the trappings of irresponsibility and put on the wise, mature ways of fatherhood.

time out

FEBRUARY 22

Life is what life is, and it's not always a series of pleasant events. We have to expect a certain amount of hardship in life and do the best we can with it. If we want the good, we have to take the bad. We know that and accept it. But when enough is enough, when February prunes our lives to the sticking point, the system breaks down. So we dig our canoes out of snowbanks, haul them to a river whose currents have cut an open-water trail through the ice, and put them in there.

It's a wonderful feeling, being on a river in wintertime. There is a holiness about it. It's like we're making progress again, as if we're on the brink of a major development. Who rides the wind? Who slips like the moon through clouds? Who flies with the soul of an eagle into the deep unclear? When we paddle into the quiet of daybreak on a river in wintertime, we do.

That's the way a movie ends, with a floating across the face of February and miles and miles of buoyancy and a blue sky supporting a distant, soaring bird, reducing the pitch and tempo of our midwinter lives. It's sooo nice. Ah, but the sticking point. Paddling a river now is no wide-eyed and boy-scout innocent adventure. The rules are hard and fast. We don't go it alone. We set definite schedules for putting in and taking out. We stick to them. We carry matches, kindling and dry clothes in waterproof bags. We dress warm and make stupidity and carelessness our enemies.

That's the story. Today is as wide as an ocean, and the time we waste sinks into the sea without a trace, or it goes up in smoke. Today's past is the dust and ashes of tomorrow, and so on and so forth.

nervous miracles

FEBRUARY 23

Like bears to honey, like hummingbirds to honeysuckles, like teenagers to refrigerators and telephones, we're hunting down the outdoor and boating and camping and fishing shows within a hundred and fifty miles, and we're going to some of them two or three times. We're doing a lot of plotting and planning, a whole lot, which has no basis whatsoever in reality.

But besides that, what's happening out there, anyway? Well, for one thing, and though it's early, horned larks are welcome-flocking to fields a bit farther south, fields that have kicked off at least some of their snow. And raccoons are somewhat out and about and pretty much for good. And woolly bear caterpillars are still hibernating, frozen solid, in barns and under bark. And maple syrup sap is beginning to work its way up and up and up, not fast enough. And praying mantis eggs wrapped in insulated foam-like coffins are beginning to feel the strength of the shining sun. And brown and purple butterflies — mourning cloaks — having slept the cold winter away in hollow old trees are unfolding their wings in an early unfurling of spring.

And as browse becomes scarce and scarcer, white-tailed deer are digging deep and deeper, and reaching high and higher for food. The shorter, smaller, weaker ones are starving. And Jupiter's the boss of the evening skies, taking orders only from a CEO moon. And some daredevil daffodils and crocuses are looking to poke through wherever they can, and so are skunk cabbages.

And most of the Valentine roses are dead and done for, and the chocolates are but memories, though the love's still there, or most of it anyway. At least that's how it is here at Lost Lake where I live, and I suppose that's how it is where you live too.

the king and i

FEBRUARY 24

The sands of time have grown increasingly frantic in the hourglass of February, and it's been a long time since we've been perch fishing on the ice, so a bunch of us snowshoe, cross-country ski, four-wheel drive and snowmobile out onto Lost Lake to do just that. There's nothing quite like fried-up perch to put February into the proper perspective. To say that, however, is not necessarily to do it, because the problem with perch, though they're out there, is finding them. Perch are nomadic. They're schooled-up wanderers, here now, over there in half an hour. But we get to thinking of a plan on how to acquire a bellyful for supper.

The way we'd always done it was to concentrate our perch-producing paraphernalia over areas with steep banks that drop rather sharply into deep water on top of firm bottoms. We'd set up there and we'd wait. We'd wait. And we'd wait. And we'd hope a roving band of perch would come to us, and sometimes they did, and sometimes they didn't.

Our new notion is to gather everybody who is perch appreciative and spread them out to work different areas of the lake. When someone, through luck, timing, skill or a combination thereof, finds a spot where a meandering school is in session, he or she signals to the rest of us, who converge on that honey hole and catch perch like crazy until it's recess time and the school moves to another playground. Then we go on our separate ways again and commence the same routine, proving again that two or more heads are better than an empty pickle pail.

winning and losing

FEBRUARY 25

We were speaking of championship fishing — Champion of Champions, The All-Time, One-and-Only — and agreed it was my grandfather, who fished nearly every day of his life. He had no major boat, no major motor. He had no major underwater network of electronic spies, no radar, no sonar and no guarantees. He had no tackle box the size and heft of the box on a pickup truck. My grandfather knew his fishing waters, and he fished them well. He knew his fish — northern pike, walleye, bass, muskie, bullhead, catfish. He understood them. He was on intimate terms with the wind and the moon. He fished honestly, and he ate what he caught. At ninety-three, he was too old to drive, yet was on his way to the lake when his car rolled over and he died. Perhaps his last thoughts were of Grandma and his daughters and sons. I think he was thinking, though, of a bouncing bobber. When I read of pro fishermen and championships based on gadgetry and dollars, I wonder.

The runner-up is my Uncle Jake. Retired, he also fishes nearly every day. His gear is better than his dad's was. His boat is bigger. His motor has an electric start. His tackle box is three times as big, but that's about all. He understands fish and prides himself on the one-on-one give and take of the ancient sport. It is a sport to him.

There's a two-way tie for third — two eleven-year-olds. They fish a lot like their great-grandfather, except what they lack in aptitude, they make up in the pure and simple joy of catching a once-in-awhile bluegill.

I don't understand the mousing around for trophies and dollars where fishing is concerned. That should be left for football, baseball and golf. Leave the fishing to the real champions, the millions of fishermen like my grandfather, my uncle, and kids who know what it's all about.

wait for me

FEBRUARY 26

Most of that afternoon, I had been sitting by the river on a sun-bleached, half-buried-in-the-sand driftwood throne near the great gray, canoe-catching rocks, watching angry, foaming currents hurl themselves again and again against the great gray rocks and then eddy around and race on down to the Big Lake. I had also been listening to the cries of endlessly circling seagulls and the wind.

I'm an ordinary guy, a dreamer and a searcher, and so, when I can, I go down to the river, where owls in faded nightgowns ask questions of one another at sundown, and hushed bats swing upside down from trees. It does something to me. I don't know what, and I don't know why.

I'm a dreamer and a searcher, but I'm a reader, too, and, sitting on that piece of driftwood throne that day, I read about wings. Insect wings. I read where the buzzings of insects are caused by their wings, and how the number of wingbeats, depending on the insect, can be as few as eight a second to as many as a hurry-up thousand. I read that an average mosquito on an average day flaps its wings six hundred flaps per second. Zing. Zing. Zing. A honeybee manages about a third of that — two hundred twenty-five or so.

I also read that the number of times per second an insect beats its wings doesn't necessarily affect its speed. A dragonfly is one of our fastest insects, zooming along at thirty-five miles an hour, yet it moves its gossamer wings just twenty-five to forty times a second. A lowly midge, on the other hand, with a thousand wingbeats every second, manages a top speed of one mile an hour. Uffda. Do I know how that feels or what?

a pilgrim's progress

27 FEBRUARY

Catching a steelhead is not the easiest thing, especially when you need to catch one more than anything. At least that's how it is with me. At this time of year especially I hunger to catch a steelhead, even in my sleep. Once in a dream I saw one and ran forward with my arms outstretched like in an old movie. But dreams like that don't work out, and I never caught it. Another time I saw one, a papier-maché one on the far side of its pasture, looking up at me. In that dream, I did a little better. I cast a chartreuse yarn fly I tied myself, a pea-sized fuzzy egg, into the seam between the current blasting downstream and the eddy along shore. I didn't get that one either, but I might have.

Once I saw a pterodactyl-looking thing with an immense smile. That time, I cast into the pocket of calm water where the trout was marshalling its strength to climb another set of rapids. Like before, it was a good cast, a nice strategy, but I caught no steelhead there. Then I saw another, taking its time, looking grand and other-worldly, strolling along a fan at the tail of a pool where the current speeds up before its next dive. I cast a slug on its nose but, like an old white-tailed buck, it disappeared as it had come.

Dreams are funny. If you dream hard enough and long enough, it's sometimes hard to tell what's real from what isn't. Once, perched below a gushing notch, I flipped a candy-coated spawnbag for the tenth time against a stone wall. As it dropped into the water, the current swung it madly downstream. The tip of my rod twitched as the split shot skipped over the bottom. The line tightened at the end of the drift. I felt a double tug. Oh man!

It was a lovely fish. I carefully backed the hook from its jaw. I cradled it with both hands and laid it amongst cowslips under a half-inch of blue sky, where it disappeared and became part of the river again, and a piece of somebody else's dream.

agony and ecstasy

FEBRUARY 28

The lopsided grin of January has been a part of my immediate, moon-drifting past for almost a month, and February is about a done deal of endless delights. It's time to take hold of myself, to set myself down and make a list of New Year's resolutions. Now is a nice time to do this, as the resolution rush is over, and I have the whole field to myself, so here goes.

In what's left of this new year, I resolve not to climb up into a tree stand with my rifle loaded, lest my future be full of holes. I resolve to set my youngsters down and explain to them that they must never, never touch any gun except under the direct supervision of me and me alone, and to quickly, quickly leave an area if another kid does. Then I'm going to double check, make sure all the guns in my house are out of reach and the ammunition locked up someplace else. I won't be left with a terrible heartache and empty cradles.

I resolve to write my lawmakers, on all levels, expressing my real concerns for environmental issues, for hunting, fishing and trapping privileges and how to save it all for tomorrow, for me and my kids, and for the sake of what's wild. I resolve not to pass a wild rose without pausing to get a whiff of it. I resolve to retrieve trash left by the I-don't-give-a-damn others of my kind at launching sites and on hiking trails. I'll become active, a mover and a shaker, in organizations that promote the general welfare of wildlife and thereby me. I can't live without wildlife.

I further resolve to miss a target without blaming my gun, and to trigger a real change by taking my kids, and somebody else's, fishing out where the air smells of pleasure all the time. If January has slipped by you and February is ceasing to be where you live too, we can do this together.

born again

MARCH 1

At the office we spend our time deciding whom to saddle with the problems we've been saddled with, seeing people we don't want to see, phoning people we don't want to phone and faxing people we wish would drop dead, and then comes March, the goose return of March, the flying Vs, the webbed feet settling into cold waters — newly created waters of muskie-becoming lakes. Then comes the chattering gossip of mergansers. Then comes the dipping, bobbing, diving, sliding, gliding pageant of incoming birds and upcoming flowers, the elegant beauty of widgeons and greenheads and greenwings and crocuses and the marigolds of marshes. Then come anthills in the driveway, and the progression of pasque flowers in full bloom, and cardinals whistling and popple buds expanding to near-explosive levels. Then the squeaking-gate squawks of blue jays melt into lovey-dovey soft and mellow music to our ears.

We pick our way through the land mines of January and February, scheduling twelve-minute chats with our children at 6:18 p.m. daily, and a romantic evening with our mate every other Wednesday when we can pencil it in. Then comes March, and the wonderfully terrible things March does to snowbanks. March winds bite a little, but they are wimpy winds whose days are numbered. Then come sandhill cranes and killdeer, making good on old, old promises. Then come babies born under the sign of Pisces — a faint constellation, but a mighty fine one.

And though we still spend our time at the office saddling people with problems we've been saddled with, and seeing people we don't want to see, and phoning people we don't want to phone, and faxing people we wish would drop dead, it's March, and we feel as good as anything.

a relaxation of tension

MARCH 2

Terror hit me hard last spring as I stumbled out of the night and into the parking lot of a famous trout fishing hot spot. There was no room for me there, nor for my pickup truck, and the shoreline was a shoulder-to-shoulder shambles. It was the craziest thing you ever saw. "Better get outa here," I thought to myself, and I went away.

Where I went to was a narrow trail, ten miles this and that-a-way, heavily overgrown with tangling tangles and strategically criss-crossed with latticeworks of blowdowns. For a half mile, on my hands and knees, I struggled along it until I came to a place where slack water off the main flow created an eddy, swirling seductively before spilling into a shortish riffle.

Small-stream fishing like this is basically an ultralight proposition for me. My rod is six feet long and has a soft tip that right away telegraphs the intent of a trout, should it make a play for my bait. My conscience dictates barbless, thin-wire hooks.

The second drift with a salmon egg — in March it's tough to beat salmon eggs as bait; the craving for spawn is inherent in trout — brought a tentative tap-tap, followed by a jerk, and at the upward flick of my rod, the trout raced toward the sanctuary of submerged branches. Denied that, it spun into the current. A spirited debate ensued, but finally, under the surface, the trout could manage only a feeble shake of its head when I reached for it. The brown was nine inches long. The vermilion and ebony spots blazed on its tawny flanks. A small wiggle loosened the hook from its upper lip, and with a flip of its tail it vanished into the shadows. Then, in this exquisite loneliness, I went and caught another one.

sparse cover

MARCH 3

Sometimes I sit and I think, and sometimes I just sit. Today, this early March day, I'm just sitting on a stump in my woods. I'm waiting for snow to melt, for sap to rise, for the sun to shine. I have a headache, and I'm waiting for it to go away. But, as so often happens when I sit, I get to thinking, whether I want to or not, and today I get to thinking about what kind of man I have come to be. I get to thinking hard on it, and to tell you the truth, I don't know.

I know what kind of man I want to be. I want to be brave in the eyes of my daughter. Fearless, daring, valiant, dashing, stout-hearted and lion-hearted, plucky, strong, unflinching, unconquerable, spunky, patient, loving, understanding and gutsy. That's the kind of father I should be.

To my wife I want to be a loving man, too. Admiring, respecting, tender, devoted, appreciative, attending, thoughtful, passionate, gentle, warm, affectionate, caring, considerate, loyal and remembering. That's the kind of husband I should be.

I want to be a kind man to my friends and neighbors. Well-meaning, pleasant, compassionate, sympathetic, understanding, generous, helpful, accommodating, tactful, easy-going, good-natured, tolerant, sensitive, courteous and thoughtful. That's the kind of friend and neighbor I should be.

I'd like to be more childlike. More innocent, honest, curious. Filled with wonder. I want to be clever. Quick and witty. Ingenious. Talented. Funny. Happy. Reliable. Good looking. Lucky. Charitable. Truthful. I want to be kinder to the universe. To the earth and its land, water and air.

As I sit and think on this stump, this stump of my making, waiting, I know the snow will melt, the sap will eventually rise to scratch the belly of the sky. The sun will shine. By and by, my headache will go away, but what's going to happen to me, do you suppose?

seedling moments

MARCH 4

They owned a house, a yard, two trees named Joseph and Clarence, a small garden and that was all. One day they decided to dig themselves out of the shallow grave of winter to secure a foothold on spring, which was right around the corner. After tea and cookies, they began wading through a fluctuating sea of water-colored seed catalogs, for it was their plan, as it was whenever they dug themselves out of the shallow grave of winter, to plant rivers of green things in their little garden, oceans of flowers and peas and carrots. It was a good plan.

But wait! Was that a meadowlark singing from the fence post? Was that a bluebird trilling in the yard? Were those nuthatches feeding upside down on Joseph and Clarence? It was and they were, which brings me to my point. As they paged through their catalogs, those wish book inventories, they took note of the meadowlark, bluebird and nuthatches, and paused mid-page to find bushes and flowers that would fill the bellies of the birds and protect them from bird-mooching predators. They found trees with leaves enough to hide the birds, with arms enough to hold their nests. They came upon grasses to plant in one corner and along a picket fence to shelter and nourish ground-eating, seed-eating songsters, too. In this green scheme of things they encountered tall and short shrubs that offered nesting places for birds of many denominations.

They went to their library, their bookstore, their extension office. There, perched on shelves, were books and pamphlets to aid them in this mission of spreading smiles with their good works, their good taste, their good judgment, and I'd say good looks, too, but that would be overdoing it, and I'd never do anything like that.

the path of enlightenment

MARCH 5

Each of us wants to be something we're not. A soldier wants to be a civilian. A civilian wants to be an astronaut, an astronaut a bank vice-president, a bank vice-president a teacher, a teacher a cop, a cop a farmer, a farmer a soldier, and so on down the line. Take me, for instance. I want to be a turkey hunter. I think about that a lot. I was thinking about it when I was poking little holes in the new sofa pillows, looking for feathers to tie flies I am inventing for the upcoming trout season. Sometimes I want to be an inventor, too, and a trout fisherman. And I get to thinking, "What is the single most important element in the getting of a wild turkey?" So I mosey over to the Elkhorn Tavern and Wildlife Museum in search of the truth.

This being the slow season, some of the boys are there already, dispensing knowledge, though it's a little early. I ask them. "What," I ask, "is the single most important element in the getting of a wild turkey?"

"Hmmm," says one, thoughtfully rubbing his chin, "I'll have to say it's scouting, knowing the whereabouts of several birds and their feeding habits."

"Hmmm," allows another, thoughtfully rubbing his chin, "I'll have to say it's knowing your shotgun, knowing where the center of the pattern is falling, and choosing the right loads."

"Hmmm, too," allows another, thoughtfully rubbing his chin, "I'll have to say it's knowing which calls to use, and when to use them, and sounding more like a turkey than a turkey itself."

"That's important," says a fourth, thoughtfully rubbing his chin, "but I'll have to say it's being dressed just so, and being able to sit for a long time without moving an eyelash."

Well, I thank the boys, and since we here at Lost Lake don't like to linger too far from reality for too long, I head back home to think about what they said and, since dreams die hard, to resume my pillow poking.

you think you've got troubles?

MARCH 6

Somewhere the secrets of spring are working deep in the bowels of the earth, but not here. That's why everybody's grumpy, and we don't care who knows it. Even me, but I've had the flu. I had it bad. First, I feared I'd die, then I feared I wouldn't. You know how it is. Today, we're taking a coffee break at Mom's Cafe over on Main Street and complaining as usual.

Uncle Jake's doughnut breaks apart and falls in his coffee. It floats around in soggy chunks the way it always does when it's spring everywhere but here. It's disgusting. He starts. "What really ticks me off," he growls, "is when I'm rowing around the lake in my boat and the oarlocks are squeaky. It drives me nuts."

"That's nothing," growls good Ol' Gladys, my usual ice fishing partner. "Slide a couple of plastic washers real snug over the spindles. But if you're talking irritation, I'll give you irritation. It's when the plastic worms in your tackle box go limp and glumpy and stick to the trays and gum up perfectly good other stuff. That's irritation."

"Shucks," growls the Professor, signalling for a refill, "that ain't nothing. Put your plastic worms in little jars filled with water and a drop of anise oil. But there's no worse affliction in the entire universe than dropping your only boat key in the drink."

"My, my," growls Ramona, the dark-eyed lady from across the lake. "String your boat key to one of those big plastic bobbers, and your troubles are over."

I think Ramona has a grievance of her own to bring before the court, but Mom comes over with a steaming-hot pot of coffee. He misses the Professor's cup by a mile, but not his lap, giving him, now dancing around with the exuberance of youth, a bit of a surprise, and such aggravation as none of us has seen before or since.

you said it, mr. kilmer

MARCH 7

I'm doing my taxes. There's nothing worse to be doing than your taxes, especially when it's late and no matter how you work the figures, you're not getting anything back. I truly believe it's the duty of every American to support the government, but not necessarily in the style to which it has become accustomed. Then I look up from the kitchen table, piled high with discouragement, and out the window into the cool gloom of a March night. The moon is caught in the brittle branches of birch trees in a corner of my yard by the swings. It's a sophisticated gathering of birch trees, and the moon pours a pool of light, a grounded halo, over them. I get all wrapped up in the night music of birch trees. The branches move and whisper of upcoming migrations, some of which are underway.

Some people, and I am one, refer to birches as Ladies of the Forest. They are. Graceful and elegant and beautiful. Their seeds feed countless birds. Their buds feed grouse. Their twigs are life-saving food for winter-poor whitetails. They are committed to holding as many nests in their branches as birds require. Indian people in Canada and up and down and all around the Great Lakes based their cultures on birches as surely as Plains Indians did on the buffalo. They used sheets of the resinous, waterproof bark to build their homes and their canoes. They used it to make baskets, buckets, trays and utensils for gathering and storing berries, maple sugar, fish, meat, pemmican and rice. They made moose calls from it and recorded their histories on it.

In the old days, as I do today and probably you do, too, they used the bark of this tree for kindling, its wood for fires, and the cool of its leaves for shade on hot summer days. Ladies of the Forest they are, and Mothers of the Forest too. There are no finer trees in all the world than birch trees.

make mine rare

MARCH 8

As they say, you can be anything you want to be — a dancing brontosaurus, a mogul or a bum. You can sell ice cream to Eskimos, speak Swahili like a native, flip burgers for a living, be an MBA, get on MTV and get as rich as Rockefeller. You can be a raving beauty, ride a rocket to the moon, grow cabbages, be a teacher or a preacher or a banjo picker, but, Pal, if you can't cook it up, you can't come a'camping with me.

You can dream anything you want to dream. You can dream of hot tamales, of leafy hearts of lettuce, of rosy globes of radishes and sea-green celery all mixed together — a medley of delight. You can dream of potatoes, of eggs hard-boiled, scrambled or over easy, and of bacon, but, Friend, if you can't cook it up, all by yourself, don't you dream of coming camping with me.

If you can't bake the beans, if you can't griddle the goulash, if you can't make the biscuits, if you can't slice the cheese, if you don't know what to put here or what goes there and how to make it sizzle like chocolate bits in trail mix, you can't come a'camping with me. This isn't only food for thought or spaghetti for your mind; I mean it. You've got to sear it, braise it, broil it, brew it, roast it, bake and saute it. You've got to deep-fry, pan-fry, stir-fry, French-fry and fricassee it over charcoal, propane or wood. You've got to heat it up, warm it over, cool it down. You've got to rehash it with ketchup, with onions, with salt, with chili powder and caution.

Don't let it get you down, don't let it break your heart, but, Compadre, if you can't cook it up, you can't come a'camping, you can't come a'camping, you can't come a'camping with me.

a beauty in baggy clothes

MARCH 9

For a long time there, we thought we knew all we needed to about coyotes. They were no good and that was that. Cussing them out was a favorite pastime, and killing them rated a close second.

"You dirty, low-down coyote" is what frontier sheriffs called dirty, low-down horse thieves. That's not fair, and coyotes must do a little dance of anguish at the thought of that. All they've got in common with no-good horse thieves is they don't wear suits on Sundays.

Coyotes are used to it. They're acquainted with intolerance. Do they complain? Do they sing the sorry songs country music hall-of-famers do? They do not. They reproduce. When one coyote is swatted down, a dozen more — smarter, bigger, stronger — jump in to take its place. Coyotes spend their entire lives dodging dogs, guns, poisons and traps. Do they go around with tear-streaked faces because of it? Do they wrinkle their brows and wring their hands crying, "alack and alas"? They do not. Despite the best efforts to erase them from the face of the earth, they thrive, clinging to their solitude even in people-thick urban areas. They don't care what's on the menu. They'll eat just about anything, dine just fine on things dead, though they prefer mice, birds, rabbits and squirrels on the hoof. They're satisfied with fish, reptiles, insects and berries, when that's all they can get. To lay something special on the table, they might team up and fill up on venison. They steal chickens regularly.

So. Everybody hates coyotes with a grave devotion, except other coyotes, of course, and those of us who have ridden their lovely, lonely cries on journeys to the moon, or heard them call out a lakeful of stars on a night that had theretofore known only darkness.

nine one one

MARCH 10

I dial God in a hurry but get Wichita instead, whistling a tune everybody knows and likes, but I go ahead and ask my question anyway. "Is it true," I ask, "that ten percent of the fishermen catch ninety percent of the fish?"

"Yes," says the voice on the other end, hovering like an airplane over a runway in fog. "It is so. It is so because the ten percenters know ninety percent more about fishing than you do, and because they go fishing ninety percent more often. Need I say more?"

"Yes," I say, emitting a signal of distress, "Yes."

"Okey dokey," says the voice, like a shadow, searching its pockets for parking meter money. "Some of the ten percenters are out there now, for example, sunfish fishing with fly rods, and they're having a wonderful time. Sunfish. Sunfish with a fly rod. That's the ticket.

"Sunfish take a variety of baits," the voice goes on, so clearly you'd think it was in the next room. "All of them small. Some flyfishing, sunfishing fishermen," says the voice, toying with my emotions and the English language, "fish with flies, of course, wet and dry. Others use leggy little rubber bugs and tiny, shiny spinners. The ten percenters fish near the bottom in six feet or more of water, though later in the evening they might go at it closer to or right atop the surface. They fish their flies in quick little jerks, with heavy pauses in between. And fun? Sunfish fishing like this is as much fun as ... well, it's as much fun as a plateful of chocolate chip cookies on a cold day."

"Gee, thanks," I say with an enthusiasm surprising in a man my age. "S'okay," sighs Wichita, and hangs up.

easy does it

MARCH 11

Though danger looms everywhere, "There is no time so dangerous," says my melon-bellied second cousin Matilda, "as when there is no hint of danger." She proved it last Saturday. Waltzing along as nicely as you please, coming from the mall, her upper body camouflaged with the pile of her purchases, she put her foot on a patch of ice. On going down, she instinctively threw out her left arm, losing a pretty vase and three goldfish. She also sprained her wrist, which got me to thinking.

While there were people there to help her out, what in the world would have happened to her had she put that foot down on a slippery rock getting out of her canoe in the middle of nowhere, or tripped on a root and her packages were packs, and she was far from first aid? So I ask her.

"Cousin," I ask, "what in the world would you have done had you put that foot down on a slippery rock getting out of your canoe in the middle of nowhere, or tripped on a root and your packages were packs, and you were far from first aid? What would you have done then?"

She looks at me and says I have birds for brains and that the first thing she would have done was nothing, not moved her wrist at all, that Georgie (Georgie's her live-in) would have applied a splint of a tent pole, paddle or blanket from her elbow to her fingertips, fastened it securely at both ends and at both sides of the fracture with tape, rope, handkerchiefs or belt, and supported the arm with a sling slung from her neck, thumb up and hand slightly higher than her elbow. Then she cites another of her favorite sayings (she is so much wiser than I at such things): "It's not so much how far you fall, but how high you bounce that counts." Wow!

patience, my friend

MARCH 12

With your eyes crinkled in small wrinkles like that, I know what you're thinking. You're thinking winter has a burning greed for profit that goes beyond reason, self-control and conscience. You're thinking it will last forever, but it won't. It never does. March, born in high meadows and snowfields, has, nonetheless, a gleam of sunshine in its eye, and spring is coming like an Angel of Mercy. Yes, it is, and the topsides of lakes will grow liquid once more and crappies, those wonderful crappies, will slide again up out of the dark deep and into the warming-up shallows, and some of the year's very finest fishing will commence. Yes, it will.

Water temperatures will rise to the magical fifty-four to sixty-four degrees, and crappies will move in close to feed on minnows feeding on insects in the new-thawed oozy ooze, first in small, shallow lakes, then along the northern shores and protected bays of bigger ones. I know that you're thinking your life no longer has wings but tentacles, and it will never, ever be, but it will, and if you're going to launch yourself into this kind of crappie fishing, and of course you are, you'll want to use, as my Uncle Jake uses, the classic bobber rig — a small hook, one-inch minnow and little bobber. He says you might want to try 1/32- or 1/16-ounce jigs, too. Light and ultralight outfits make for good sport. Fly fishermen experience unspeakable joy. This is up-close fishing, fishing in three to ten feet of water. Imagine what kids can do with fishing like this.

Even now, the rivers are whispering of mountains they have come from, and wind and snow they so intimately know. March, as we speak, is transforming the universe into a frying pan of unlimited opportunities, and you'll be surprised at how full of silent prayers your life will be, how full of grace and meaning, so relax.

raising a stink

MARCH 13

As plain as the nose on your face; can't see beyond the end of your nose; count noses; cut off your nose to spite your face; follow your nose; keep your nose clean; have your nose in a book, in the air, in somebody else's business, to the grindstone; led by the nose; look down your nose; no skin off my nose; thumb your nose; pay through the nose; win by a nose. Our noses are indispensable to our language, essential for the completeness of our face, necessary for the sifting of scents, but I am getting ahead of myself.

Labeled *Mephitis mephitis,* a Latin phrase meaning noxious gas, skunks have a reputation with noses that both precedes and follows them. It is this reputation that allows skunks to walk the earth with impunity. I was reminded of that this morning when a team of skunks arrived at 3 a.m. to play tiddlywinks with the lids of my garbage cans outside my bedroom window. I awoke with a start as I recalled an incident that I refer to as "Please, God, Not Me."

I had not been seeing eye to eye with skunks since they began blowing holes with pellet guns in the compost bins down in the garden, so I devised an apparatus to catch them. I took a 15-gallon can and on the open end attached a wooden frame that enclosed a sliding trapdoor. I put pieces of raw chicken liver in the far end of the can — this is a fine thing to do with chicken liver — and I strung a trip rope to the house. After dark — I have never seen such darkness — I saw what I thought was my neighbor's cat sneak into the trap and instinctively jerked the rope. In my robe and slippers I went to dislodge the cat and to give it a kick, whereupon it flicked its tail and ejected, in an arc of 180 degrees, a secretion at me so potent, I nearly died.

My robe and slippers are buried beneath the tulips over there, and skunks are playing tiddlywinks with the lids of my garbage cans, but me, I'm keeping my nose out of it.

a metaphor for life

MARCH 14

Georgie is very like me. He is a trout fishing kind of person. And like me, he is also a walleye fishing kind of person, and northern pike, and bass and crappie and bluegill and bullhead, but that's where the similarity ends.

One day he's fishing; his line tightens, and a lump in his throat grows hard as it always does in a situation like that. He's got a fish on. This fish is doing a fine job of resisting arrest, but it doesn't feel quite like a trout, or a walleye or a bass, though pretty close. When he gets it up to where he can see it, he lets out a string of cuss words. "Gosh darn stinking fish," he says. "It ain't nothing but a stinking sucker."

What Georgie doesn't realize is that some people go fishing for suckers and mean it, especially in the spring. And when they catch on to a few, they often soak them in brine and smoke them. There is nothing quite so good as a slab of smoked sucker alongside a cool brew and three aces. Some people go a bit fancier. They take about a pound of the smoked fish and flake it up good. Then they chop it very fine and mince two tablespoons each of onions, celery, fresh parsley and sweet pickle and one clove of garlic. They add one tablespoon of prepared mustard and a fourth tablespoon of Worcestershire sauce. They mix this up with a cup and a quarter of mayonnaise, put it in the fridge for a bit and then spread it on crackers or dip potato chips in it.

I let Georgie try this a couple of times, and he overcame his fundamental intolerance of suckers, and he finds himself doing what so many do, which is to go fishing for suckers on purpose, and like it.

historically speaking

MARCH 15

Ours is a government of the people and by the people and if we aren't able to speak out about what we believe in, somebody else will, and then we're sunk. That's why we've written into Lost Lake's Fish and Game Club bylaws that every once in a while one of the kids has to give an oral report on something important. At the last meeting, eleven-year-old Dusty drew the short straw, and he was stuck. Unable to think of a topic by himself, he naturally came to my house for help.

It just so happened, I'd been going through my camping stuff when he came. I've always had the problem of taking too much on my camping trips. I can never judge how much is enough and how much is too much. When I sleep out where coyotes howl at the edge of smoky fires and rain drizzles on my sagging tent, I want to go as light as possible, yet I need to go as right as possible, too, but I can never find that middle ground. So I handed the boy an encyclopedia.

"Speak to us," I told him, "about how much camping stuff to take along and how much not to." And he did, at tonight's meeting, and it went something like this.

"One day Julius Caesar was planning a campout. He took a look at what he had and saw that too much was too much, and it was taking the sparkle out of his life. So, he heaped his gear into three heaps. In Heap 1 was what he used and needed all the time. In Heap 2 was what he used occasionally, and in Heap 3 was what he never used at all. What was in the first pile he packed. What was in the iffy pile he put away to see if he would miss it. With everything in the third pile, he had a rummage sale. He was so pleased he said, 'I came, I saw, I conquered,' though in a foreign language. The problem was that some of the third pile belonged to his buddy Brutus who did not like his stuff being sold without his say-so, and said so on the Ides of March some years ago."

rising to the occasion

MARCH 16

It was dawn. The sun was rising with the living, shimmering colors of an oil slick on the water, and I was on my way to Inspiration Point to fish for trout. A tree had blown across the trail and I had this terrific idea, "Look Before You Leap," which makes a lot of sense if you are a trout fisherman, which I am, and I'll tell you why.

Usually, when I get to the river, I am pulling on my waders as my pickup truck is rolling to a stop. As I am shutting off the ignition with my right hand, with my left I am zipping my fishing vest and clamping on my cap. Before the engine has fully sputtered into silence, I am grabbing my rod and racing to the water, false casting as I go, so that by the time I am at the water's edge my Elk Hair Caddis is dropping thirty yards up and across. But no more.

Thanks to that log lying in my path, from now on when I go fishing I will actually catch fish. I will go calmly. I will show restraint. I will, as all good trout fishermen do, approach the water shadow softly. Then I will sit there unseen for quite awhile. I will study the water. I will notice whether it be high or low, roiled or clear. I will note the position of the sun, if any, and the direction of the wind. If no fish are rising, I will put on my polarized sunglasses and look into the depths for them. I will focus my attention and my patience, watching for mayflies and terrestrials and nymphs and caddisflies.

Then, serenely satisfied with what I have seen, and only then, will I rise and enter the water. Thus armed with the knowledge of my reconnaissance, I will catch me a trout as big as a moose.

naked majesty

MARCH 17

One night I went down to the cellar for an old jug of elderberry wine to calm my nerves. Actually, only the jug was old. The elderberry inside it was as new as last October. As soon as I popped the cork, Robert Burns showed up. I was surprised. I'd been expecting Walt Whitman. We had a so-so conversation, the gist of which was, *O wad some Pow'r the giftie gie us to see oursels as ithers see us,* but you've already guessed that, and you know how true it is, especially if you're talking about bowhunters.

If you look, for instance, into the souls of bowhunters, you see people with the patience of oak trees, people who sit still longer than fence posts. You see humility, too; braggarts find much easier ways to fill their needs. If you look into the souls of bowhunters, you see streams, rivers and mountains wet with dew where magical things happen. You see secret somethings nobody else understands. You see people who walk softly, who've been kissed by the sweetness of living, and whose great loves are the creatures, great and small, cuddled in the complimentary arms of a moaning, roving world. If you look into the souls of bowhunters, you see eagles. Though bowhunters stand on solid ground, their hearts fly with eagles. You see people who understand the wild voices of the woods, who glory in the glory that they see, and who are as faithful to themselves as can be.

Look and you see people who would trade, in a New York minute, the doubtful benefits of progress and the spreading wings of commerce for bankrolled dreams of hopes and maybes. Look in the mirror, and you see grand and glorious moments right before your eyes. Then Robert Burns mumbled something about *auld lang syne* and needing another *cup o' kindness*, but I won't go into that now.

pregnant moments and progress

MARCH 18

In the inflated market of March, miracles are a dime a dozen. Just look around. The winter-sameness of nuthatches is going, going, gone, and the differences between the sexes are becoming wonderfully obvious. This is, as you can imagine, a very important springtime development in the lives of nuthatches. And in a slow, deliberate tick-tocking down of the March clock, way down at the root of things, the sap in sugar maple trees is headed on up to the top of the world.

Skunks are out, smelling up the place and making the dogs nervous. And, if you can find them, trumpeter swans are trumpeting, and mourning doves are coo-cooing, and robins' songs are breaking up what snowbanks are left. And the particular marvel of the Big Dipper, the Great Bear, has swung to the east on a journey that will take it straight up overhead by the middle of summer. And that's not all. The white winter hair is falling off the backs of ermines, and the browner stuff of summer is reappearing on the hindmost parts of weasels. Is there more? You bet there is.

Have you noticed the renewed ooomph of the sun? The bloom-willingness of pussy willows? The abracadabra of red-winged blackbirds staking out homesteads in cattail forests? Have you heard with your own ears the chattering of brooks, flood-planning, licking at the ice on their banks, lunching on stream-fattening ice where there is any? Have you ever in your life heard popsicle-frozen frogs thawing out and croaking? It's almost supernatural. Baby otters are born. Wood ducks are back. Salamanders are moving from wherever they spent the winter to wherever they'll spend the summer. And the needle's gone from the haystack, the skeleton's come out of the closet and the fly's flown the ointment, if you know what I mean.

striving for immortality

MARCH 19

Saint Patrick, that wearin' of the green Irishman, cast snakes out of Ireland. Saint Urho, that Finn, vanquished grasshoppers, except a couple dozen for bait. I love those guys, and I wish there were some awful somethings, some vile somethings, for me to trounce. Maybe you are thinking that I am thinking too big. Maybe you are thinking that I am a weenie or too old for this. Maybe you should keep your nose out of it.

Wood ticks. I've been thinking of wood ticks. Wood ticks are not snakes, nor are they grasshoppers, but if I eliminate wood ticks from stream banks and riversides, fishermen will go to taverns and drink beer, food-colored with my special color, a nice magenta.

No, not wood ticks. Mosquitoes. It would be better to have at it with mosquitoes. Mosquitoes are not snakes either, nor, of course, are they grasshoppers, but they are troublesome nonetheless. If I eradicate them, from dawn's early light to the twilight's last gleaming, think of the parties people will throw on my birthday, October 24.

Dandelions, when I think about it, though not wood ticks nor mosquitoes, are easier to catch. Stomping out dandelions, nipping them in the bud — I find I am being consumed with a vision of manifest destiny — frees up fishermen to fish more frequently and hunters to hunt when seasons open like sweet promises.

On the other hand there are fleas, mites, crabgrass and boll weevils, too, which seems like too much work for one fellow. And those of you who know Saint Patrick know that I am no Saint Patrick, nor am I a Saint Urho, and Saint Jerry sounds left-handed and lumpish, and the crappies are biting on Whatchamacallit Bay. Maybe tomorrow.

the sunny side of paradise

MARCH 20

I know you, you have all the luck. Your soul's where it's always been, but your heart's staggering around somewhere between a hot flash and a four-pound walleye when the alarm clock goes off at six. You bend one eye open; a sunbeam slips in and points a finger at you. It curls upward, beckoning. Inasmuch as this is what you've been waiting for, you get up, pull your pants on, hunt down a pair of socks, step out the door and sniff the wind. As you hoped it would, it smells of mint and wild onions. You check the sky for clouds that flow like rivers. Satisfied, you turn up your collar, square your hind end on the worn seats of your pickup truck and go.

It's not quite the season of ferns nor of wildflowers nor butterflies, but you drive through the dark music of potholes and pine trees — it's a mildly established habit with you — to a cove on the north corner of your lake. In the water there is the fishy cover of sunken brush and fallen timbers. There is an inflowing of water there, too, though not much, and a gravelly bottom, sort of. It's this cove on the north corner of your lake that absentmindedly loses its ice before the rest of the lake does, and that's where you go when the air smells of mint and wild onions, and a beckoning sunbeam warms the water to fifty-something degrees.

A bundle of nerves, you wind four-pound monofilament line to your ultralight outfit. You tie on a number eight hook, and above it pinch a split shot, and well above that a pencil-type bobber that eagerly transmits to you any monkey business going on down there in the water. To the hook you apply a two-inch shiner minnow just ahead of its dorsal fin. You experiment with the depth until you get it right. Then you cast for crappies, and more than I can tell you, I envy you your good fortune.

the golden age

MARCH 21

A thought drifted into the harbor of my mind, tied itself up there and wouldn't go away. It was that life is nothing more than a collection of memories. That's not a deep thought, but for me it's not bad. I don't know where it came from, but it made me edgy. Up to now I haven't accomplished much. The album of my life is nothing but a scribbled pad, a little book of scraps. That's not much of a life.

Then, spring sprung. I wiped the cobwebs from my glasses and raised the shades on my kitchen window for a look-see. "Aha," I said, "So it has." The river that runs by my house was getting fat with the juices of melting snow. That made me feel much better. My river and all the rivers around here will now be warming with the persistence of spring, and steelheads, which have been wintering in the waters of the Great Lakes, dreaming dreams of green, will get the itch that eventually will bring them upstream to spawning beds, and me.

Though the leaves of trees are as yet only budding fantasies, it's the steelheads' turn to spawn. They'll have no choice but to leave the Great Lakes and make pilgrimages upstream to do it.

I looked again. The ice in the river was breaking up into chunks. The chunks will shoot downstream like rudderless canoes gone mad; the fish will hold off and off. They'll stack up until the signal comes, the stage is set and the curtain rises. Then they'll move. Slowly, slowly at first, then more and more-so toward the watery, higher-up breeding grounds to me and to men and women eager to fill their creels with memories enough for a lifetime, maybe five lifetimes, maybe more.

you and me, kid

MARCH 22

It's a smooth sound — somewhere between a fluttering buzz and a soft whine, a fluttering buzz and a soft whine — this sound of kids sleeping in a tent. Eagles are riding on currents of air. Big old pine trees are rock-and-rolling it in the breeze, and your kids are sleeping in a tent. With you. You are camping, canoe-country camping with your kids, because canoe camping with kids has it all.

When you hand a kid or two a paddle or two, you hand them a dream, and their lives will never be the same. And yours won't either, because this isn't the canoe camping of your kidless days. For this to work, you bet your rain fly you've got some adjusting to do. Gone are the days of going at the drop of a whim. Here are the days of careful, careful planning. Gone are the days of hop-skipping over long portages. Here are the days of rock-skipping, of stopping to catch a frog. These are days of family building, of good-kid building. These are days of the zump-zump-zump of canoes scraping over water-wet rocks. And back-slapping loons' calls. And wrinkled clothes. And walking paths leading to wide-eyed wonders. And smells of campfire-cooking bacon and round tin bowls of oatmeal. And smoke in your eyes. And the radiator rattle of popcorn popping. And crickets twanging banjos to the tune of sighing moons. And goofing off. And laughing. Laughing. There's nothing sweeter.

If you don't do it now, it'll be too late, and in the late afternoons of your life, you'll find yourself sitting in a rocking chair, looking through the crimson shadows of your past, surrounded by loneliness, wondering where the time has gone.

the abcs of trout fishing

MARCH 23

One of the greatest abilities a person can have is the ability to be a good teacher. At least the English teacher over at the high school thinks so. But these days he's having trouble keeping his mind on business. He's had Saturday morning running through his head ever since last Sunday night, when he took his heart off the riffles of his favorite trout stream and traveled the long and winding road back to the hard-core here and now. But time was, time is and time will be, and the teacher's time comes again with the tolling of the last bell on Friday afternoon, when he rushes again to the river in his rusty pickup truck that lists a couple of points to starboard.

The English teacher isn't exactly the Ernest Hemingway of fishermen, but he is committed to the sporting life. Now, however, as luck would have it, he isn't having any. After a couple of hours he's sort of licking his wounds, when he looks up to see somebody looking down at him. It's a boy from the high school, a boy who never allows his attendance at school to interfere with his fishing. Or his hunting. Or his camping. Consequently, the relationship between them is somewhat strained, to put it mildly. 4-F, to put it precisely.

"You gotta learn how to read the water," the kid says. "The water right along shore here runs slower. Where the slow water along the bank meets the faster water out about a foot, that's where an eddy forms, and along that line is where trout like to lie in the still water and sneak out into the currents to catch food drifting by."

Then the kid, who had said more in that breath than he had in the two years as the teacher's sometime student, neatly drops a nymph on the money and proves his point, which just goes to show you, though what I'm not sure.

getting in shape

MARCH 24

We liked winter well enough — the coldness and the whiteness of it. We liked the fishing on its hardness and the skiing on its softness. We liked the glidings and the slidings of winter. We liked the snuggling opportunities. But enough got to be enough, and winter became a weather-beaten thing, and our soul hammered like a fist against the wall to get out of it.

Then, like a donkey on fire, came the explosion of spring and, like pitchers getting catcher-signs from everywhere, we are into spring training. We are laying out old tires on the lawn or on golf courses if that's all we've got. We're backing off a ways and casting fly rods and spinning outfits into them until we hit them dead center every once in awhile. We are devising methods of building the upper body strength we need to row our fishing boats when the motors, like black metaphors, go kaputski and to hoist canoes onto pickup trucks with ease.

With bows, rifles and shotguns, we are shooting at lifelike targets until we hit them where we have to from here and from over there, sitting, standing, kneeling and belly-flat. We are practice-jumping as best we can over mud puddles to aid us in upcoming stream crossings. (Just kidding.)

We are developing stalking and sitting-quiet skills and improving slinking abilities by arming ourselves with cameras and going hunting with them. Since it is spring, you will note (heh-heh-heh) that none of this is taking place indoors. At least it doesn't here at Lost Lake where I live, and I suppose it doesn't where you live, either.

harmonious developments

MARCH 25

The collective experiences of my past have enabled me to become a more effective human being. Only this morning, as I scratched at the itch of March, I took a map and wrapped some about me like a church-going aftershave. With the index finger of remembering, I traced the red lines of highways over to the blue lines of roads and up to the pothole-dotted trails that lead to the river from which I often launch camping attacks.

I've been waiting and waiting for enough of a spring to come that would let me ride that river down to where I can lay my head in a tent, where I can listen to the racket of angels' wings in pine trees, where I can read by lantern light, where I can trigger attitudinal changes in my winter-weary kids by making them make cookies where the extension cords of life have fallen a couple hundred miles short. Yes, cookies. Kids need to be needed, no less when they're camping, and they always need cookies.

These are cookies they can make by themselves while I cast about for supper. I'll have two sticks of butter in a plastic bag, but my responsibilities end there. To that bag the kids will add half a cup of powdered sugar, two cups of flour and half a teaspoon of baking powder and salt. The kid not worm fishing will get in there and mix it into a smoothish dough with her hands while others pull up the canoe and roll it over. On the bottom they'll form big cookies and put them on a cookie sheet leaned sharply toward hot coals. They'll umbrella tinfoil over it to reflect their own beauty and the heat on the cookies. When they reach a straw color, they're done (the cookies).

Experience has taught me that as with any camp recipe, the kids will need to experiment with this one at home before they try it in the bush, though how they'll get the canoe into the kitchen, I have no idea.

of rivers and things

MARCH 26

The greatest right of a free people is the right to make fools of themselves. That is why there are rivers like the one not far from here. You can't go to it without thinking of woodsmoke and quite places. This river sings. Its songs are sung in the riffles and runs. It dances over stones buried there. It's where you go when you've nothing to lose and you've lost it anyway. The river lets you forget to be ashamed when you have need of that. At the long table of this river, you can curse your enemies without being afraid; you can curse fate, if you must. You can sing your songs of sorrow. You can gossip with the ghosts of lovers. Sitting on the banks of this river, in the lush stillness of this river, you can remember false midnights, the dingy light of false midnights. Of cold fires. Of lean and hungry springs. Of going crazy.

This is a river with the wings of the Milky Way, a river as intimate as the lights of the Milky Way, where the sky and the earth and the moon and the clouds and the sun and the trees and a million wildflowers speak in the one voice that is you. It is a river where you see yourself or your reflection, and you know you must take the utmost care of things. And you breathe in, knowing this is what you are made of.

This is a river you go to when maybe you did and maybe you didn't (You open your eyes wide at that, for you see the possibilities). I once knew a young man; his shoulders were broad, his cheeks ruddy, his hair fair and long. His body spoke of strength, and good nature shone from his eyes and lurked about the corners of his mouth. His heart was good. Today he goes to this river, this river with time on its hands, when it gets so bad he can't stand it anymore, for he has songs of his own to sing, and because it smells of wind and woodsmoke and quiet places.

discretionary penance

MARCH 27

We're smack dab in the middle of Lent, a time when we ordinarily do without and don't mind a little inconvenience here and there. But we've been suffering from a particularly acute strain of cabin fever, so we flirted with hypothermia this morning and went crappie fishing. It was nice. Then we made our way back to Mom's Cafe over on Main Street for coffee. We had a piece of hot apple pie, too, fresh from the oven. We take our apple pie with a slab of cheese because Mom doesn't let you have his apple pie unless there's cheese on it. All the food's pretty basic here.

We had fished the little bays that were free of ice, and we had the lake mostly to ourselves, which was the topic of our conversation. We were not comprehending why more people weren't cashing in on this crappie bonanza. At this time of year, when it's immoral and illegal to fish for so many fish, action-needy anglers need look no farther than the nearest lake to satisfy the need for good fishing, good crappie fishing, Lent or no Lent, as long as you don't overdo it or enjoy it too much.

Crappies are usually open-water fish, but once ice-out happens, they move into the shallows that warm up the earliest, say into the mid-forties, mostly along the north shores. There it is that crappies come to feed and gather strength for the soon-to-be spawning season. As the sun warms the water during the day, afternoons are often the best times to fish, and in the covers of fallen trees, reeds and submerged brush are the best places. Crappies are hungry now, but in this shallow water, we take special care to be quiet, and with their paper mouths, we're careful to set the hook not with a jerk, but with a sweeping motion. Then we spent a couple of hours wondering why croppie is spelled crappie, but came to no conclusion whatsoever.

masterful strategies

MARCH 28

Here at Lost Lake, it's almost time to shed the mackinaws, mufflers, sweaters, wool overshirts, undershirts and long underwear; the wool pants, overalls, sweatpants and blue jeans; the arctic socks, heavy wool socks, light wool socks and cotton socks, and get down to the basics. It's also time to get our tackle boxes in order. We'd rather be bullhead fishing or frog hunting, but it's too early for that, so we'll have to get our tackle boxes in order. I say have to because it's not an altogether pleasant business. You open the box, and you're faced with those empty bins and jaded, faded and twisted pieces of junk that constitute your fishing tackle.

Money isn't everything as long as you've got dough, but you weigh the pennies in your pocket against the price of two-by-fours, and milk money for the kids, and new sneakers, and you find yourself wedged between half a dozen hard places. The earth is spinning on its eternal rounds and you find yourself wedged tightly between half a dozen hard places or more.

You decide maybe it's time to make your own fishing tackle to save some money. If you're the cautious type, like me, you'll want this metamorphosis to go okay, so you'll start simply, with jigs. First, you'll get a few pre-painted jig heads and some hair, feather and plastic skirts and assemble them into fabulous fish-catching machines. Then you'll probably take the daring step of buying unpainted heads and painting them yourself. Then, in a move not short of heroic, you'll get your own molds, and on and on. Before you know it, you'll be a fisherman with a tackle box fulfilled, a Rockefeller of a fisherman, a J. Paul Getty, a Donald Trump of a fisherman — and which of us presumes to hope for anything more?

upping the ante

MARCH 29

If there's one thing I've learned in this life, besides "He who hesitates loses his parking place," it's "Knowledge is Power." I have further learned that with the possible exceptions of hunting and five card draw, limit three, nothing wild, in no other thing in this world is knowledge so directly equated with power as it is in fishing.

Take my Uncle Jake. I don't want to beat this steelheading thing over the head, but as rivers and streams feeding into the Great Lakes warm up somewhat and relax their somersaulting mode somewhat and settle into a more meandering state of mind, steelhead, heretofore impatiently waiting for such a sweet situation to occur, begin to do-si-do up into the flats in preparation for a mad crapshoot of a spawning run that will carry them jolting up to more pregnant waters. Uncle Jake takes his knowledge of this and his waders and sets a course for the river. Earlier, when the water was higher, cloudier and more troubled, Jake used a three-way swivel and a dropper rig with a fairly weighty bell sinker to hold the bait in more-or-less one place. Now, he keeps the swivel, but he replaces the sinker with a string of split shot, adding or subtracting shot to regulate the speed and depth of the bait, which in Jake's case is now a spawn bag. He wants to keep that dropper just tick-ticking the bottom.

From where he stands in the water, he casts across and up, taking in slack as the rig settles. Any hesitation on the part of that spawn bag on its downhill run is a signal to set the hook, bringing the kind of expression to Jake's face that he gets when he's betting on a pair of twos, and the bluff appears to be working.

a legend in his own time

MARCH 30

I am reading a book of pests, of mosquitoes and how you can avoid them somewhat by choosing campsites removed from swampy ground and stagnant pools. How you should set up on a site where steady breezes blow mosquitoes on over to campers camped near swampy ground and stagnant pools, if you can find a place like that.

I am reading of the inconvenience of deerflies, midges and no-see-ums, of wood ticks and the need for vigilance in keeping them at arm's length. I am reading of chiggers, the six-legged blood suckers. I am reading of spiders — black widows, brown recluses and tarantulas — all not so bad according to this book, but bad enough to me. I am reading of scorpions, ants and snakes, of poisons ivy, oak and sumac, but nowhere in this book am I reading about my second cousin Howie, a flyfishing purist.

Like most flyfishing purists, Howie drinks scotch and martinis with little or no vermouth. He detests worms, spinners, spoons and those who use them. He resents aquatic insects because they are imperfectly tied, inexact imitations of themselves. He is convinced he is Chosen. He is secretive. Unsharing. Above all, he is preoccupied with tippets, water temperatures, double hauls, leader straighteners and hatches. All kinds of hatches. If he catches a fish, he releases it, even if it is a trophy. He insists everyone else do likewise, even those who have not caught a trout in a while and need a little taste now and then.

When we die, he and I, says he, people will come to the graveyard and say, "Who the devil was Jerry Wilber?" But they will point to his stone and say, "There's Howie, a flyfishing purist. Ain't it grand?" So beware, my outdoor friends, of mosquitoes, ticks, chiggers, spiders, poison ivy, skunks, and my second cousin Howie. He's a germ.

# of bangs and whimpers

MARCH 31

At what age, I wonder, do old people stop sleeping on the ground in a tent at night? At what age do they stop dreaming of hillsides where the earth rolls on and on and on with trees and stones and winding streams?

At what point in the lives of old people do the steel bars of their age keep them from rivers whose waves are white-winged eagles that fade into the light of the sky? When do they become deaf to the songs of moons as yellow as butterflies' wings? When do they cease to need the sun and thundering grouse? When does the honest hope of campfire smoke fail to move them? When do they no longer look out an open window at the Great Bear, climb upon its back and ride it into gray clouds? When do they quit struggling to free themselves from the glue of the earth to run and dance in cornfields where pheasants roam, to go where the wind riffles and dimples lakes?

Though gold remains gold even after it's broken, when does the strength of old people shatter? When do they no longer challenge the truth of a river? When do they give up swimming against the current in waters swift and cold and clear, always changing and always fresh, where they chased each other full of sparkle and stars and flashing laughter? When do their eyes dim to the piercing strength of green valleys and to snow-topped mountains under winter stars, and to the rustle of oak leaves pieced together in long bridges? When do they grow numb to the sky-blue kisses and deaf to the whispers of holy April days? When is the problem of choices taken from them? At what age do they give up on their souls and fall like feathers? And bound to them by the same sacred blood, at what age, I wonder, must I?

MACIEJ

solid as a rock

APRIL 1

Last night a flock of frogs flew over, honking in the way of frogs on the lookout for open water. Some crickets came into the pond, too, and this morning woke us with their splashing and quacking. We wouldn't have minded if a pussy willow hadn't wandered in around midnight with an armful of firewood and a six-pack and kept us up with its chirping. We got hardly any sleep. June bugs howled at the moon. Ants yip-yipped to the twang of Orion's bowstring, which is nothing to get excited about.

Truthfully, April doesn't affect me like it does some people. I can take it or leave it, unlike my brother. He's a merganser. Ask him to supper, and he shows up at lunchtime. He's always early. Yesterday we got his Christmas card in the mail and my birthday present two years in advance. He's got his trick-or-treating done through 2001. Mergansers are like that. Especially in the spring, they're hurry-up birds. They're here already doing startling exposes for the newspaper. But I don't go in for stuff like that. Do you? However, you can't argue with a merganser on April Fools' Day.

I went trout fishing and heard a voice coming out of a Gothic twilight rich in the elements of April. It said, "You will find what you seek with long leaders and drag-free lines." I've got an ear for things like that, and April hasn't got a thing to do with it.

I said good morning to a fisherman next to me. "Good morning!" she said. "Is that all you can say about the first day of April?" Then she poured a cup of guerrilla coffee and pounced on the opportunity to inform me that April was something out of Heaven, living gold spun with sunlight, marsh marigolds drinking up the moonlight, whimsical vistas of green and stuff like that which is far beyond anything I would have thought of, but then, as I said, April doesn't affect me, doesn't affect me, doesn't affect me like it does some people.

a world apart

APRIL 2

For some people, fishing is everything. Fishing is life. But not for me. For me, fishing is relaxation, an island of peace in a headless world gone mad. For me, fishing is tranquility in a universe grinding its gears. It's a period in a rambling paragraph going nowhere. I mention this so you'll understand why I fish with less, let us say, intensity than I would if I were defending myself in a sword fight to the death, with less vigor than I would if I were trysting in the cool gloom of the Northwoods, with less zeal than I would escape a burning building. But not my Uncle Jake.

"Look at it this way," says he one day last spring, as if he's talking to a little kid, because I'm having a little trouble in the walleye-catching department and don't seem too nervous about it. "To be a walleye fisherman," he says, "you've got to be a jiggin' fisherman, and you've got to have good jigs, none of that cheapo stuff. You've got to let the rod be like it's a part of your arm. And since there aren't many weeds yet, and the fish aren't too deep yet, we're going to cast because we cover a lot of water that way. And when you're bringing in the jig, point your rod tip directly at it, so you can watch the line real close for any twitching. And when you're bringing it in, move the tip from a nine- to an eleven-o'clock position and back so you're bouncing the jig a couple of inches off the bottom, and when you get it under the boat, stop and hop it a little in case a fish followed it in and can't decide if it's worth the trouble to bite it. Now, have you got all that?"

"Well, Uncle," says I, trying to tune in a ball game on my transistor radio, "I got it all up to where you said something about jigs." And that's when he uncorks his medicine jug and takes a long drag off it.

See what I mean?

small fry constellations

APRIL 3

I have taken kids fishing — my own and other peoples' — many times, and I believe the philosophy of it to be a sound one, but now it's their turn to take me. It won't be easy, this kid-fishing, I know that. I vaguely remember the tic-tac-toe business with sticks in the sand, and how to follow a wave out and race the next one in, but it's been a long time since I've built a castle in the sand. If they go at it remedially, maybe I can get the hang of it again. It's a prerequisite for kid-fishing trips. I've never been good at skipping stones — three, four at the max. That will take longer. I'm nervous about stripping down, cannonballing off suicide leap and yelling "Geronimoooo!" My voice cracks at the thought of it, which is good.

I can roast marshmallows. I can handle that. I'll have a problem, though, with the lighting logs without kindling part, and the part where you bang two rocks together for sparks to ignite soggy sawdust hacked up with smuggled-out hatchets. We're not allowed to use matches yet. It'll be hard for me to choose up sides and scramble up and down the shoreline blasting each other with cap guns, but this is, after all, a fishing trip. They'll make me be the bad guy. I hate that.

I might be okay at mumbletypeg. My jackknife's dull enough. I'll beat most of them at arm wrestling, I hope, but I'll lose at holding my breath under water. If my slingshot holds together, I'll get my share of frogs. Is it paper covers rock? Rock breaks scissors? Yet, like them, I'll probably be reluctant to call it quits when Mother's voice goes hoarse from calling us in to supper, and Dad, who knows something about getting us home on time, comes looking.

A person can do worse, I suppose, than go fishing with kids.

shining headlights

APRIL 4

Where there once were few or no signs of life, there are now full-throated robins claiming territorial rights, getting very serious about this when the average twenty-four-hour temperature gets to be thirty-five degrees. They think they own the world, and basically they get away with it, since they're such enormous piles of raw material.

Where we once carried the remains of winter wrapped in brown paper bags, we now nearly die of excitement because the business of April is booming. Dandelions are marshalling the strength to march over fields and lawns and back and forth. Chipmunks, recently marooned under oceans of ice, are stuffing themselves with sunflower seeds spilt from bird feeders. Stocky, secretive, Wilson's snipe are settling in on marsh and bog breeding grounds. Time-lapse tulips are filling in the shallow graves of our recent past. Rivers of migrating ducks and geese are reaching the high-water mark.

The birth of beaver kits? It's happening now. Hepatica is blooming on rocky hillsides. It's a nice flower and a heck of a word. Gardeners are flocking to stores sprouting the wonderful tools of the gardening trade. Bobwhite quail are calling the sweetest calls ever called. Persistent peepers have been frosted into silence a couple of times and snowed on more than once, but they've finally broken the back of winter with wild celebrations. Aspen, popple and alders are full of bee-beckoning pollen. Belted kingfishers are calling with loud, rattling calls. The mating dance of woodcocks is in full swing. And Castor and Pollux are two of the brightest stars in the night sky, and so on and so forth. Not every month can accomplish all this, but by God, April does. At least it does here at Lost Lake, so I suppose it does where you live too.

a little knowledge is a dangerous thing

APRIL 5

I'm reading a book: *The Compleat Canoer*, but it's a disappointment. It's incompleat. "The portaging procedure," it says, "is a piece of cake. Turn the interior of the canoe away from you, bend over and grab the center thwart as low as possible. Simultaneously thrust your knees against the bottom and pull on the center thwart as if to throw it over your shoulder. If the action is perfectly coordinated, the canoe will fly up to your head and settle on your shoulders."

Ha! Nowhere does it tell you to position a doctor at each end of the portage, especially when your canoe is an older model, as mine is, made of scrapped World War II battleships and weighing two thousand pounds. Nor does it mention that to "bend over" is dangerous for portagers who can only do this ten degrees windward. To "grab the center thwart as low as possible," they must get to their knees, which causes grass stains on their pant legs as they make their way across the portage in that position. Those able to "grab the center thwart as low as possible" from a standing position are faced with the need to "simultaneously thrust their knees against the bottom." Such simultaneous thrusting of the knees can cause you to become momentarily airborne and end up with the canoe in your lap. "The action must be perfectly coordinated" is a term of unknown origin and one I am unfamiliar with. "The canoe will fly up to your head." As it does this, it will remove your head from the main trunk of your body.

Nowhere is it written, either, or implied, that once the canoe is "settled down on your shoulders," black flies and mosquitoes crawl up your nose and into your ears, and that with your head stuck into the bottom of your canoe, you cannot see where you are going. None of this is meant to discourage you; but, the written word being what it is, writers should strive for the highest degree of accuracy, as I do.

i quit

APRIL 6

I'm not going to reach the end of my life with nothing to show for the experience but whiskers; consequently, I've decided to become a bump on a log, and that's about it. I'm going to nip the stress of my life in the thorax, tension in the bud. I'm going to calm the ripples on the surface of my existence by simplifying my life, by denying myself all but the barest of essentials — oatmeal cookies, popcorn and beer. I'll strip my tackle box to its naked fundamentals. Angleworms and leeches. When I write a letter, if I do, I'll sign it anonymous, unless it's asking for specific fishing information. My garden must grow its own weeds.

I'm going to stop living life on the edge of loss, which flags my energy and taxes my nervous system. I'm tired. Except when trout rise to mayflies, I'll subside into a slow-moving orbit. I'll have no opinions on anything except migrating strings of geese. I won't make a single impression — good or bad — on anyone at any time, except when I see an eagle, I might say, "Look at that!" The only seasons that affect me will be hunting and fishing. The only questions I'll answer will be theoretical ones like, "Do you want another cookie?" and "Who's got the bug dope?"

Each day of my life will be nothing not dictated by the solunar tables — and I mean that — with no arbitrary beginning and ending for no apparent reason. I'll spend hours and hours perched in maple trees in endless, aimless service to my soul. If I have to express myself, it will be in italics. This is a reckless course of action, but rather than passively await the gradual approach of my disintegration, I'm going to meet it head-on. I'll be starting this a week from tomorrow (what's an April for anyway?) or the week after that, and when I do, there will be no stopping me, so thank you very much, good-by.

literary obscurity

APRIL 7

I'm trout fishing in a little stream not far from here, but hard to find, and what good does it do me? I'm up to my eyeballs in lousy, cloudy, foggy, rainy, basically miserable weather. This makes me feel a little tired and hungry, so I scrunch under a neatly gnarled cedar tree to munch on a peanut butter and jelly sandwich and take a nap. I'm wishing I'd saved some coffee, and I'm dozing off when I get this idea to write a book on trout fishing. I'll start out by calling it *Ninety-nine Sure-Fire, Super-Duper Ways to Catch Trout*. A catchy title is seven-eighths of a best seller.

I'll begin by telling how to dap for trout, which is the fishing of a fly without the casting of it, not a new technique by any means, but one often overlooked by anglers in their haste to wade deep and cast long. I'll write about stalking within a rod's length of a trout without spooking it, usually by creeping on hands and knees in a very sly manner. I'll write about slowly extending the rod with three to nine feet of leader dangling from the tip, through camouflaging cover, and gently placing a fly on the nose of an unsuspecting fish. I'll include the information that any bankside trout can be dapped, but the procedure really comes into its own when a particularly super-duper fish hides out in dense tangles of brush or under overhanging branches, convinced no mortal human will deliver danger to its being in a place like that.

I'm beginning to get quite excited about it, too, but before I get to the other ninety-eight chapters, the clouds part, a ray of sunshine lights the water, and two trout rise to the surface, so I say the hell with it and go fishing.

see you later, alligator

APRIL 8

Though we've passed to the promised land of April, it's too early to know if this spring is going to come out easy or come out hard. It's the topic of our pow-wows when we gather at Mom's Cafe over on Main Street, as we do this morning. We're well into conjecture and second refills when in comes the Professor, acting mysterious and profound. When he's like this, he's been up to something, but we don't ask.

It only takes a couple of sips of coffee and half a doughnut before he clears the hurdle of silence when he says kind of casual-like as we know he will, "Sure had some fine fishin' this mornin'." He doesn't stop there. We know he won't. He says, "These late-snow runoffs and early spring rains that have turned our fishing waters a cream and coffee color have also apparently transformed outdoorsmen into indoorsmen" — meaning us — "because you have the mistaken notion fish don't bite under these conditions. But," he says with the condescending air so typical of him, "some fishermen fish no matter what."

He says fish see about as well in these muddy, off-colored times as people do in pea-soup fog. So, he says, he eschews live baits, relying instead on fishes' keen sense of hearing to find meals they can't see. He says he goes artificial and uses baits that give off the most vibrations and wiggles at barely moving speeds. He retrieves them, he says, very slowly, giving fish every opportunity to strike, which, when they do, is no gotcha, dramatic jolt, but a meaningful mouthing, as if the fish isn't quite sure this is going to taste as good as it sounds.

As he winds the story down, the Professor looks up from his coffee and doughnut to discover that for the last fifteen minutes, he's been addressing an empty table, since we, of course, have sneaked off and headed for the river to test the theory.

pangs of regret

APRIL 9

We've been holding out high hopes for April, but so far the month's been a dud, somewhat depending on who you are and your mental disposition. Mostly, we sit at the kitchen table, staring wistfully out the window, though sometimes we stop at Mom's Cafe over on Main Street. That usually makes us feel better. It did yesterday. That's when Mom announced he was closing down for opening day of turkey season. We said that was probably okay, since we'd be out there too.

"Well, be careful," he said. "and remember that turkeys see ten times better than we do and hear eight times as well." That put a little sparkle back in our souls, and it showed.

"That's for sure," said the Professor, coming to life and seizing the lead-in to display his incredible accumulation of knowledge. "Therefore, as you're going out to your blind, act like a turkey. Make like a hen in pursuit of her daily duties."

Even here at Lost Lake, competition is the spice of life, so my Uncle Jake, getting a feel for the conversation and not wanting to be outdone, jumped in. "Yes!" he said, "take three steps and stop, wait, take another and then three more." He demonstrated and did a fine job of it.

"You bet," said the English teacher, "and cluck and purr as you go along like a satisfied, untroubled feeding hen, and scratch in the leaves as she does.

"Right!" said Ramona, the dark-haired lady from across the lake. "And if you make a bad call, keep on calling, because none of those birds listen to the same tapes we do, and maybe they'll think we're okay if on the uneducated side."

"Enough," moaned the Professor, becoming a little unbuttoned because we'd stolen his thunder, "Let's get out there and do some scouting." Which we did. All except the English teacher who, under the thick veil of a metaphor, drifted sadly like a derelict back to the backwash of his classroom.

the beginning of a beautiful relationship

APRIL 10

It's April, four in the afternoon, maybe five. A cocky northern pike, smelling of stale beer and cigarette smoke, works a key from the front pocket of his blue jeans hanging low and tight. He fumbles at the lock and swaggers across the kitchen linoleum. A tired Joe, he scrambles half a dozen eggs, brushes his teeth, kicks off his shoes and hits the hay. It's ice-out time, and for northern pike every day's a Saturday night, all night. He needs his rest for the feeding frenzy ahead. He's a twelve-pounder, but that will change.

As the ice rots and weakens, and for the two or three weeks thereafter, northern pike of the male persuasion slick back their hair and hit the disco joints in weedy bays or dance halls with video screens that play nothing but country. They're looking for girls. In lakes they cruise to marshy places featuring jazz or bluegrass, or to karaoke dives in dead-water sloughs and creek-fed cattail ponds. They're looking for sweeties to make out with in the backseats of their convertibles. They listen to Bruce Springsteen on the radio, real loud. You've seen their souped-up wheels and how they cruise up and down Main Street raising hell. At the drive-in they eat enchiladas and make phone calls to breathtakingly beautiful females. They're no better, the females. Mascara'd meter maids. Secretaries. Social workers. School teachers. Looking for guys in honky-tonks, listening to heavy-breathing piano players, bleary-eyed banjo pickers.

Northerns lay their eggs, depending on latitude and weather conditions, from late March to mid-May, after which they lie suspended or near the bottom (when they've hit bottom) in three to fifteen feet of water to recuperate. Then they feed heavily, ravenously, to replace weight lost to carousing, which can be of interest to you fishermen moving urgently to music of your own.

a question of necessity

APRIL 11

The antlers of a deer hang on my dining room wall. A set of moose horns is nailed up above the fireplace, and the fan of a partridge tail decorates an otherwise grim corner of the woodshed. Though I have long ago eaten the last of the sausages, the last of the steaks, the last drumstick, the antlers, the horns and the feathers are still there. I need them to make me feel better when the grimy scraps of days make tatters of my life. I need them when my mind is a crumpled Sunday paper blowing around on a dead-end street. I touch them, and their strength becomes my strength.

They hang there both terrible and wonderful. When I touch them, it's spring again, full of hope and promise, and I'm sitting on a hilltop, smelling the woodsmoke of campfires. When night comes and it's time to be undone, they take me to a pool of shadows and the sound of running water where the deer, the moose, the partridge dipped their heads to drink, where they brushed the water's surface and spread ripples round and round. Or they take me to quiet places where their spirits dwell just before a rainstorm. Or to sunshine splashing off waist-high yellow prairie grasses, or atop a mountain littered with Indian paintbrushes, red and yellow.

In the face of sadness, they give off the smells of rivers and emit sounds of bullfrogs brooding in shallows. When I'm tried with temptation, they sing the songs of sunrise. When I'm lonesome, they shine like long rows of wild roses and give me eagles' wings.

More than gathering places for dust and arrogance, the antlers, horns and feathers put me at home with myself. They cause my heart to skip whenever I look at them, the way a loaf of new-baked bread does, cut into warm slices and buttered as thickly as the midsection of an April day.

gunboat diplomacy

APRIL 12

Deep in the woods we came across a wood tick, or it came across us. Perhaps we had wandered between it and its young, because once it caught our scent, it stood on its hind legs, sniffed the air and came right at us. We had to kill it, later estimating it to be five years old and 580 pounds, a fair-sized wood tick for these parts.

Most everybody around here has a grudging respect for the unpredictability, aggressiveness and tenacity of wood ticks, and any approach to one of them is made with utmost caution. When someone comes across a wood tick's tracks, he is likely to leave the area immediately, returning with a group of men to hunt it down. Then, if it is found, it can be killed with a volley of bullets. People emphasize that this is a very difficult insect to kill, that one person alone could shoot it many times and still be attacked. There are many stories about wounded wood ticks charging people, though most of them end without serious harm being done, as far as we know.

I cannot overstress the caution we exercise when wood ticks are involved. In the summer we nearly always carry rifles in case we meet one. If we find their tracks, we avoid moving upwind of them, lest the ticks begin stalking our scent. Even after we locate a wood tick, we all shoot it at once from a good distance. If we are successful, someone invariably says, "We got that one," underscoring his feeling that these are menacing creatures.

A few years ago, some teenagers were charged by an unprovoked wood tick, but they got away. Later, we picked up its sign and followed it to its natural conclusion. It was in very poor condition and had obviously been stalking them. When we come across a mean one in poor condition, it's often because it has been injured. For this reason, you should always do everything possible to track down any wood ticks you have wounded.

forty-foot wide and running deep

APRIL 13

It had been a long time since I'd ridden The River so, although it was April, I threw a saddle on my old canoe, the big and heavy one, the one made from scrapped battleships, and rode it. The River was doggone high. One look at it was enough to make my head spin and my innards weak. But this was my River, and I rode it anyway, though it was spitting like a wildcat, snorting like a balky mule. It was impudent, galloping as hard as can be, but it was my River, and it wasn't fake or phony. It was telling the truth, the whole truth.

It was fat and huffing like it had swallowed a double shot of something powerful or a twelve-pack of the other stuff. It was whistling like a train. It was singing off-key with a vengeance. It was laughing. It was snarling. It was dancing when it wasn't melancholy and vice versa. It was lightning when it wasn't thunder and the other way around. It was blasphemous. It was running with a spooky confidence. It was bawdy and lusty. Its sparks mingled with the timeless sparks of revolution. It was rough, it was mean, but it was honest. It had a grayish haze hanging over it like a hair spray halo. It was snuffling like an old cow bawling for her calf. It made me feel uneasy. It was sharp. It was cold, swift, sudden and wet. It was howling like hungry wolves under a full moon. It was waving its six-gun in the air like a drunken cowboy.

I tried to read that River. I tried to judge it by the whiskers on its chin to see if I could beat it, but it was tough. It was raw. It was an irate buffalo with a knot in its tail. It knew no fear and its fists were law. If I'd known all that — after all, it was my River — I'd have gotten myself more involved with the whole idea of sanity. That was last week. I'm feeling better now.

piscatorial delights

APRIL 14

The Elkhorn Tavern and Wildlife Museum isn't the social center that Mom's Cafe over on Main Street is, or the Post Office, but it runs a close fourth behind the Town Hall where the volunteer firemen meet every other Tuesday. The beauty of the place is that you can be yourself there, which doesn't help my situation.

I'd been there about an hour, thinking, when I interrupted a dart game to bring up the subject of sucker fishing. The season isn't open here for the real fishing, walleye fishing, but fishing for suckers gets you in the mood and helps keep the sucker population where it ought to be, which is low.

"Let's go," I said. "Phooey on you," everybody said, so I went back to minding my own business and concentrating on letting normal thoughts run through my head, when a redhorse sucker kicked the door in and made disparaging remarks about my character. I swung around, looked it in the eye and said, "So what?" It wore its gunbelt low and slightly forward like the fast ones do. Like I do. To make a long story short, I plugged it and was faced with the eternal problem of, doggonit, what do I do with a dead sucker? "That's sure a pickle you got yourself into," said Harold. "Good idea," said I and headed for the door.

At home I took three quarts of filleted sucker cut up in one-inch by two-inch pieces and put it in a plastic ice cream pail with half a cup of non-iodized salt and enough water to cover it. I refrigerated that for a day and a night, drained off the liquid, dissolved three cups sugar in one of white vinegar, heated it and cooled it. I added a cup of white port wine, two hefty sliced onions and half a cup of pickling spices. I brought it to a boil and cooled it again, put the fish and onions in alternate layers in jars, poured the solution in and stored it in the fridge. This tastes so good it's almost sinful, and like many things of a nearly sinful nature, you can have fun doing it.

i ask you

APRIL 15

I'm confused. It's the middle of April, the Opener's in the almost here and now, and I'm riding the horns of a dilemma, asking the question, seeking the answer: Did I choose fishing or did fishing choose me? Is it my fault, and mine alone, that soon I will fish day after day after day and some nights, too, while the millstone grinds on without me? Am I to blame for the dollars I cast aside in pursuit of fish instead of storing them away for an undisclosed and bothersome old age? Or am I but a poor pawn, an unwitting victim of fate and circumstance? It's a good question, a fair question, in the middle of April with the Opener in the almost here and now.

If the answer to the former (did I choose fishing?) lies in the affirmative, that's one thing. If it lies in the latter, however (did fishing choose me?), that's something else again. It's a baffler, and I'm plagued by cutworms of doubt. The boss is interested in the answer, as is my wife, so I can't puff myself up and say, "God made me and God made the world," and let it go at that. It doesn't get me off the hook. If I look to my heart and let my head take care of itself, I lean one way, and if I look to my head and say horsefeathers to my heart, I still lean one way. If these were the olden days, without telephones and automobiles, and trains ran slow and mail came once a week, I'd have time to look for the answer in the stars, but I'm living in the here and now, and the Opener is days away.

What came first, the chicken or the egg? Can God make a rock so big He can't lift it? How many angels fit on the head of a pin? To be or not to be? And, hell's bells, did I choose fishing or did fishing choose me? It's a Humpty Dumpty of a question, an absolute Humpty Dumpty of a question.

mean affairs

APRIL 16

I wish my Uncle Jake wouldn't take everything so personal. Like this morning, we were having coffee at Mom's Cafe over on Main Street, and he was reading the morning paper. All of a sudden he looks like he's going to pull a Mount Vesuvius.

"Notwithstanding football, basketball, baseball and softball!" he spouts. "Notwithstanding YMCAs, libraries, museums, concert halls, art galleries, gyms, golf courses, bicycles, bowling alleys and tennis courts, schools, churches, scouting, 4-H, youth leagues, band, choirs, theaters, parks and nature trails!" he says like a bubbling coffee pot gone mad, "it says here that today's kids have nothing to do and have consequently gone berserk. It says kids need a place of their own!"

"Do you mean, Uncle," I ask, "that if kids have places of their own to cha cha in, and fluorescent pool tables, they'll quit turning the country into breeding grounds of the outraged and ravaged?"

"That's what it says," he says, spraying me with emotional spit, "but what these kids need is more time well spent with their families and fishing!"

"Fishing?" I ask.

"Yes!" he says, "When you take kids fishing, you wash their souls with pure air and sky-blue sky. With fishing come meekness, humility, inspiration, patience, tolerance and a quieting of hate. Fishing creates wholesomely imaginative minds. Besides, it's fun, it's cheap, and it's easy!"

"Are you telling me, Uncle," I ask, "that if I take kids fishing, they'll feel no need to burn the place down or join gangs; they'll grow into fairly well-adjusted, reasonably pleasant human beings; they'll learn to laugh in all the right places?"

"Certainly," he says with a simple dignity so typical of him.

"Wow!" I say, realizing he has said it all, and from now on when I think of progress, I'm going to think of that.

etc. & etc.

APRIL 17

"Alas and horsefeathers," he sighed to himself one day last summer. "There is no joy unmixed with woe." He liked a good poem as well as anyone and found himself quoting one when he couldn't think of anything else to describe the fix he was in and to show off a disposition for things literary. At the time, he was orally contemplating a cheerless reality, which was that fish were biting, but he wasn't catching any, and you know as well as I do why. His hooks were dull.

Before you get to feeling smug, so are yours. Yes, they are. Borrow Junior's magnifying glass or the one Grandma uses to read her Bible, poke a precautionary paw into your tackle box and scrutinize the business end of the lures and flies you find there. You'll bristle with disbelief. We know, you and I, the need for sharp-as-anything hooks. Every fishing book and magazine reinforces the practical philosophy of it. Even new hooks should be run over a whetstone, and surely those that snag up on tree limbs, bounce off rocks and get chewed on by willing-enough fish.

But the difference between knowing it and doing something about it is the difference between the honeymoon and the marriage. It's not then that we're uninformed or asleep at the wheel. It's that we're too busy to busy ourselves with the hunting up of a stone or file with which to do the job, and that we lack a third hand with which to do it.

Then, last fall, an old guy told the aforementioned fellow to epoxy a good stone to the side of his boat, back where he sits, so between casts he can take a swipe at it with his hooks. He did that and can modestly report he's caught, oh, half a dozen fish so far and feels positively wrapped up in the mantle of salvation. For similar results, you should follow suit.

if variety is the spice of life ...

APRIL 18

I've always thought I should be a philosopher, but it takes too much time. When I think, one thought generally leads to another, and I never know when to quit. Like the time somebody said it's better to go fishing on Sunday and think about God than it is to go to church and think about fishing.

That got me to wondering. Does six of one and half a dozen of another mean a twelve-mile portage to the river goes uphill both ways? And in the middle of that portage, isn't it the heat, or is it always the humidity? Does it take two to tango, even when your wedding anniversary falls on the opening day of dove season? Isn't it truly more blessed to give than to receive when you own a cornfield in pheasant country and I don't? A bird in the hand can't be worth two in the bush twenty minutes before the opening of partridge season, can it?

Is a good time had by all when you attend thirty-seven Ducks Unlimited banquets and never win a darned thing? In an age of catch and release, is there such a thing as a fine kettle of fish? A poor excuse has to be better than none when you don't get your deer three years in a row. Is a fool's paradise forty acres and a trout stream owned by an anti-hunter? Do you continue to be your brother's keeper when he asks where you caught the biggest muskie of your life? If it's different strokes for different folks for canoers, too, is that grounds for divorce?

Isn't an angel in heaven nobody in particular? If you cross a man with a black Lab, we agree it'll improve the man, but won't it deteriorate the dog? Isn't the best time to repent a sin just before you commit it? When you call your partner crazy as a loon, aren't you being a little unfair to loons? Do rolling stones gather no moss because they're the ones you keep tripping on with a forty-pound pack on your back? Aren't a reasonable number of fleas good for a dog if for no other reason than to keep its mind off being a dog? If all good things must come to an end, does that go for me, too? Okay.

perpetual winners

APRIL 19

Nock, fire. Nock, fire. Nock, fire and fetch. It is pride that makes us do something well. It is love that lets us do it to perfection.

Nock, fire. Nock, fire. Nock, fire and fetch. Therefore, it ought to be a rule that only bowhunters who love the animals they hunt be allowed into those good positions from which to watch the stars. Nock, fire. Nock, fire.

Bowhunters not able to hit the mark every time, all the time, under any and all circumstances, should not go out to where the only sounds are sounds their hearts can hear. Hitting bullseyes is an all-the-time thing, and that takes practice — hours, days, months of it. Nock, fire and fetch.

The snow has melted from the hay bales stacked out by the woodpile, out behind the garage, so now in the dappled shade of leafing-out trees is the time to begin the journey that will carry you into the circle of wine and roses. Nock, fire. Nock, fire. Nock, fire and fetch.

It's not so bad, really. The hours, the days, the months of practice need not be boring. Make a good time of your practice time. Join a league and shoot competitively. Nock, fire. Set up a mini-course in the backyard with small-animal targets mounted on cardboard boxes. Nock, fire. Hang plastic bottles from thickets and half-hide life-sized targets in brush. Nock, fire and fetch.

Put targets in tires and have a pal in similar circumstances as you roll them bumpety-bump from over here to there. Turn loose a flock of half-filled water balloons on kite-flying afternoons. Swing targets from old oak trees.

Be creative. Nock, fire. Shake the boredom of bad habits. Nock, fire. And come next fall, when sunsets fade beyond dark pine trees, you will tell us the news we have been dying to hear. Nock, fire and fetch.

gloomy days

APRIL 20

Nobody's fishing. It's the third day of rain in a mean and rutted row, and they are playing checkers — my Uncle Jake and the Professor. Jake is black as always; the Professor is red as usual.

"Those cashews you're eating belong to the same family as poison ivy and poison oak," says Jake, moving diagonally and forward toward the Professor's well-provisioned line of defense.

"Chain stringers with individual hooks keep fish alive longer if you hook the fish through the bottom lip or both lips and not through the gills," counters the Professor with a similar though opposite move toward Jake's army.

"About the best way to make toast over a campfire is to put a buttered slice of bread buttered side down on a frying pan over coals. When that side's brown, flip it over, and … Look at that!" says Jake, pointing out the window with his right hand and sliding a checker up and over with his left.

Keeping his eyes on the board, the Professor jumps two of Jake's men and says, "Researchers have found that some fish can detect such substances as sunscreen and bug dope when there's only one ounce of it per 100 trillion gallons of water."

"Bingo," says Jake with a horizontal leap of his own. "If hunters would fill the pockets of their wool hunting pants and coats with cedar chips and shavings before putting them away for the season, it would keep moths at a distance and give them a pleasant and natural scent besides."

"Cows' tails to the west, weather's best," says the one. "Cows' tails to the east, weather's a beast," sighs the other. "There are over 7,000 species of grass," says the one. "What in hell's that got to do with anything?" says the other. "Nuthin'," says the one, "but it's lunchtime, and I gotta go." "So it is, so it is," says the other. "So long," says the one. "G'bye," says the other, and makes his way across the shortcut, mean and muddy trail to his house.

satisfaction guaranteed

APRIL 21

When you're ill at ease in your heart, don't abandon it. Take a walk. Take a walk where oak trees grow light as air, where bright, clear water flows weaving bandages to mend the tears in your life. Trust the whispering voices of oak trees and water that comes on shadowed wings like feathers softly falling. When your life gets to be a hard-edged one of clocks and steel, of street lights and highways that slice your days and nights into hard-edged pieces, take a walk. Take time for a walk on the welcoming stones of the earth. Feel the wind on your skin, in your hair. Take comfort in your dreams, in the small warming fires of your dreams.

When sharks close in around you, take a walk. Forgive yourself the sins you've committed. Build a nest under pine trees like a sleeping fawn's. Follow a set of wolf tracks for a little ways. Follow the call of a roosting hoot owl. Ease the weight on your soul with a walk. When your faith grows grizzly, take a walk, free and floating, to maple trees and wild roses. To sagebrush. When failure flames your cheeks, when everybody doubts you, take a walk, any kind of walk, along streams laced with trout and moose.

Walk barefoot in the sand. Lean over and whisper "Yah-hoo" to a baldheaded turtle. Write a ten-thousand dollar check to a chickadee. Sit spraggle-legged across a mossy log and match calls with a loon. Chip a chunk of strength off a fluorescently shining moon. See the humor of it. Adjust your soul to the light. Drink the wine of the great outdoors. Don't waste it. Take only what you need.

When you're ill at ease in your heart, don't abandon it. Take a walk, free as a bear, tall as a redwood, to find the truth of you, the indisputable, rare and wonderful truth of you.

hunkered down to serious business

APRIL 22

Too many people live the lives of moths, fluttering in foolish persistence against a back porch light, but people who paddle canoes don't. They live lives of drama and excitement, experiencing first hand the great out-of-doors. They share in the drama of it and relive the sensations of those who paddled centuries ago.

Lest we get carried away with this, you should understand there's more to paddling a canoe than dipping a ladle into a potful of oatmeal. If you don't master certain techniques before you go, you'll end up like a moth fluttering in foolish persistence against a back porch light.

If there are two of you in a canoe, that's one thing. But one of you in a canoe is something else again. Alone, you kneel amidships slightly toward the stern. The more weight up front, the farther back you slide. The basic stroke of a lone paddler is a J-stroke. Here the paddle is drawn back. As it passes your hipbone, you feather it, turn it on its edge, draw it all the way back and hold it for a moment, then withdraw it from the water and return it to its original position. If well executed, this stroke will keep you on a straight and narrow course quite unlike the willy-nilly ones of moths fluttering in foolish persistence against a back porch light.

The C-stroke is commonly used to turn the canoe. Here, you immerse the blade on its edge like the oar of a rowboat and sweep away from the desired direction. A reverse sweep is done with a forward draw. To slow the canoe, drop the blade into the water perpendicular to the canoe and hold it there, or employ a backward stroke.

There are other strokes for maneuvering in fast water, but not until you are expert in placid, slow-moving water should you attempt them or, like an overworked and all-wet metaphor, you'll become like a moth fluttering in foolish persistence against a back porch light.

a musical interlude

APRIL 23

Kicking up old illusions of grandeur, I go trout fishing. On this day, I go trout fishing later than I should, and somebody's already there where I want to be. But the river looks especially lovely, smiling a pretty smile, so I sit back to watch the maestro at work in there where I need to be. His back cast begins slowly enough. He lifts the rod with his forearm, his elbow acting as a hinge, his wrist unbending, his upper arm not moving — the fairly standard gesture of a conductor cueing up a Vivaldi concerto.

When his forearm reaches forty-five degrees above the horizontal, he begins moving his elbow forward, his upper arm swinging forward, smoothly integrated with the forearm flexion of Schumann's Symphony in D minor. He continues to close his forearm against his upper arm as his elbow flows forward, so that his hand continues smoothly up the stroke line like the functional harmony in Bartok's *Music for Strings*.

His forward cast is as utilitarian as Tchaikovsky's Symphony No. 6. His hand moves halfway down along the stroke line, his elbow leading, his wrist not tipping forward, his forearm not hinging forward from the elbow, his grip as comfortably tight as Handel's *Water Music*.

After his elbow begins to move rearward, his forearm begins hinging forward, reminiscent of Wagner's *Tristan und Isolde*, and every bit as catchy. As his hand reaches the midpoint of the stroke line, he smoothly flips his wrist forward, the rod becoming an extension of his forearm. As his wrist is tipped fully forward, his arm stops (adagio?), while the line falls as softly as the finale to the second act of Mozart's *Le nosse di Figaro*, whilst I sit banished to an aisle seat in the balcony.

i'd appreciate it

APRIL 24

It comes as no small surprise to me that you take a certain delight in the fishing for walleyes. How can you, when fishing for walleyes is such a grim and losing proposition? Why do you, ordinarily of such sound mind and body, even consider fishing for such a fish? It is easier, it seems to me, to move the mountain to Mohammed, to fit a rich man through a needle's eye, than it is to fish for walleyes on purpose.

I can tell you several reasons why. For one thing, walleyes don't stay put. This means you have to go hunting after them. If they're not over here, you have to try over there. If they're not over there, you've got to try over here. Also, just because you caught one in one place last week or yesterday or an hour ago, it doesn't mean a thing, though it can. Furthermore, if you sincerely want to catch walleyes on a consistent basis, you have to fish for them at night. Have you ever gone fishing alone at night? You get the heebie-jeebies once in a while, don't you? And are you aware, though walleyes feed at any temperature, that they harbor a strong preference for water about sixty degrees? Do you know how hard it is to find sixty-degree water down there? Do you know that during daylight hours yellow seems to stimulate more strikes than all other colors combined? Is your tackle box very full, then, of yellow jigs, yellow diving lures, yellow nightcrawler harnesses, yellow floaters, and yellow deep divers? I didn't think so.

Consequently, if you've got so much as one live, working brain cell in your noggin, say the heck with it. Stay home. Relax. Take a load off. Turn on a ball game. Devote your attention to things more spiritual and leave the walleye fishing to those of us who don't know any better.

as easy as 1 ... 2 ...

APRIL 25

In mastering topwater tactics for largemouth bass, it is essential to master stickbaits, among the most difficult topwater baits to master, since the angler must impart the action from his or her catbird seat, if you know what I mean.

"Walking the dog" is a term that describes the basic stickbait retrieve. In his or her struggle to master this technique, the novice may experience a small amount of frustration. Not to worry. Essentially, he or she holds the rod tip close to the water and alternates between jerks and pauses. The lure should swap ends and glide with each jerk. Stickbaits that have no propellers are more responsive and glide farther than those that do. The angler should take up line, of course, after each jerk, but a little slack must be left so the lure can glide without hindrance. Depending on the rhythm and force of the jerks, he or she, with practice and dedication, can make stickbaits walk with everything from my Aunt Fern's wayward shuffle to the splashy dash reminiscent of my second cousin Howie at a wedding dance.

Stickbaits, especially those with propellers, are also effective with twitch-and-wait retrieves. The blades on these stickbaits turn each time the lure is moved. A gentle twitch causes the blades to flicker, while a hard jerk, as you can imagine, kicks up quite a ruckus. A slow twitch-and-wait retrieve closely resembles a dying minnow and has its place, though a noisy, more aggressive action often triggers more strikes. A word of caution: Bass are easily spooked when fished shallow, so the angler should keep the boat noise down and stay back from the cover. He or she should cast beyond the cover and work the lure up to the fish. There it is. What more could I have said, and how could I have said it more simply?

mixed blessings

APRIL 26

It has always been satisfying to me that I don't live where rattlesnakes do. They make me nervous. There are no rattlesnakes in my county, or in the surrounding counties, which pleases me, unless you count the two safely caged behind thick glass doors in a zoo thirty-five miles north and east. Dressed in day-glow outfits, they eye me with furtive eyes, as I eye them in return, measuring the distance between me and certain death. In hurried trips through rattlesnake country, I have seen the sideways waltz of their having been there and quickly high-stepped it in another direction.

Imagine my surprise then when I learned that of the 8,000 people bitten by all kinds of snakes each year in this country, including rattlesnakes, only ten to fifteen die. This isn't so good for the ten to fifteen, but mighty fine for the 7,985 to 7,990. But that's not all I learned. Rattlesnakes go out of their way to get out of the way of human beings, electing to retreat or remain as quiet, camouflaged observers when people pass. It's only when they're poked at or stood on that they defend themselves by striking. Their eyesight is very poor, and they don't smell, so they have to use their forked and flickering tongues for those purposes, which is gross but not fatal. And not all rattlers rattle before striking, but when they do, it's probably to warn you away without a fight if they can. And the distance a snake can lunge at you is only a third to half its length. This is a relief to me.

Rattlesnakes, then, are not as bad as bats that suck your blood and get tangled in your hair, or wolves huffing and puffing around for a taste of human hot dish, but nonetheless and notwithstanding, if I spot one messing around my woodpile or cabbage patch, I'm moving to somewhere where they're not, and that's the truth.

thank you thank you thank you

APRIL 27

As the Earth spins on its eternal rounds, groaning with the labors of spring, as it does that, there happens a most remarkable thing — the mayfly hatch. Nobody wants to trade places with mayflies.

Mayflies begin life simply enough, plainly enough, as nymphs, as wigglers, lying politely on lake and river bottoms in tiny U-shaped burrows. There they grow, fashionably changing coats to accommodate the growth. Then, on magical, warm evenings in late spring, just before the rise of a soul-dissolving moon, they break from their dens and swim to the surface. There they struggle to free themselves of the confining skins to become — as caterpillars become butterflies — large-winged, beautifully fragile duns.

Briefly, breathing the fresh air of freedom, they ride atop the water until moonbeams dry their angels' wings, and with the glint of ambition shining in their eyes, they float up into nearby trees to think things over. In a day, maybe two, the purpose of their pilgrimage becomes clear to them, and in a blessing that is also their downfall, they change into spinners and abandon the leafy hiding places to gather over the water they've so recently abandoned. In magnificent mating flights, they move upstream in hovering, swarming clouds. Softly, the females drop to the surface to lay eggs that sink again to the bottom. Their mission completed, the future of mayflies assured, exhausted males and females, wings outstretched in final surrender, fall to the water to die, and the entire trout population rises to the occasion.

it's worth a try

APRIL 28

Every once in a while, like a wood duck molting, like a weasel alternating colors with the seasons, like a tadpole moving into frogdom, I undergo a metamorphosis. Last week, as I was wiggling through the course of April, it happened again, and it happened like this.

Down by the garden a partridge drummed, followed by another one to the south, and yet one more off to the north. It was quite a deal, being one of the few people in the country with stereophonic partridges, and it got me to thinking how much I love that sound and that bird. Then it hit me. Old-time writers and old-time hunters in old-time partridge country spoke and wrote and thought of partridges as pa'tridges. It sounds so much softer like that, so much prettier, so like the birds themselves. I decided then and there that I am going to do that, too, whenever I speak and write and think about partridges, as I so often do. From now on, it's going to be pa'tridges making those wonderful drumming sounds. It's going to be pa'tridges aggressively dominating and defending their six- to ten-acre homesteads against interlopers. It'll be pa'tridges laying eight to fourteen buff-colored eggs that take two weeks to lay and twenty-four days to hatch. It'll be baby pa'tridges that are thumbnail-sized when they're born, that leave the nest and start feeding themselves as soon as they're dried off, that fly a little bit already when they're five days old. Remind me if I forget.

And what, you ask, will I do with the leftover Rs?? I'll give them to Butch, my dog. Heretofore too congenial to be a good watchdog, his ruff-ruffs at things that go bump in the night will henceforth become rruff-rrruffs, more straightforward and effective, don't you think?

in golden glitter and brightness

APRIL 29

I have been plucked from certain death. Where once I was wandering in the wilderness, I am now found and revived by the arrival of fishing season. The sun has risen on a new dawn, and before it slides down into the night, I will be well-seasoned and browned on a lake, on this one or that one or the one over there. I will be suckled like a babe at the breast of a river, of this one or that one or the one over there. It will be one long, rugged ritual of a picnic. I will fish, therefore, I will be.

The fishing season is upon us, and I am burning like pine pitch. My heart is heaving, is heaving, like a toad's on tarmac. I am a blazing gun, a time bomb ticking, unblinking and full of hope. I'm a fat-petaled chrysanthemum in hot-house heat. I'm a full-blooded mango on a mango tree.

The fishing season is upon us, and I am the legs of a centipede. I am yeast. I am the dry essentials of pancake batter in a Duluth pack. I'm sharp as an ax bit. I'm a train whistle, blowing and coming on strong. I'm the musical music of a white-throated hound dog. I'm the face in the crowd, the frosting on the cake, raw cookie dough, a gleam in the eye of God. I'm a Monet, a Stradivarius, a '69 Mustang convertible, a rookie Mickey Mantle in mint condition, a baited hook, a full tank of gas, lasagna. Health insurance. A belly laugh. A back rub. The color of a wood duck's wing.

The fishing season is upon us, and I'm a bank president, a county fair, a good-night kiss from my kid, a photo album of silver recollections and the woo-woo of an owl at midnight. The shade of an apple tree. Some scrap of poetry that would pass for the lyrics of a country tune. A paid-up mortgage. The fishing season is upon us, and the enormity of it is just sinking in.

a rose by any other name

APRIL 30

The natural flow of the universe has dictated that we rise out of April and climb into May, so, like stirring Rip Van Winkles, that's what we're doing, and everything's proceeding more or less as expected. In fits and starts the grass is growing, a little here, a little there. In froggy swamps and bogs, marsh marigolds (you might call them cowslips) are spilling out deep-yellow flowers. And rototillers are migrating from garage-corner hibernation to feed on garden soil. It's hard not to be poetic when we rise out of April and climb into May.

Wood ticks are starting to waylay woodcutters and rosebush pruners. We're careful around wood ticks, as you know. Otters are giving birth to two or three blind and helpless kits in riverbank dens. Walleyes are spawning. Cackling, clucking, kuk-kuk-kuk-kukking coots are back doing coot things in Whatchamacallit Bay. And where we've got red maples, we've got red buds opening on red branches. Great Lake steelhead are running, crappies are moving into the shallows, and mosquitoes are up and at us. The Big Dipper, The Great Bear, is riding high, and Mars is a morning star. Aphids, caterpillars and beetles are popping out just in time and none too soon for meat-eating, migrating birds. In another nice piece of coinciding, the first batch of bumblebees wait in their eggs and will hatch just in time to pollinate the first batch of apple blossoms. And dandelions, flowers now, are brightly blooming in a basically colorless world. In a week or two, they'll be weeds.

And down at the Post Office, Gladys said she saw food-hunting sparrows scratching the ground with both feet at once. I've got an uncle who dances the schottische like that, and I suppose where you live, you do, too.

a sentimental approach

MAY 1

May is a verb — an action, action, action verb with many subjects. It's a transitive verb, and we, the upright two-leggeds, are the lucky receivers of that action, and I'll tell you why. It's the lawn mowers moving out of hibernation. It's the swallows inhaling newly hatched mosquitoes. It's the wild-blooming blueberries. It's the blooming pincherries, which are nice, too, but not quite as exciting. It's the reckless strawberries blooming sweet possibilities. How right you are, Walt Whitman. How right you are!

It's the sandhill cranes — trust me, it's the sandhill cranes by the pair and by the flock, dancing breathtaking dances of courtship. It's the leafing-out basswood trees. It's the hunting red-tailed hawks. It's the crappies moving into shallows and skunks giving birth to little stinkers and gray squirrels nursing their young. It's Spica, a very nice star, shining tonight just above a Captain-May-I moon. It's another rash of spring fever, a voodoo malfunction of May, a malingering malady of May. It's the morel mushrooms and the open season thereof — fried in butter. Rise up, mushrooms, rise up and sing.

It's the silent stampede of wildflowers, the dandelions massing for lawn assaults. It's the bluebirds. It's definitely the bluebirds. It's the wood turtles slowly mating. It's the flute-like whistles of orioles. It's the vireos, the sulphur butterflies, the dragonflies, the sun-coated buttercups, the trilliums, the whip-poor-willing whip-poor-wills. It's the hatching mallards getting a taste of the real world. It's the seniors over at the high school graduating in a couple or three weeks, and how we're hoping all their dreams come true. It's the world turning green again. We here at Lost Lake get a kick out of things like that, and I suppose where you live you do, too.

small miracles

MAY 2

Fishing in May is such a grand, go-it-alone thing. The aloneness of fishing in May is wonderful. It's outstanding. It's incredible, just incredible, but you know as well as I do that a good fishing partner in May, in the green, green days of May, about doubles the pleasure of fishing.

I've had a couple of fine fishing partners, but people change and move away and things like that, and for a long time there, I didn't have a fishing partner. That hurt. It's one thing to fish without a fishing partner when you've got the option, but quite another hill of beans when you don't. But then something happened, and I got me a new fishing partner. Unlike the others, this one's a she and, to tell you the truth, I'm not sure how it's going to come out. We've been taking it slow and careful. We've got our differences, I can tell you that. She's not very good. She doesn't cast too well, though she's okay at trolling if she's got a book along. She has a different set of priorities. A school of bass can be tearing up the lake and she'll want to stop and eat. She likes to eat. Or go to the bathroom. She'd rather catch bluegills than walleyes. She doesn't care to bait her own hook. If it's cold or rainy, she'd rather stay home. She's afraid of the dark.

We do have things in common. She sometimes cries if a nice fish gets away. I have a tendency to do that too. And every fish she catches, she figures it's a trophy. That's me all over again. Like a lot of partnerships, this one's iffy, but I think it's going to work out okay, especially now that she's eight-and-a-half and heading into the third grade.

so much for sympathy

MAY 3

The opening day of fishing season has come and gone, and I have come off the lake to wallow in the mud of it at Mom's Cafe over on Main Street. What tension I had felt. What anticipation! The opening day of fishing season is what got me through January and February and March and April and every day since the day after Christmas. The weeks of getting ready were like waiting at a drawbridge for a ship that's never coming in. I hardly slept. I dreamed of water furnished with the most unusual fish. I told fish stories at breakfast. You should have heard the prophecies I made. Maybe you did. Then it came.

It was cold in the beginning, but I was eager. I was willing. I was confident, but I didn't get a bite. Sometimes you have to search a bit harder, travel a bit farther. I know that, and I did it. Confidently, I hunted for fish-bearing clouds. Confidently, I searched the curves of long, fish-empty swells for the least riffle of a nibble, while my luck sat still. Confidently, I waited. I reckoned. I figured. I computed. I multiplied and subtracted, yet the shifting ciphers came to zero. There is much to be said on both sides of confidence. Though I knew better, I began to cast without confidence. I cast thoughtlessly, mechanically. I told myself — and what choice did I have — that I'd never catch a fish, and I didn't. I lost my edge. I lost my faith, and when you lose your faith, you've lost everything. You might as well pack it up and head it in, so I did.

I came to Mom's. Now I order my fourth or fifth cup of coffee and my third piece of peach pie, and Mom tells me okay, but he'll have to shut me off soon because I'm starting to slur my words and repeat myself. And then he tells me to take it easy, and that I shouldn't devote more than one lifetime to an opening day of fishing season, which helps, but not much.

unscheduled departures

MAY 4

Around seventy percent of all boating fatalities are caused by capsizings and falls overboard. The solution, then, is simple. We duck hunters, we fishing people, we canoers, shouldn't tip our boats over or fall out of them. When we make our escapes from the prisons of our triple-glazed offices and the iron bars of responsibilities, we should be careful. Sometimes the waters we ride on are windswept and wild. This is okay for you with boats big enough to hit bully waves alongside the head and tell them to behave themselves and they do it. It is not quite so okay, however, for those of us making our getaways with littler boats — twelve-, fourteen-footers, and canoes. In those windswept and wild waters, no matter how macho we are on the inside, on the outside we're tippy, unstable and weak.

In the freedom flights we make on weekends and days off, we should stay alert, even if we've done this a thousand times. We should remind ourselves of our little crafts' limitations and fight off the universal but self-defeating impulse to take them for granted. We should set up a plan in our heads, if nowhere else, on what we'd do in a goose-bump and chilblain set of circumstances that could put us overboard.

The moral of the story is this. After we've tended our factories, milked our cows, vended, merchandised, escrowed, bought souls or sold them, after we've done whatever it is we do in the prisons of our dog-eat-dog daily lives, we water riders should pay attention to what we're doing when we hit the water, when we make those great escapes, lest too, too soon a pulley cranks us down the dark shaft to a cell from which there is no escaping, no matter who we are.

clear to partly cloudy

MAY 5

I fall asleep in front of the ten o'clock news dreaming big-fish dreams and hearing my Uncle Jake calling me. "Hey," he is saying, "are we going fishing or aren't we?" Then he pulls on my big toe, causing me to lose the nicest fish you ever saw. We're going walleye fishing, and you're thinking I haven't woke up yet, and anybody who goes fishing after the ten o'clock news is a few feathers short of a molt. But this is spring, and these are walleyes.

You'll find a lot of birds like us when you get into serious walleye country. It's no secret among this crowd that good, shallow-water walleye action comes after dark, though Jake, who's retired, goes them one better. They launch their boats at sunset, which isn't bad, but by midnight they're back home. Not my uncle. He's found that walleye feeding activity is often the greatest after midnight, especially during the last couple of hours of darkness, so we're hauling his boat out when the others are bringing theirs in.

Walleyes are skittish in shallow water, so we approach cautiously, shutting off the motor and drifting into position or maneuvering in with Jake's electric. Sometimes we hear the fish taking minnows close to the surface. The sound is like the one Jake makes at his morning toast and coffee before he puts his teeth in — a loud slurping. Big browns taking mayflies sound just like it. We use shallow-running floating and jointed minnows retrieved slowly, with just enough speed to throw a little wake on the surface. Walleyes chase their food neither fast nor far here.

Now, if you'll excuse me, I'll get back to the TV. Jake is due to pick me up any minute, and I'd like to catch the weather report before sign-off.

a hell of a deal

MAY 6

First you're born, then you die, and you're riding a canoe down the River of No Return to the red-hot gates of hell and playing twenty questions with a joker who wants to know if you're the one he's been waiting for. You figure your goose is cooked and the jig is up, so you more or less nod in the affirmative to the scorecard he lays before you.

"It says here youse is da guy," snarls the joker, his face in your face, "dat's forgettin' ta pack toilet paper on campouts, and dat's never believin' da direction indicator on his compass and gettin' hisself lost." The poor devil is obviously a high school dropout.

"It says youse is da dope," he goes on, "dat backs his boat inta da water wit da plug in his pocket. Dat youse is da dimwit who leaves his fishin' pole on da kitchen table when he goes to Canada on fishin' trips. Dat youse is da one fergettin' ta patch yer waders till yer in da river. And in da summertime youse leaves cans o' woims in da trunk of yer wife's car and leaves egg salad sandwiches in da pocket of yer huntin' coat in da hall closet. And youse don't clean yer shotgun. Don't sharpen yer huntin' knife. Don't change da spark plug in yer motor. Can't tie a decent nail knot and exaggerates da size of fish youse catch. It says youse misses easy goin'-away shots on rooster pheasants. Are youse dis guy?"

You know how it is. When your goose is cooked, it's cooked. When the jig's up, it's up. "That is I," you say. "What in hell!" scowls the gentleman behind the red-hot gates, picking his teeth with a poker, "Youse is a regular fella. We got no use fer ya down here. Now scram."

"Gee, t'anks," you say, and do.

passing to the promised land

MAY 7

Sometimes we pass through life homesick for something without being able to pinpoint what it is we're homesick for. It's like when you open the refrigerator door and stand there trying to recall what you're looking for. It's a lonesome feeling. Then along comes fishing season, and you remember, and you mount a great white horse, and you ride it into rose-colored clouds. I know you're thinking that sounds like a twenty-five dollar exaggeration, and I'd be the first to agree with you, because I know as well as you do that sometimes the clouds are purple-colored or red or yellowish or blue. And sometimes the horses are black ones or bays or paints or palominos, though they're all fast and wild and wonderful.

And sometimes when we ride, we arm ourselves with cane poles and braided line or tin tobacco cans of angleworms. Sometimes it's with stout casting rods and tackle boxes five miles across. Sometimes it's with sleek fly rods and inexact imitations of hairy little insects. Sometimes we ride casting. Sometimes it's trolling. Sometimes we ride wading or motor-driven or paddle-propelled in still waters, in rivers, in great salty seas or tiny, nameless streams.

A fishing season helps a little in our mortal lives when a little helps a lot. When somebody sighs and says life is hard, when fishing season's upon us, we ask, "Compared to what?" When somebody grumbles that roses have thorns, during fishing season we say, "You're a little out of line there, Pal. Be thankful thorns come covered with roses." And when they tell us the chance of a slice of bread falling with the buttered side up is directly proportional to the cost of the carpet, we'd say they're probably right, except during fishing season, and then it doesn't much matter one way or the other.

the bitter and the sweet

MAY 8

I stopped by Mom's Cafe over on Main Street. At the counter was a kid. School was in session, but he wasn't. Most everybody here in Lost Lake knows everybody else, and this was no exception, so I said, "Hey, Kid. How come you're not in school?"

"I quit," he said. "They don't learn me nothin' to help me succeed in life."

I called him a dimwit and pointed out how through the study of biology he'd learn the life cycle of a mayfly and how *Ephemerella guttalata* is really a green drake, and a *Stenonema vicarium* is in actuality a March brown, and without that information he'd find himself out on a trout stream with nothing to do. I told him in history class he'd learn about Dame Juliana Berners, who wrote the first recorded book on fishing more than five centuries ago. If he didn't study his accounting, I told him, he'd never learn to squeeze a new shotgun out of a household budget and make it look like bread and porkchops.

I discussed how people with no knowledge of geography couldn't tell the Mississippi Flyway from the capital of North Dakota, or read topographical maps, thus spending a greater portion of their lives lost. In shop class he could build tree stands and duck blinds and fix his little five-horse for practically nothing. With math he could score his deer antlers and calculate ballistics.

"If you don't learn to write," I told him, "you can't sell your hunting and fishing stories to outdoor magazines, and if you don't learn to read, you can't enjoy books like *The Adventures of Huckleberry Finn*, a great and helpful story of camping out, and "To Build a Fire," a wonderful how-to story, though it ends on a sour note, and "The Big Two-Hearted River," by Ernest Hemingway, which has no plot and needs none.

I could have gone on and on and nearly did, but the kid bolted for the door and headed up the street toward the school at a real good clip.

a quiet place

MAY 9

This happened last fall, but it seems like only yesterday. I was crouched in a bomb shelter of birch branches when I saw him. He was climbing out of a ditch of daisies and sapling spikes toward me. I got so excited I could hardly breathe. He was moving slowly and carefully the way they do; then he stopped. He was a real tomato, that one, and my heart beat like crazy. I could see only a little of him where he stopped, and that with some very cautious leaning out, but I could feel the oceanic possibilities even so. He stood absolutely still for a minute, maybe two, then he flared his nostrils. Geez. He had caught my scent. That had to be it, though I had taken such care with my smells. You should have seen the glory of those nostrils and how his breath hung there like a cloud.

I didn't dare move. I didn't dare set my rifle down or raise it up to where it would do me some good if he'd come a little closer. The world filled with his breathing from those nostrils. Leaf-shadows skittered like mice on his body. His ears flickered and burned with his listening. He leveled his look at where I was hanging numb in the birch branches, tight as a wrapped cocoon. I didn't put my eyes on him too hard, lest he read me. I would not give him that. His antlers — I can still see what I saw of them — were golden like a grandfather's wedding band. I couldn't count the points. He wouldn't come far enough out of his own bomb shelter of daisies and sapling spikes for me to see them all. What I saw clearly was the awful beauty of his nose and ears working me over in the wind.

His muscles were bunched. He was poised like a bird to fly, and for me there was both joy and terror in this. Then, like a feather plucked and tossed away, he was gone. Watching him closely, I didn't see him go, leaving me in the birches and the silence.

back in circulation

MAY 10

As usual, it's the Professor who has got there first, to Mom's Cafe over on Main Street. This gets him the front page of the newspaper and dibs on the topic of the day's conversation, something he cherishes. The rest of us straggle in from the lake, finish the sports page, comics, crossword puzzle, want-ads, horoscopes, TV section and two cups of coffee, while he tut-tuts and shakes his head and knits his brow before mosey-ing into his morning monologue.

"I don't get it," he says at last, firming his grip on section A of the tabloid. "All this fuss about kids and gangs." That's the opening we were waiting for, and everybody jumps in, the gist of it being that we agree with him. Here at Lost Lake, we more or less encourage our kids to join not one gang, but three or four. Last week some signed on with the Greenwings, their equivalent to Ducks Unlimited. We've got kids in Trout Unlimited, Whitetails Unlimited, Pheasants Forever, Ruffed Grouse Society, NSSF, NRA, 4-H, YMCA, and Scouts. About all our boys and girls, knock on wood, are bona fide members of our Fish, Game and Cribbage Club. It's our conviction that a family that stands together butt-deep in pretty little trout streams pulling up beer cans somebody on their way to somewhere else put there is a family indeed. They help us build bluebird and wood duck houses and a million other things. Early on, they learn the awful responsibilities of gun ownership.

It's not that we don't worry about the kids; it's that we do, and when one of them gets into trouble, we're by God going to be right there to take some of the blame for it. That's about it, except that my Uncle Jake unwraps a dead fly he carries for the occasion and sneaks it into the Professor's coffee. The ensuing pandemonium causes him to release his hold on the newspaper and put it up for grabs.

innovative adaptations

MAY 11

I believe as much as I believe anything that it's not absolutely necessary to catch fish when you're fishing, that there's plenty of pleasure in the artful art of fishing all by itself, although, to tell it truthfully, I suppose it increases my sense of well-being if I do catch fish. That's why my Uncle Jake and I were out there on Lost Lake, doing our darnedest to nail a brace of walleyes for supper.

This was the post-spawning period, which is why we were postponing the catch-and-release portion of our dyed-in-the-wool philosophy, and we weren't supposed to be having quite as much trouble increasing our sense of well-being as we seemed to be having. The food chain was coming alive, and walleyes were about to be blessed with a feast of insects and minnows. Oxygen in the water was abundant. Sunlight wasn't yet a factor. Walleyes were, in fact, in walleye heaven, though we were not. Underwater rock piles were absorbing the heat of the sun, attracting schools of bait fish. Twice a day, walleyes come there to feed. So did we. Zilch. Occasionally, they were dropping deeper to snag easy meals. So did we. Nothing. At times, they were sliding up into shallow bays to feed on perch fry. We slid, too. Zero. We fished here. We fished there and everywhere. We studied our map. We fan cast. We drifted. We used jigs and minnows. We used diving lures, deep diving lures, rattling lures and nightcrawlers pinned to nightcrawler harnesses. Leeches. We hopped them. We bounced them. We skipped them on one leg and two, fast and o-o-o-h so-o-o slow. Nothing.

"Oh, piffle," said Jake, "Whattya say we increase our sense of well-being up at the Elkhorn Tavern and Wildlife Museum?"

"Bingo!" said I, thinking up a lie for later, and started the motor.

all fired up

MAY 12

When daylight fades like a casual pigeon sinking downward on extended wings, I can't help it, I get an urge to build a campfire. There is something about a campfire, a small and pleasant campfire, that kindles my spirit and cleanses my soul. A campfire, a small and pleasant campfire, is a companion and friend that lets me feel quite right at home when darkness holds me in its grip. It transforms grizzly bears, hunkered hungrily between me and my escape canoe, into big and bouncy boulders. Without a small and pleasant campfire, I find more holes in my confidence than I do in a pair of cheap waders rolled up and stored wet for the winter. There's a spirit in a fire, a small and pleasant one, that talks to the spirit in me. It reassures me when I'm hanging, dangling — strictly speaking — by my fingertips and a toe from the North Star, all alone at night. A fire, a small and pleasant fire, comforts and inspires me. It cooks my beans, boils my coffee, gives me light and dries my socks.

But a big fire, a great big fire, an ugly, forbidding conflagration of a fire, does none of that. Rather than cleansing my soul, it sends clouds of smoke into the pulsating generators of my lungs. It is neither a friend nor a companion, but a selfish beast, demanding, demanding to be fed. It blinds me to my surroundings. It lets hunkered grizzly bears slip to within arm's length of my throat. Its flames fly out of control into trees that wide-eyed owls call home. It drives me from its heat. It scorches my food. It dries my socks to ashes.

So you see, then, a great big fire, an ugly conflagration of a fire, is of no value. What we want is a small fire, a pleasant fire, a cuddling fire, the kind of fire we can gather around and sing the old campfire songs to and roast marshmallows. Got that?

exploring the primitive state of consciousness

MAY 13

Sometimes I think fishing is a metaphor for life, for the only real stumbling block in fishing is the fear of failure. In fishing, as in life, you've got to have a what-the-hell attitude. Take my Uncle Jake. When the water here at Lost Lake reaches a fine fifty-two degrees, give or take, then perch come floating across the face of the underworld and move into the shallows to answer nature's call to propagate. This is very good, much-anticipated news to Jake and the rest of us who pursue wily walleyes whenever we can.

Though walleyes are seriously considering major moves back into deeper waters to escape from the ever-climbing sun, they're not about to abandon the smorgasbord provided by their spawning perch cousins. When Jake finds these aggressively feeding fish, he usually nabs a couple right away, especially in the low light of sundown, on overcast days, when the wind kicks up and cuts light penetration, in the dark of night or under the cover of thick weeds, which are scarce right now, or fallen timber. Near prime perch-spawning beds, Uncle Jake tries small golden shiners or two-inch fatheads. In darker waters, he might give mud minnows a shot, or the artificials that resemble them. He saves crawlers and leeches for later, after a spell of warmer weather. He uses the lightest weights possible to the depth he needs, and small, number eight hooks, keeping the whole business simple. A lot of these walleyes are males, on the smallish side — one pound, two pounds, three — but they're fun to catch and so good to eat.

On the outside chance Jake can't locate any spawn-feeding walleyes, he figures "what the hell," and settles for a nice mess of perch. And on this side of Heaven, I don't know how we could ask for anything more.

dream makers

MAY 14

You know how it is when you've got a kid who's eleven years old, and it's spring, and you're stretched out together under the stars. It's the kind of spring night that hovers around you like an awkward angel, and when you close your eyes you can't help feeling like some kind of true-blue historical figure, and when your kid who's eleven years old asks you how the stars got that way, and a couple of coyotes cry somewhere off in the moonlight, what can you do but tell her the truth?

You say: Once, as far back as the beginning of time, there was a meeting of all The People. Our Mother gave each of the four-legged and two-legged and flying People jobs to do to make The Earth a pleasanter place. To a two-legged she gave a jar full of stars and told him to arrange them in a suitable fashion in the sky. This he did, setting out the Great and Little Bears and Orion and all the constellations. By and by, the two-legged got a little hungry, and even though he was only half finished, he set the jar down, put a big Do Not Disturb Or Else sign on it, and went home for a sandwich. Along came Coyote, as curious then as he is now, and saw the sign. Naturally, his curiosity was aroused, and he looked around and looked around and then he sneaked a quick peek. Before Coyote could slap the lid back on, the stars jumped out and scattered themselves up there all over the place. As you can imagine, Our Mother was quite unhappy about this and scolded Coyote and told him from then on the only kind of luck he was going to have was bad.

Then you look over at your kid, who's fallen asleep, and even though she's eleven years old and much, much too old for this sort of thing, you pick her up and carry her softly to the tent and snuggle her into her sleeping bag while the scattered stars wink good night and a couple of coyotes cry again, off somewhere in the moonlight.

field notes

MAY 15

You have met, I believe, my second cousin Howie. He's the dry fly-fishing purist. I was reminded how good he is last Saturday night at the Elkhorn Tavern and Wildlife Museum. They had live music. Howie, who has heretofore been unmarried, became smitten with a dark-haired lady from the other side of the lake. Howie's approach to a trout stream and his presentation are impeccable. His placement of the fly on the water is delicate, light and quick. He wades carefully so as to avoid alarming the fish. This was all evident when the band struck up a schottische, and Howie headed for her table.

On the stream, Howie wastes no time over refusals. If a fish has not risen at the third presentation, it is because, at that moment, it is untakeable. He considers the loss of time occasioned by continuing to try stubbornly for acceptance is not worth the effort. From my vantage point — I am married and do not dance — it seemed the lady rose at the second cast. Howie lands most trout very quickly. They slide across the surface, and as soon as they are within reach of his landing net, down they go. He was holding her pretty close for a schottische.

Somebody sprinkled something slippery on the dance floor, which Howie seemed to appreciate. When he walks on the slick bottom of a trout stream, it seems like he has eyes in his feet. As on the dance floor, he never makes a false step.

Howie's instinct for conservation and strict adherence to the rules of catch and release are legendary. When he catches a fish, he takes the leader in one hand and the fish in the other. While holding it in the water, he removes the hook and waits until he's quite certain the fish is okay before he lets it go. So, you can imagine our surprise when, after the schottische, a bunny hop and two waltzes, he and the dark-haired lady slipped out the side door, and we haven't seen either one since.

illustrating the close personal relationship between you & me

MAY 16

Once you have heard booming prairie chickens, it's unlikely your life will be quite the same. Once the sweetest sound in all the world — Bob-WHITE! Bob-Bob WHITE! Ah-Bob-White — drifts into your bloodstream, you can't get it out. When you have talked with turkeys under rustling oak leaves crusted with crystal beads of sweat or, better yet, conversed with elk, mountain high, other conversations are just gobbledygook. Are you confused by that? You look confused.

You can't sleep on an island, sprawled before a fire, without the memory of it stretching and pulling inextricably around you. You can't say goodbye to it. You're shaking your head. Nor can you hunker over a pot of bubbling beans and bacon, smelling of woodsmoke, and not be touched forever by the piety of your doing and being. You're shrugging your shoulders. I almost got you on that one, I think.

Have you noticed how some things can't die? How no one ever tires of trees? How there are no meaningless clouds? How no one ever quarrels with the idea of partridges? How you can't let your soul stroll a beach and not be captured by the sea and the earnest sounds of measured surf? They hold promises of eternity, and we believe what we hear. You can't look up at a night sky without thinking it's okay the stars are like that, and feeling a little luckier because of it. You can't — it's not possible — paddle some oxbow bend of a river, or stare into the wise, black pools of a river, and not have the elegance of it rub off on you. Hear it once — the slip-slap of water on the bottom of your boat, or a wild goose honking on a tin harmonica — and you hear it for a lifetime.

You smile at that one because you've been there, too, and you know finally that I know what I'm talking about.

insights into the human condition

MAY 17

I live at the end of a dead-end road, so imagine my surprise when a fellow stopped by, hunkered down next to me planting peas, and said, "May I smell that rosebush over there? May I get a whiff of that flaunting lilac yonder? Inhale the apple blossoms in your backyard? May I borrow your canoe, your paddle and your life jacket? May I tune in to the middle of that robin's medley, that robin hunting worms in this garden of yours, that robin blazing away in the middle of this day? May I? And may I go with you to that secret trout stream I've heard so much about?"

I smiled at him and said, "Yes, you can smell my rosebush. Breathe it in all you like. You can whiff my yonder flaunting lilac, inhale the apple blossoms in my yard. You can borrow my canoe, paddle and life jacket. Be my guest. You can even tune in to the middle of that robin's medley, that robin hunting worms in my garden, that robin blazing away in the middle of this day. But can you go with me to the secret trout stream you've heard so much about?"

He said, "May I use your dock, that strewn wreckage of a dock, to cast for twenty-pound northern pike? May I have a close-up look at your tackle box, at the contents of your lunch bucket? May I take a bite off this chicken leg? Or two? And may I ride a ways with you on the wings of your canoe to the hidden waters of that trout stream you've talked so much about?"

"Yes, you can use my dock," I told him, "this strewn wreckage of my dock, to cast for twenty-pound northern pike. You can take a close-up look at the contents of my tackle box, of my lunch bucket. The chicken leg's on the house. But can you ride with me a ways on the wings of my canoe to the hidden waters of the trout stream I've talked so much about? Go to hell."

a pot of gold

MAY 18

You won't believe this. I hardly believe it myself, but I have become invincible. It's true. I wouldn't kid about a thing like this. It was last Sunday, an on-again, off-again rainy Sunday. Foggy. Windy. I was standing on the north shore of Lake Superior in Duluth, Minnesota, huddled against the rain, the fog, the wind, when the sun broke through, and there it was, the rainbow. It wasn't a big rainbow. It wasn't a double, which is not a bad rainbow at all. But there it was. I could touch it, and it spanned maybe a couple hundred yards. It was between me and a close-by fishing boat. It was between me and a ship from the Far East. A seagull swam through it to snag a crust of bread from a little kid on the beach. I was right there. I could touch it.

You smile, but it's no laughing matter, standing at the end of a rainbow. As an average outdoorsperson, you may have a very meager understanding of the importance of rainbows, especially to someone who hasn't exactly made a big splash at this point of his life. I'm going to get lucky any day now.

My fishing boat, which has heretofore leaked a gallon an hour, will henceforth be limited to a trickle. The endless array of defective sporting equipment that is mine will last me one more season. I'll get another hundred thousand, at least, out of my four-wheel drive. At least. I may become irresistible to women; I haven't decided yet. Any day now my compass will point true north, and I will accept that. No more will I fear being mauled by grizzly bears on sleep-outs, nor will I ever again sit down on poison ivy. Snakes won't crawl into my sleeping bag. I needn't fear quicksand any more, or lightning, or thin ice, or rapids, all because on the north shore of Lake Superior in Duluth, Minnesota, I have stood at the end of the rainbow, and my luck, she is a'changing.

and lead us not ...

MAY 19

The Devil is walking to and fro upon the earth, considering how he might do considerable damage, for it is the nature of the Devil that he goes about tempting mankind to do his fiendly pleasures. This time, however, as the Devil so walks, it is the opening day of trout season. Whereas at other times it is the nature of a man to be filled with envy and worldliness, on the opening day of trout season, his heart overflows with charity and love. Thus, on this day, the Devil becomes more diabolically minded than ever to work his unclean will. He girts about himself a fishing vest and chest waders so none will see his cloven feet and poison tail, and he hums a country tune as though he is indeed fishing for trout instead of men's souls.

Now, it befalls that on his way to the river, he meets a fisherman known for deeds of charity, Godliness and uncompromising philosophies of catch and release. The Devil asks if he can bear him company, to which the unsuspecting fisherman says, "Sure."

Then, while they journey together down the trail, the Devil discourses of theologies and mysteries and of the taste of trout fried in butter. The fisherman becomes troubled by the abominable argumentations and begins to waver, and to be filled with miserable doubtings because, by the Devil's trickery, he begins to smell the smells of frying fish.

Yet (and now I tell you of a special Providence that befalls fishermen on opening days), while the Devil whispers in his ear, there comes unto the fisherman a certain power to resist evil and, casting misgivings to the wind, he falls upon the Fiend, crying, "You are the Devil." And he plucks the vest and waders from the Devil, exposing the cloven feet and poison tail, and the Devil runs away. Whereupon the fisherman continues down the path with thanksgiving and praise, and all the great fish that are in the river before he gets there are also in it when he goes.

quote/unquote

MAY 20

"How old would you be if you didn't know how old you was?" That was Satchel Paige. I'd been fishing all day and came home pooped out, so I went down to the cellar for a jug of elderberry wine to refuel the fires of my ambition. A little while later, Satchel came by with half a gallon of morel mushrooms. It was after I enumerated the aches and pains that hold me back in life, and mentioned a couple of times how unfair my situation was, that he put the question to me.

A few days later, I was thinking about what he'd said, and one thought led to another, until I got to "a rose is a rose is a rose," something I'd read. I could tell right away whoever wrote that wasn't a fisherman or she would have written "a fish is a fish is a northern (pike)" instead. I was fishing at the time.

You're thinking I was still under the inspirational influence of the elderberry. "A trout is a fish," you're thinking. "A bass is a fish, a walleye is a fish, even a bullhead is a fish, but a northern (pike) is a snake, a hammer handle, a low-life creature of teeth, bones and bad manners."

But no. To have more fun than you can have fishing for this fish, you'd have to be on medication. The northern (pike) is a wonder of creation, an able adversary and an aggressive hunter. We fish for it early in the morning because it doesn't feed at night, and its belly is empty then. Afternoons are good, too, because it has to eat enough then to tide it over until dawn. Hooked, it lets us lead it quietly to the boat, then takes one look and blasts off and our tackle with it. The northern (pike) is a fish of history, a fish of myth and legend like no other fish. Fried, baked, smoked or pickled, few taste better. On second thought, the northern (pike) is not just a fish just a fish; it's a celebration, a celebration, a celebration, though who said that I have no idea.

a slice of life

MAY 21

In this life that's been allotted to us, we're doing okay, because money's the root of all evil, and we sure don't have much of it. We don't worry about it more than half our waking hours because, where money's concerned, a lot of time is wasted in the making of it, and we're not guilty of that. To prove the point, we're about to take a short, skittering leap into the hushed and breathless fresh air of freedom. We're about to foreswear the doubtful benefits of progress. We're about to give up greed, ambition and the lust for power and preference. We're about to, as you have guessed, go camping.

We're heading into the wilderness, and ain't it grand? And we're going at it with the careful confidence of campers who've been there many times and forgotten stuff before they went. For instance, we're taking the tent out of mothballs and pitching it in the backyard before departure, and we're missing three of the stakes that hold it and us to our Mother Earth. And we're finding them in the sandbox.

To check out the camp stove before the old pickup truck is due for take-off, we're preparing supper in the backyard, too, and we're discovering that the BakePacker is missing. That's a trademarked term, I believe, and I'm getting, surprisingly enough, no cash whatsoever for mentioning it, though I would if I could. It's reward aplenty for me if you should never go canoe camping without one. Anyway, we're finding it in the playhouse on the cardboard cookstove and, here in the backyard, we're chuckling at the experience and joshing the little Dickens who pilfered it from the cook pack for mud pies.

And then we can't help but notice how bright the stars are, and how close, and how there's no accounting for our considerable good fortune.

build it and they will come

MAY 22

You are dreaming, and the telephone rings like a lame love song at the crack of dawn. You don't have a fishing trip planned and hunting's illegal, so you answer it with your heart skipping a beat. It's trouble all right. It's your aunt. "Hurry!" she cries, "It's Uncle Jake." Needless to say, after a hurried breakfast, a quick glance at the morning paper and a speedy stop in town for gas and oil, you rocket right over there.

In a minute, you see the cause of your aunt's concern, and your heart goes out to her. Uncle Jake, in the middle of the night, has been jolted by an inner voice. "Raise your own fishing worms," the voice said. And there is Jake, knee-deep in sawdust, mucking up your aunt's happy home and peace of mind.

"Grab a hammer and get busy!" Jake says, and heck, building a worm-growing box seems like a good idea, so you join in. You put it together like a peach crate, six inches deep. You drill holes in the bottom for drainage and lay in layers of newspapers. Over that you spread an inch of dry grass clippings. In your aunt's big bread-making bowl you mix three gallons each of store-bought cow manure, topsoil and peat moss. You stir in a cupful of cornmeal and a canful of coffee grounds and you pour it all into the box to within a couple inches of the top. You dig worms, dump them in, add another inch of bedding and one of grass clippings, cover it with burlap that you'll keep damp and store it where it's sixty-five to seventy-five degrees — like in your auntie's fruit room.

Say, where is she anyway? We've made an awful mess here, and, Neighbor, don't look at me like that.

expedient ideologies

MAY 23

Whether one reaches the sublime by fleeing the real world or by hunting it down like a mad dog, I have no idea, though I have lived long enough to see many things.

I am crappie, whispers a voice like a unicorn's, watching the ark disembark to my Uncle Jake and me. Come to me. Thus, we are crappie fishing, though that is an exaggeration, since the crappies aren't aware of it or, being aware of it, don't feel the need to participate.

As you know, I like fishing as much as anybody and better than some, but it's not my religion or anything, like it is with Jake. Consequently, I don't mind taking a snooze now and then if the situation calls for it. So, I'm stretched out in the front of the boat with my baseball cap sort of pulled down over my eyes, about to doze off, when I see my uncle giving me a sideways glance of owlish contemplation. Then I see him sneak a pouch of cornmeal out of his tackle box and, every once in a while, toss a handful overboard. As it settles into the water, down to the brush pile over which we are parked, it triggers considerable feeding activity (I am cornmeal; come to me) on the part of minnows in residence there. Naturally, the many close-by crappies (I am minnow; come to me) reach out for the minnows.

The old man starts hauling in crappies like crazy. "What's happening?" I yell, as if I don't know. "Nothin', and go back to bed," he says. But of course, I don't, and I don't mind sharing his secrets with you, either, though I'd rather you didn't mention it to him. As usual, I owe him a couple of bucks and like to keep his spirits up.

food for the body, food for the soul

MAY 24

We are strung out at the counter of Mom's Cafe over on Main Street like birds on a telephone wire when the conversation takes a sudden, though not unexpected, turn toward fishing. "Cherish the loveliness of it," says someone working on a BLT. "At this very moment, some fish somewhere is biting on a piece of pork rind."

"How right you are," sniffs Mom, taking a panful of his homemade caramel rolls from the oven and smelling up the place something wonderful. "In this technical world gone goofy with gadgetry, you'd think a thing as commonplace ordinary as pork rind would have gone the way of other, less sophisticated stuff."

"Agreed," agrees the Professor. "For the last sixty years, pork rinds have kept my nervous system from shorting out." I agree, too, as I'm sure you do, that this is no suntan-oil philosophy, either. I, for one, am devoted to the rabbit-foot powers of pork rind. It gives fish the taste, smell and texture of real meat. It's tough enough to use and reuse.

"It's effective as a go-it-alone bait," says my Uncle Jake, eyeing the buttering-up progress of the rolls, "but I prefer to hook it to the hooks of other lures as trailers. It often improves the action of the originals." He's got that right. Speared to the business end of wobbling spoons or wiggling crankbaits, a strip of pork rind can increase the wobble and multiply the wiggle. And it comes in sizes small enough for flycasting to bluegills and lunker enough for trolling after muskies.

Ol' Gladys points out that with a sharp knife, come-as-is pork rind can be customized. "Surely," says Mom, beaming like a deacon and distributing at last the rolls to the assembled, "a tackle box lacking pork rind is a tackle box unfulfilled."

"Amen," we say, and dig in.

a jumping off place

MAY 25

There were jagged scars on its jaws and old wounds on its flanks. Its fins were frayed. There was a gouge on its tail where something had taken a bite out of it. That was a long time ago. Now, at the top of the food chain, it lay like a satisfied lion in its den alongside a log at the bottom of the lake. Its dark brownish sides and back blended perfectly with its background, so perfectly it appeared to be a log in a sea of logs to the muskrat passing over it. With eyes as large as humans' eyes, it looked up at the muskrat swimming, a yearling muskrat with adult possibilities. The log of the muskie rose from the logs where it lay. An empty hole opened on the surface, and only a faint swirl marked the muskie's eating place.

From weeds sticking out where water met sky, the muskie ambushed suckers grubbing along the muddy bottom, and yellow-sided bluegills and perch. With a missionary's zeal, it grew fat with its eating. It grew long. From lily pads it curled upward, dropped its lower jaw — undershot like a bulldog's — yawned open its cavernous mouth lined with cutting, grabbing teeth, and only downy feathers floated where mallard ducklings had been. It grew old. Then came a day when a chub, red and yellow, flushed from the weeds. As was its way, the muskie smashed it, sank its teeth into it, swallowed it. The sting of the hooks was real, and the fish could not get rid of it. It jumped clear of the water, swinging its long head and rattling its gill covers. It turned again and rushed the other way and leaped again. And again. For half an hour it fought a good muskie fight, but there was no escaping the steady squeeze of fate and the spring of the bent rod. Spent at last, it only half-felt itself lifted up out of the water like a slow-dancing shadow into the land of exile.

transcendental meditation

MAY 26

Too often, the camping experience is associated with adversity and hardship, calamity and grief. It began, as so much does, with a caveman who, hoping to unclutter himself of the cynicism and false sophistication of his daily life, planned a simple weekend getaway into the breathless, marveling out-of-doors. "Come," he said to his little extended-family clan huddled over bowls of dinosaur soup, chewing on dinosaur bones. "It will be better than anything at the movies, and fresh air is good for the soul."

It was not to be. The balloon of his cheerfulness burst when someone — each blamed another — forgot to pack a sharp rock for scraping things and a pointy stick for poking and jabbing. It has continued to this day. Not once — you can relate to this — in the whole history of getting away from it all has any camper gone camping without leaving a piece of equipment back at the cave. Not once. Not ever. It'll be a tent peg, toilet paper, stove fuel, salt, spatula, flashlight or rope. It'll be duct tape, saw, biscuit mix, peanut butter or fishing pole. It'll be hot dogs. It'll be beans. It'll be matches, bug dope, frying pan, rain fly, aspirin, tackle box, map, canteen, underwear, first-aid kit or sleeping bag, but it's something, and it gets left behind, and I'll tell you why. People don't make a list. Too many rely on their memories to get them safely and comfortably into, out of and through campouts. Campers have to make lists and check off each item as it is packed.

Moreover, there's not an outdoor writer worth a hoot who doesn't supply his readers with a list of essentials that should be taken on campouts. Many put little squares next to each item for checking-off convenience. I should be doing that for you; I want to be doing that for you. I want to be worth a hoot, but I've gone and left my list at home.

preoccupied with the truth

MAY 27

Most people believe, as I do, that a fishing expert is a fisherman more than twenty-five miles from home. That's rather bad luck for me, because I'm almost never allowed to stray more than half a dozen. I have to fish where everybody knows my name, and any exaggeration one way or another makes their blood boil. This is why you won't find my name in the Fishing Hall of Fame.

Once, however, I did find myself on a lake that was not only the expert-producing twenty-five miles away, but almost twice that. On this special occasion, I was fishing floating jigheads for walleyes. Floating jigheads can be trolled nearly anywhere that's wet or cast into thick weeds or still-fished. My Uncle Jake uses them for trolling or suspending baits just above walleye-hiding weeds and tangles. We usually tip them with leeches or minnows. It's too bad he wasn't with me that day, since I had good luck.

I caught lots of walleyes — smaller ones in the three- and four-pound class, and some eight and tenners. I also lucked onto some very nice northern pike — floating jigheads are that versatile. There were smatterings of crappies and bass, too, as you're beginning to suspect. It was almost as if God was providing and I had nothing to do with it. I'm a pioneer in the practice of catch and release; still, I thought it wise in this case to bring them home with me as enthusiastic witnesses to my uncharacteristic success.

In my zeal to do this, though, I overstepped the dock, lost my balance and dropped the fish into the water. As you can imagine, the experience was enough to make an infidel out of the most ardent believer, so I've hardly mentioned it to anybody but you. You don't know me.

a pretty pickle

MAY 28

Happiness is an inside job. In our adulthood, we get so snarled in cosmetic struggles for success that we go about unremembering what it was like being encircled by the magical mysteries of childhood. We have little choice in this, but if I let my imagination float a bit, I can admit to being reminded of my boyhood recently when we were visiting the kids' grandparents as close to Father's Day as we could get.

The grown-ups were concentrating on essential grown-up matters when the kids came busting up from the dock, in the way of kids, a'dazzle and full of bloom, with an ice cream bucket full of bluegills. These were dock-caught bluegills, not bluegills of size, and most of us didn't want a thing to do with them. But Grandpa, in the way of Grandpas, filleted the tiny fish and handed them over to Grandma. And Grandma, in the way of Grandmas, rinsed the five cups of fillets, put them in a quart of water and a cup of non-iodized salt and refrigerated them for forty-eight hours.

We had to go home then to continue our struggles, but when the time's up — I remember this clearly — Grandma will rinse those fillets again, pour a couple of cups of white vinegar over them and put them back in the fridge for another forty-eight. Then she'll pour that off and cook up two cups of white vinegar, one-and-a-half of sugar and one teaspoon each of mustard seed, whole black pepper, allspice and cloves, and four bay leaves. When that's cooled, she'll pour it over the fish and top it off with lemon and onion slices, and back in the fridge it'll go for five days. After that, she'll take out the spices and put it back for five more.

Right on time, we'll be back, and Grandma will let us at them. Goodness, they'll be good, and it brings back memories of a not-quite-so-old twosome doing the very same thing when a little boy, not so long ago, came busting up from that same dock with an ice cream bucket of baby bluegills.

observations on society and human nature

MAY 29

They say love makes the world go 'round, and so it does. Less often do they say that a good swallow of hot mustard does the same thing, as do the soft, breathtaking possibilities of a sunrise. It's tempting to read all kinds of meaning into a sunrise, but to my Uncle Jake, a sunrise means only one thing. It means little food fishes — basically called minnows — voraciously begin to forage for the littler bitty stuff that is their breakfast. Jake, as you know, is no romantic.

This commotion triggers a follow-up reaction as bass (sometimes big bass), smelling the coffee, the bacon and eggs, the hash browns, slide up and out of their overnight resting places to meals of their own. And eat they do, on minnows breakfasting on their breakfasts until, bellies filled, they slip back down and out of circulation to sleep it off.

There's more. As the sun rotates behind the pines on the west end of Lost Lake, it starts again. Nighttime bugs bestir themselves and begin to locomote in and on the water. And when that happens, you guessed it, little food fishes — minnows — left over from breakfast, hustle in for big bug suppers. And when that happens, bass (sometimes huge bass that haven't eaten since morning) shake the sleep from their eyes and slide up and out again into suppers of their own.

That's why my Uncle Jake, a bassin' man, a man who knows his bass and measures the high-water marks of his life by the bass he catches, is on the lake before the first light of the soft, breathtaking possibilities of sunrise and again from the time the sun settles on the pines until it's well out of sight. If you're the kind of person who needs to have a little fun once in a while, that's what you should be doing, too.

where do we go from here?

MAY 30

Nothing much bothered Milton McCool. Nothing much scared him. He was fond of saying he'd graduated from the school of hard knocks — magna cum cool. What he didn't tell us was he failed the course in Common Sense I, which is why he isn't with us anymore. He came face to face with a drowning machine, took a last gulp of air, filled his lungs clear full of water and got lost among the stars. Here's how it happened.

One day, a day that started out like any other day, Milton crowded the current flowing over a lowhead dam in his fishing boat. It wasn't much of a dam. Ten feet, maybe less. The dangers of getting too close were clearly marked, but you know Milton. He got swept over it and became trapped in the mess below. Water poured over the dam, of course, and created a churning backwash, an unforgiving, recirculating agitation of current. The roiling water took Milton to the bottom, then released him to the surface, then sucked him back to the face of the dam, then pushed him down again. And again. And again. It could have gone on forever, and it did, though Milton could not and did not. Branches also trapped in the water posed additional hazards. Cold water decreased his survival time. Air bubbles mixed in with the water decreased his buoyancy, lack of life jacket notwithstanding, by a full one-third. Anyone coming up in a boat from downstream to rescue him would have been caught up in the same no-win maelstrom, but Milton died alone.

What happened to Milton McCool wasn't a freak accident. Graveyards are crowded with people like him, people the world couldn't do without, people better educated and smarter, people like you, like me, who do crazy things but have so far gotten away with it.

a sort of love story

MAY 31

Hers is an ageless beauty, and love is a funny thing. The minute I saw her, how she looked, how she carried herself, I knew I had to have her. It was as if I'd stumbled across a charm woven by a fairy queen, or drunk a potion with my coffee, or got hit squarely in the heart with an arrow. I don't know. I'd had many before her, but never like that.

She'd been around, too. She knew the score. She knew me, knew how I was. She knew what I expected of her, yet she came along willingly. Many times, especially at first, I was proud of her and showed her off whenever I could. There were times, too, when I treated her bad, real bad, took her down some rocky rivers, but that's life. That's the way things are. There were times I left her for others. I'm not proud of it, but I've got a roving eye and an itchy soul that needs scratching from time to time, and that's the way things are, too.

But, as I say, love's a funny thing, and I've always come back, and we've always been able to pick up the pieces. It wasn't all thistles. We've had plenty of sunny times, like when the wind comes up softly off the water and kisses you on the cheek, and you climb the cloud-memories of your dreams. And we've weathered stormy seas, that's for sure, and long, long dry spells. And don't forget, she's dumped me once or twice.

All in all, we've done about as well as we could. We've done okay. Of course, she's not as young as she was. I've had to patch her bottom a few times. She's popped some rivets, but she performs like she always has, give or take. You're thinking I'm not the man I used to be either, and I'll agree with that, so when magic things need to be put in their places, if I can, I put myself back into my good old canoe.

room with a view

JUNE 1

My second cousin just had a baby. She named him John. John's a nice name, but every Tom, Dick and Harry is named John, and how was May for you, anyway? Was it a month of May baskets or of troublesome Maydays? I guess it doesn't matter, because May's a done deal and hello June, and what's happening out there?

Well, for one thing, my cousin timed it perfectly because, despite the calendar, it's summertime, at least some of the time it is, and when it's summertime in the great outdoors, the party for the most part is over. All that riotous living of April and May, all that courting rigamarole, all that showing off, fighting for position, mating, nest-building and egg-laying is over or much of it is. June's a family month, a quieter time of protecting, caring for and growing. The first baby chickadees of the season are about to leave the nests of their birth and babyhood. Do you remember that "fee-beeing" of chickadees last February? Well that was what this is all about. Nearly odorless fawns are lying still as death, hidden from wolves and coyotes and she-bears with babies to feed. Grouse hens are dust-bathing little ones on lonely backwoods roads. Mother mallards are herding newly hatched ducklings through dangerous forests of fields and cattails to the relative safety of open water. Bluebirds are fetching grasshoppers and beetles to their babies at about one every twenty minutes per. Baby loons are hitching rides on the backs of their mamas and papas, who are catching for their babies' breakfasts baby perch and insects.

Otherwise, fireflies are lighting lanterns over flowering laurels and rosemary. And we call this moon of June the Strawberry Moon. ("Doubtless," wrote someone, "God could have made a better berry, but doubtless God did not.") At least that's what we call it here at Lost Lake, and I'll bet that's what you call it where you live, too.

that's my mom

JUNE 2

Not too long ago, I made some noises about the importance of taking your kids fishing. "Take your kids fishing," I said, "it'll do them some good." Imagine my surprise when somebody did. It was a week ago last Tuesday. The telephone rang. "Be here at dawn, Dear," my mother said. It had been a long time since I'd been fishing with my mother. I have no idea why. "We'll go bluegill fishing," she said. "It'll keep you occupied and pleasant to be with."

We boarded her fourteen-footer as the sun was cutting a swath through the mist on the lake. She was using an ultralight outfit strung with very light line. "Let's begin," she said in a tone I hadn't heard in quite a while, "with artificials because they work so nicely, and kids feel so clever when they do." With that, we put tiny curlytails on teeny jigheads and swam them around in all kinds of cover. We probed the shallows on down to ten feet, keeping a keen eye on the lines and setting the hooks the instant we saw movement or felt weight, and I had fun. We fished tiny spinnerbaits, plain and skirted, shallow and deep near weedy covers. We tied on spongy spiders, size tens. We worked them slowly, and we did okay. We looped redworms on number six Aberdeen hooks and attached pencil-thin bobbers and enough split shot to all but sink them out of sight. We kept adjusting the hooks to keep the baits close to the bottom while we probed weeds, lily pads and brush piles. We rigged crickets by pushing the barbs downward through the chest shells and then burying them in their back ends. ("A dirty trick," Mom said, "but a necessary one for catching bluegills.")

My mother is to be envied for what she has sought out and learned about the nature of things, quite unlike so many of her cronies who, as they grew older, gave up fishing, got into golf, went insane and died.

american history 101

JUNE 3

Pemmican has changed the course of history numerous times. Pemmican, as you know, is a Native American concoction of dried, powdered meat, dried berries and melted fat. Stored in animal intestines and kept dry, it lasted indefinitely. In the early days, it provided energy and sustenance when other food supplies failed. It was pemmican, for instance, that gave Lewis and Clark the nourishment and stamina necessary to complete their trip into the trackless wilderness.

It was pemmican that gave the besieged defenders of the Alamo the fortitude to hang on as long as they did. And John Paul Jones could not have said, "I have not yet begun to fight," had he not stored barrels of pemmican on board. When MacArthur said, "I shall return," it was pemmican that brought him back. On Lindbergh's flight across the Atlantic, high octane fueled the plane; pemmican fueled the pilot. The Doughboys of World War II could as easily have been dubbed the pemmican boys. His health failing, Edgar Allen Poe fed ravenously on pemmican to finish one poem after another. To this day, pemmican gets many hunters, fishermen, hikers and campers through long stretches of fast-food famine.

You may ask in wide-eyed wonder, "Can this be? Can pemmican have done all this?" Let me say, I have no concrete and irrefutable evidence, but I am versed in pemmican, and I'm sure as hell it can.

To make pemmican, grind in a grinder (but not too much) one cup each of dried apples, dates, prunes, peaches, peanuts and raisins. Add a cup each of currants and coconut flakes. Thoroughly unite this in a big bowl. Melt a half-cup of margarine and mix it with a half-cup each of peanut butter and honey; mix all this with the other stuff. Form it into bars. Roll them in powdered sugar or graham cracker crumbs. Instead of animal intestines, wrap them in waxed paper and freeze them until needed.

back to the basics

JUNE 4

This was last Friday. It was late in the afternoon. The sun was bringing the day to its knees. My Uncle Jake and I were catfishing on this little river that feeds into a bigger one that feeds into Whatchamacallit Bay on the north end of Lost Lake. We're not ordinarily the type who confuse good fishing with easy fishing, and we were doing our darnedest to catch us some catfish. We were using our never-fail, secret-recipe stinkbaits with downright enthusiasm. We were tossing them into deep holes we knew were there, into tangles we could see with our eyes, and under the undercut banks on the opposite shore, like we always do. And, to tell you the truth, we might as well have stayed home and played pinochle at the Elkhorn Tavern and Wildlife Museum.

But my Uncle Jake said, "Guess again. We're not going anyplace until we've got catfish for supper." Then I got edgy and, seeing this was becoming an emergency, he ambled over to his pickup truck and fetched back a can of leeches and a bucket of three-inch shiner minnows left over from walleye fishing earlier in the week. "This'll do the trick," he said with a smugness so typical of catfishermen. He tied on a number four long-shanked hook and just enough split shot to keep the bait in place, more or less, on the bottom. He put on a minnow and handed me a leech which, as a measure of blind faith, I attached to a similar hook and split shot.

We'd been fishing with our never-fail secret-recipe stinkbaits for so long, I'd forgotten that live bait is a natural catfish food. It should come as no surprise, therefore, that we caught a mess of fish. I even had to apologize a couple of times because I accidentally caught two walleyes, but Jake said it was okay if I didn't get uppity about it.

aye, aye captain

JUNE 5

Everything in life is either swell or lousy. Take the other day. I was caught up in the quarrelsome confines of June, spending too much time on the job, too much time trimming the crab grass of my lawn, pruning dandelions, enlarging the woodpile, which had shrunk to nothing. I was a mess. Imagine my joy, then, when my Uncle Jake asked me to go bass fishing with him on the day after tomorrow. This was last week.

I jumped at the chance. Then I got to thinking. I am no raw beginner when it comes to bass fishing, yet I didn't want to take a chance on this day off of mine. I wanted to — no, I needed to — catch fish. I needed it bad. So I strategically placed a call to a guy I know who had been bass fishing earlier in the week and did very okay. Sure enough, he gave me the lowdown, dished me the dope, handed me the keys to the Cadillac of his fishing success.

The day came, and Jake and I headed out. For once, I'm as sure as a hound dog on a hot trail I'm going to show the old boy up and have me a whale of a day, but Jake starts to catch fish, and I don't. He tells me I'm doing it all wrong. "Don't worry, Uncle," I say, smiling like a fox with a mouthful of feathers, and I tell him what I did.

"Don't you know," he says, "that you've got to read the water each and every time you go fishing? Don't you know bass waters are always changing, that it's cooler today than it was yesterday, that it's overcast, that the wind's coming from a different direction? Don't you know," he goes on and on, "you've got to read the day, process the info in your head, and only then come up with a plan of action?"

Well, of course I did, and I understand the wisdom behind it, though it made me long for the days when all I needed to catch bass was a hook and bobber, a cane pole, a worm and a warm school day to skip out of.

my tin cup runneth over

JUNE 6

If you fear less and hope more, and talk less and say more, and hate less and love more, then, they say, the world is your oyster. I hope so but, to tell you the truth, I don't need it. I am, you see, in canoe country, and I'm perched on a rocky ledge that juts into the water perfectly. I'm watching the sun come up into what's going to be a humdinger of a day. The lid on my battered and bubbling coffeepot is doing the hootchie kootchie atop a small campfire, the smoke of which is mixing itself up with the percolating smells of coffee and pine trees wet with rain and steam coming off the lake. The jiggling lid of the coffeepot is echoing the fading rumble of thunder running just ahead of the rising sun and this new day. This is the stuff of life. This and fireflies.

Fireflies. Lightning bugs. They're not flies at all; they're beetles. And, of course, they have nothing to do with lightning, except they're racing to catch the thunder now and the disappearing night. Near breathing tubes, fireflies carry something called Luciferin. This stuff combines with something else called Luciferase to produce instantaneous light, far more efficient than anything mankind has manufactured. Lightning bug light is light without heat, nearly one hundred percent light energy. By contrast, our old-fashioned, ordinary light bulb is about ten percent efficient. In fireflies, both sexes flash to attract members of the opposite sex, which must produce a certain amount of anxiety in the rolled and twisted turbulence of night.

And besides the fireflies of this almost summer morning in canoe country, I've got bacon sizzling in a frying pan and loons calling like bits of ragtime and the murmur of the west wind passing by in dreamy, whispery whispers, and I don't know how I could expect more out of life than that.

sneak and release

JUNE 7

To be a consistently good bass fisherman, you have to do a little scouting, so I slicked back my hair, put on a clean T-shirt, paid out good money for a new pair of sunglasses, dangled a cigarette out the corner of my mouth (though I don't smoke) slapped a James Dean sneer on my kisser and slipped into a jumpin' kind of joint on a Saturday night. I walked up to the bar where there was a line of big ones drowning whatever ailed them in various and sundry potions of poison. I bought 'em a round and, casual like, asked 'em if anybody knew a hot spot close by where a guy like me could get a little action.

This one fish, a two-, two-and-a-half pounder, gave me the once-over. "Aftah tinkin' it ovah," he said, "I tink youse might try Undercut Banks, especially doze extendin' back a foot or t'ree, if you know what I mean."

"Nah," said a tough-looking four-pounder with a scar running from her left eye to the corner of her mouth. "Ah personally prefers Riffle Holes where fast warter runs into slower warter, digging into the bottom and pushing against the rocks. Ah like ta lie in the still warter behind the apparent obstructions. And ah sometimes like ta catch mah breath where trees and brush slow the warter down."

An older fish in a threadbare suit huffed on his monocle, wiped it off with a soup-stained tie and said, "My good fellow, go to Feeder Streams that bring in fresh minnows and crayfish daily. And I find the quieter waters of Cutbanks suitable resting places."

An eight-inch kid — he had no business in a place like this — said, "Go to Overhangs, man. Lots of us go there for frogs and insects, and to Deep Runs where currents have pushed through long channels. And oxbows, man, they're cool."

Then a cloud passed over. They gave a little jump and looked at me hard, like they were seeing me for the first time. Then they scattered. I gave 'em fifteen, twenty minutes to get settled, and did likewise.

... till death do you part, etc.

JUNE 8

Weddings in and of themselves have terrified more than one soul and, to tell you the truth, the ones I attend, I attend with a certain skepticism. But we went to one last Saturday that wasn't bad. It was my niece's, my sister's daughter's. She was so beautiful, so full of hope, of promise, so like her mother. The drive down there was nice. I took the back roads. The ponds and potholes and ditches along the way were filled with water, and in each were mating and nesting ducks, and I like that. In the sky were Vs of geese heading this way and that. In the cornfields, geese were picking over what farmers missed last fall. The ceremony itself was also nice but, five minutes into the thing, my mind went back to the ducks and geese.

Most ducks have different mates in their lifetimes, different ones each year, usually. Once they've mated and brooding begins, the males leave. The hens then have to incubate the eggs and raise the chicks all by themselves in the face of a thousand dangers. But with geese, it's different. After mating, they stay together to care for the young. The males are fiercely protective of their families until, at the very least, they reach their wintering grounds. Swans are like that, too. I was starting to think about swans when I was jolted into the here and now with an elbow-jab to the ribs just in time to join the reception line.

I suppose I should be able to come up with an appropriate ending for this — something that sums up the points I made, something inspirational and, above all, cute, but when I got to the youngsters, I wished them happiness and expressed the hope that in their married life they'd be more like geese and swans instead of ducks. This brought blank stares from the kids and prompted another jab the likes of which you wouldn't believe.

there's more to fishing than fishing

JUNE 9

There's no such thing as a bad day of fishing, even if you accomplish only half what you hoped you would. This basically is a story about life and river fishing for smallmouth bass, and here's how it goes.

A couple of our younger fellows home from college for the summer, and pretty good softball players by trade, came to my attention when I heard they'd rather river fish for smallmouth bass than you-know-what. Since knowledge is the cement that holds my life together, and I know only a little bit about river fishing for smallmouth bass and nothing whatsoever about you-know-what, I asked them one day if I could join them. My reputation on the river is well known, but they said I could come along anyway, so long as I didn't ask too many questions or get in the way.

These kids wade the rivers they fish for smallmouth bass in. And they wade simply enough, in sneakers and cut-off blue jeans. They carry their fishing tackle in little boxes stuffed in their back pockets and their baits in small baskets wired to their belt loops. In case you can use the added information, they use six-pound monofilament line and set their drags perfectly.

Once they (we) got to the river, they (we) moved as quietly as could be, hunting for submerged rocks in the faster currents, deeper backwater pools and shaded honey holes under bridges and fallen-in trees. They (we) hooked lively crawlers once through the collars and cast upstream and let them drift effortlessly down. Boy, oh boy, did they (we) catch fish.

Once I had it figured out, I launched into the second phase of my plan and asked them what they could tell me about you-know-what. They took one look at me and left me high and dry. Apparently, where you-know-what is concerned, it's every person for himself.

running out of time

JUNE 10

Fishing encourages both solitude and society. The act of fishing is practised in lovely, wild surroundings, giving each of us who fishes the opportunity to be alone, if we want to be alone, with a stream, river or lake, and with ourselves. But, at the same time, we are gregarious. This social side of us, this getting-together side, this need to compare notes, to enjoy each other's company, is sometimes as important as is the solitude. That is why a bunch of us have come off the water and gathered at Mom's Cafe over on Main Street.

The fishing has been good here at Lost Lake, but the catching has been lousy, so the conversation naturally centered around when we could expect improved conditions. Some said the best time to go fishing is when the barometer is rising. Some said just before a storm. Others said just after a storm, during the dark of the moon, or when the sky is overcast. We pretty much agreed with that. Uncle Jake and the Professor, in a rare display of unity, thought the best time is when cattle are up and feeding, and when deer are moving, and the hour or two before or after dark, and right after a rain or just before one, or during a drizzle. That sounded good, too.

Ol' Gladys liked the period just before the spawn, or just after, and when the water is rising or as it begins to drop. "Here, here," someone said, and we nodded. Mom came over with refills and opined that the best time is in the middle of a hatch, any kind of hatch, or when Jake complains of a crick in his back, or when his knees get stiff. There was no denying that.

After considerable discussion, however, we came to the unanimous conclusion that the very, very best time to go fishing is today. Because if we waited for tomorrow, we'd find out they were biting yesterday, which is ... well, you get the idea.

coming to terms with an out-of-body experience

JUNE 11

Yesterday I was down at the garden, digging worms for the kids to go fishing with, when the crabapple trees got in my way, and I had to sit down to think about that. They were loaded with blossoms and the whole place smelled like Grandma's bathroom. If each of those blossoms generates one crabapple, we'll be filthy rich with crabapples come September, which is okay.

We don't usually let our crabapples fall off the trees and just lie there to ambush passing lawn mowers. We don't rake them up into fuel for the compost pile, either. Some go into wine, of course, and some we turn into stuff so fine it would wide-open your eyes and big-smile your grin if you should come over and try some. It tastefully decorates baking powder biscuits and freshly-baked, new-toasted toast. It deliciously glazes smoked turkeys and venison roasts. Slathered between omelet layers for campout breakfasts, it's a kiss from heaven. It's called, though you've guessed it, crabapple jelly, and we (meaning she) make it all the time.

We pick about five pounds of the little apples and wash them off with the garden hose. With a jackknife, we cut off the stems and blossom ends, cut the apples in half, put them in a kettle with eight cups of water and boil them mushy. Then we strain the goop through a jelly bag without putting too much pressure on it. For each cup of juice we stir in three-fourths cup of sugar and boil it fast to 220 degrees, skimming off the foam. Finally, we add a teaspoon of vanilla (though some don't) and pour it into hot little jars.

The kids like it on crackers. It makes nice Christmas gifts for people who like things homemade and perfect and, as I say, in camp and at the deer shack or ice-fishing shanty, it's grand stuff. But let's not think of that now in June when the sun's shining, and the whole place smells like Grandma's bathroom.

a treatment program

JUNE 12

Each time any of us goes fishing, it's like the coming of spring again. It's refreshing, and it's revitalizing. The thought of it is enough to set the fast pace of life into low gear. For nothing else do we leave a warm bed before the sun rises. For nothing else do we drive a hundred miles to stand chest-deep in freezing water. For nothing else do we get our feet wet, our fingers hypothermic, in the name of pleasure. For nothing else do we suffer mosquito bites and bloodshot eyes so willingly. Which brings us to the subject of wobbling spoons.

Wobbling spoons come in sizes from little one-inchers to those big enough to interest barracudas. They're a most versatile bait, fishable on top of the water or all the way to the bottom. Wobblers are perhaps most effective, though, when fished over and through thick weed beds where the darn things usually get hung up and tangled. Even those with built-in weed guards get caught on something.

Glory to him, then, who thought of this. Single-hook wobblers, the only kind to be chucking into the fish-hiding jungles you're fishing in, can be greatly improved with a small rubber band and thirty seconds. Take the hook and bend the point down a little so it's out of a direct line with the eye. Put a rubber band through the eye, pass one end of it through the other end and pull, leaving a loop, which you stretch to the barb and hook under it. With a little piece of pork rind added, you can cast it into the thickest weeds. Keep the rod tip up so the line doesn't get caught, and reel it in slowly, stopping now and then to let the fluttering motion of the tail and the wobbling motion of the spoon drop into the thick of things.

And when a long dark figure swings up with the fully loaded intention of taking a bite out of it, and every nerve fiber in your body tenses with anticipation, tell me it's not a sure-fire cure for whatever ails anybody.

upstream/downstream

JUNE 13

Each of us canoes for reasons of our own. Some of us like to ride with eagles down slippery slopes into morning suns. Some of us like to sail with the wind Mariah at our backs or in our faces as we rearrange reflections of gray-white clouds in the water. Some of us like to hitch rides on loons' calls and wolves' cries and full half moons. It doesn't matter why, and it doesn't matter how, each of us mounts our canoe and rides it heaven-bound according to our individual natures, simply for the jazz of it. But I write too much about canoes, and don't think I don't know it, so this isn't about that. It's about paddles.

When we choose our canoes, we do it with campfires dancing in our eyes, with loons' calls and wolves' cries ringing in our ears, as well we should. But when we pick our paddles, we usually do so as a laid back afterthought. It shouldn't be that way, because a canoe without a paddle is like a bird with a broken wing. It's like a butterfly clinging lifelessly to the radiator of a '58 Chevy. (That probably sounds like I'm overdoing it again, but I'm working on that.)

Generally, in-the-know stern paddlers prefer paddles that reach up to their eyeballs or noses at most, while those whose favorite thing is to be crouched up front pin their hopes on paddles that reach chin high. Wide-bladed paddles are more efficient than narrower ones, but they're more tiring to use. Kids should have their very own paddles, perfectly fitted to them. Paddles should be straight, unpainted, unvarnished, with no knots or burrs, and evenly feathered.

New, synthetic paddles are making splashes here and there, but most of us prefer to screw our souls to the old-fashioned ones of maple or ash to bring us, hearts thumping, over jumpy waves of gladness and down rolling rivers of hope, and, darn it, there I go again.

hot flashes and cold feet

JUNE 14

We're playing poker in my neighbor's garage when somebody wonders aloud where the fifth guy is. "He's probably lost again," someone else says, which sends my mind reeling.

Not everybody who's been lost has lived to tell about it. It's that thought more than any other I think about when I'm direction-confused in the out-of-doors. I've spent the greater part of my life not knowing where I was going or what to do when I got there. Through the fourth grade, I was lost somewhere between the house and the bus stop down by the mailbox. Once, as a teenager during the smelt run, I slipped into the woods for one minute and disappeared for three days. Give me a fishing pole, aim me down a well-traveled path to a crowded river bank, and I'm gone for a week. Put a gun in my hand, walk arm-in-arm with me through a thicket, and you'll come out alone.

That I've thus far managed to emerge from my encounters with the unknown, I owe to the greatest of all motivators, which is fear, and I was blessed with speed. It's this combination that has allowed me to outrun wolves that howl in the night. There is no record in all of history of wolves attacking human beings, and I aim to keep it that way. Fear and speed have allowed me to scale mountains at a pretty good clip when I've come betwixt she-bears and their cubs. They've permitted me to leap rivers and climb trees, deciduous and coniferous, with ease. Fear of starving to death and sleeping alone with nothing between me and the cold ground has led me hot-footing it over deserts and has got me, with a lusty yell, through blizzards.

Do I avoid panic when I'm lost? Do I keep calm? Do I assess the situation and plan a strategy? I do not. Alas, I am very like those who perpetually believe their pair of aces can beat somebody else's three twos. Poor souls, they are lost forever.

now, in june

JUNE 15

Here at Lost Lake we don't live so much by the calendar as we do by the barometer and thermometer, so the outlook is especially bright for us in June. We're squeezing as much out of these long days as we can, making time for picnics and walks along the beach.

Before and after work, we're tying flies for trout and building poppers for bluegills, reloading shotgun shells and darned near wearing out the porch swing after supper when things cool off. The kids are roasting wieners and telling ghost stories around campfires down by the pond, and eating strawberry shortcake like it's candy. We're weeding and mowing and weeding and mowing, not quite sick of it yet, but getting there. Any day, we're going to fix the sagging dock. We've been going to do that for two or three years. We're canoeing as often as we can, and hiking if you can call it that. We're probably strolling.

We're skipping stones on Whatchamacallit Bay, swatting mosquitoes and cussing out black gnats and deer flies who don't appreciate a good bug dope when they see it. Walleyes are down deep, so we're teasing crappies from dark holes and luring northern pike out of weed beds. Bass fishing is not bad and, as usual, we're muskie-hoping. In the shade of a big, flat rock in the tail of an eddy just upstream from a riff we know, there's a nice brook trout. It keys on anything that moves, but it's still there. We're shooting at clay pigeons once or twice a week, and sticking arrows into hay bales stacked three high out behind the garage.

It's time for lemonade and iced tea and cold beer. Hummingbirds are draining the feeder on a regular basis, and we're making all the time we can for our kids and the older folks, because this would be an unhappy world without our kids and a desolate one without our older folks. At least that's how we feel about things here at Lost Lake, and I suppose that's how you feel about things where you live, too.

when less is more

JUNE 16

Things are run-of-the-mill quiet here at Lost Lake, except for the daisies. They're making a stand against time, as are monarch butterflies in flowering fields of clover. Painted turtles are laying eggs; bobolinks are hatching theirs in saucer-like nests. June bugs are lying upside-down in futile attempts to swim dry backstrokes across the summer-sandy kitchen floor, and muskie fishermen think they've died and gone to heaven.

Muskie fishermen fish for the awful wonder of it, because they so admire and delight in muskies. It's remarkable. Most muskie fishermen around here are like Native Americans who counted coup. They merely touched an enemy in the heat of battle without killing him. It was the greatest of honors to do this. Our muskie fishermen are like that. They believe a muskie is too honorable a fish to be caught only once, that it should be judged only on its value as a challenge. For them, the thrill lies in the chase, the catch and not the kill. To that end, we use artificial lures to avoid deep-hooking fish. Muskies can swallow sucker minnows, hook and all, a long ways into their bellies, making it nearly impossible to remove them without risking the life of the fish. Despite the pleasure we feel at hooking such prizes, we stifle an urge to prolong the excitement by overplaying them, tiring them to where they can't recover. We likewise suppress an eagerness to bring them in too quickly.

How many muskies do we need to catch? Not many. Sometimes none. We don't expect a lot of action. We count our successes in other ways, in reaching for the high challenge. We're fascinated by the pursuit and are sweetly enough hooked by the pleasure of it. To us, there's more satisfaction in fishing for muskies and catching nothing than there is in fishing for anything else and catching ... nothing.

it's not my fault

JUNE 17

People sometimes ask me, "Are you a fisherman?"

"I am," I say.

"And how many fish have you caught lately?" they sometimes ask.

"Not any," I say, "but countless thousands have caught me." They look at me then like I'm putting them on, but it's true, and it's driving me crazy.

I may look fine at this moment. I smile. Courteously, I answer the telephone. My shirt is buttoned. My shoes are tied. But the vacant look, the wide-eyed, walleyed cant to my eyes and the tight little lines around the smile are signals that not all is well with me. I am losing control. I may look okay to you if you see me stopped, white-knuckled, at a red light in heavy traffic, or picking over picked-over tomatoes at the supermarket, or in the garden cutting weeds off at the knees (using a very sharp hoe) or hacking heads off dandelions (even now I smile at the thought of that), but I am as tight as fence wire.

There is the sense of a tic incubating on the left side of my face (my good side) and a juggling bounce to my knees. As I said, I am losing controlll. Forgive me for inflicting this on you, but if I seem all right, if I seem to be holding my own when you see me hunkered over my desk, or shaving in the morning before the mirror with a keen razor, then you should know that I have not been fishing in a week. Because of that, blood is rising in my temples, and I am slowly losing ccontrolll.

You should know, if you see me appearing quite normal, that the fingers on the hands in my pockets are clenched. Have I mentioned, have I told you, it's been a week, seven days, since I've felt river currents washing against my legs, and visited tree-darkened, fog-enshrouded islands thick with fish wishes? Have I mentioned that? Have I told you I'm dizzy? That I can't breathe? That my vision is limited? That I'm becoming unmoored, and inch by inch I'mm llosingg cconntrrolll?

we can't take it with us

JUNE 18

I obviously can't write from a mother's perspective, and the days of my childhood are too long gone for me to come from that angle. Consequently, it's a father's point of view — for better or worse — that I'm stuck with at this time of year set aside for fathers, of all things. Can you believe it?

So, happy Father's Day to you and to you and to me, too. What'll it be? Neckties? Socks? Hugs and kisses? We'll take it. But Father's Day isn't a day exactly; it's a seasonless, everyday kind of thing, not for getting gifts but for giving them before we vanish like snowflakes.

Fathers' days are the days, every day after day, when we tell our kids old stories that swarm off cool waters on summer nights. When we give them clouds and constellations. When we teach them how to perfectly lose a day here and there, and flow like rivers. When we give them lessons — being very patient — in the practical realities of overhand casts. When we teach them how to love wild animals and how to hunt them with honor.

Fathers' days are days after days of showing our kids that their survival depends on blue waves washing upon clean shores. The days we teach them to shrug off early frosts and laugh at mosquitoes. The days we demonstrate leaping over creeks and whistling like swans. When we give them a continued interest in living, like revved-up motorcycles, with time-outs for woodsmoke and quiet places. When we show them how to be guardian angels and to plant fairly straight rows of onions.

Fathers' days are days after days of teaching our kids to give generously to their kids, when the time comes for them to have kids, so such gifts as we give them don't go up in smoke when the arsonist of flesh puts a torch to us, and we dissolve into nameless bits of wildflowers.

thanks, dad

JUNE 19

The answers to so many questions can be found in the out-of-doors if we but look, and look in the right places, but who can explain such a complicated thing as a father? Not the poking-along moon, which keeps its secrets so well. Not small-fry constellations swimming in the dark, or, if they know, they're not telling. Who can account for this man who gave us life, this man who protected us when we were weak? Even clever ravens go silent at the question.

Who can explain a man who carried us giggling on his back, who helped us grow and grow, who loved us? Not the pine trees with their piney smells and heads bowed with the weight of knowledge. Who can explain a man strong enough to be gentle, a man who taught us to love, to work, to answer for our deeds, who kissed scraped elbows and dried wet tears? Who can explain that? Not the mountains or valleys or all the rivers flowing to the sea. Who can account for a fellow who was a Santa Claus, an Easter Bunny, the Tooth Fairy, rolled into Dad? A fellow who set aside his life for ours and helped us unravel the tangle of the universe? Ask the old owl when the night comes on, and the owl can't account for it, either. Who can understand this man who gave us the power to hold on to the true things of the earth, and the courage to join eagles in high flight? Not the soft mystery of twilight, or the woodsmoke from campfires riding in on spirit winds. Who can figure the guy who gave us his giant steps to follow?

Who, then, can fathom such a thing as a father? As we warm our hearts from the fire of the life he has given us, only we can. Only we. So, on that special day in the late-middle of June, embrace the man, or the thought of him, or, if that's all you have left, his memory.

teddy and me

JUNE 20

Though I am fiercely independent with a mind of my own, it has always been a comfort to me that many of Teddy Roosevelt's theories are also mine. So it was no surprise last Thursday, when he stopped by to sample a new batch of dandelion wine, to learn that we share similar versions of life in the Great Upstairs. He started it

"In my version of heaven," he said, blustering like a bull moose, "all hunters are accurate in their aiming, clean in their killing, persistent in their tracking and wise in the ways of the wild."

"Here, here," I said.

"In my version of heaven," he said conservatively, "no hunters shoot at road signs, overshoot their limits, leave wounded game without extending every effort to find it, blow away so much as a porcupine for the hell of it, nor shoot at a chipmunk to sight in a 30.06."

"Righto," I said.

"In heaven," he said, "there are no slobs who litter, who trespass, who shoot unless they are certain of their target and well beyond it. In heaven, no one makes a mistake with a gun. With guns, there can be no mistakes. All hunters understand that hunting is a privilege, that killing is only a small part of the hunt, that killing is merely proof of a skillful search. No one ever breaks game laws, but goes beyond mere laws."

"Here, here," I said again.

"In heaven," he said, "adults take kids into the woods, into the fields and mountains and streams, and patiently, lovingly teach them to hunt and pass that lore on forever."

"Here, here," I said sounding uncomfortably like a yes-man. I added, "Though heaven be a mystery on the wing, that's as much a heaven as with a straight face we dare hope for."

"Tally-ho," he said, walking softly away, grabbing the twelve-foot popple stick he always carries, mounting his horse and riding roughly through the garden.

hook, line and sinker

JUNE 21

We are mourning the loss of my second cousin, Petie. Not that Petie has died, of course. His is a fate worse than that. He has, in effect, gone from the frying pan into the flames of a living hell, if you can imagine that!

Petie was a fisherman obsessed. He lived it, breathed it, ate it, drank it. He fished for walleyes, for muskies, for northern pike and crappies, for perch, trout and catfish, for bluegills. He fished with worms, with minnows, spinnerbaits, crankbaits and stinkbaits, with flies wet and dry, with pork rind, it didn't matter. He nymphed. He fished in the winter, in the spring, in the summer and all fall, while his wife stayed home. She changed diapers and wiped noses. She hung clothes out to dry. She scrubbed, dusted and cooked. She pulled weeds out of the garden and canned tomatoes. She got to where she couldn't stand the sight of Petie. To rescue himself and his marriage, Petie suggested to his Snookums that she come fishing with him.

"But Petie," she sighed, "I don't know fishing from beeswax."

"I will teach you," he said, and he did.

She took to fishing as seagulls take to popcorn and has got to where she is obsessed with it. She lives it, breathes it, eats it, drinks it. She fishes for walleyes, for muskies, for northern pike and crappies, for perch, trout and catfish, for bluegills. She fishes with worms, with minnows, spinnerbaits, crankbaits and stinkbaits, with flies wet and dry, with pork rind, it doesn't matter. She nymphs. She fishes in the winter, in the spring, in the summer and all fall, while poor Petie stays home. The last we saw of him he was changing diapers and wiping noses. He was hanging clothes out to dry. He was scrubbing, dusting and cooking. He was pulling weeds out of the garden and canning tomatoes. Poor Petie.

life after death

JUNE 22

Before you know it you die, and you're standing on a cloud. A white-robed old fellow hunts up your name in a big book, studies it awhile, points thataway, and off you go into eternity. You're headed down a trail — a very nice trail without blackberry bushes to scratch you, without rocks to trip you up, without low branches to knock your cap off, without quicksand.

By and by, you come to a lake with a sandy beach all around it. There's a fishing pole there, all rigged and ready to go, and a tackle box that's loaded. You cast. You're a little surprised you didn't hook up in a tree on your back cast, but then you notice the trees are set a dozen or so feet from the water. You are further impressed at the length of your cast — it's way out there — and the lack of a backlash.

The bucktail lands with a soft kerplop, and before the ripples settle, a muskie, the likes of which you have seen only on the wall of the Elkhorn Tavern and Wildlife Museum, grabs it and clears the water by three feet. You start to reel it in, and it comes a little easier than you expected it to. You release it and start over. You make another excellent cast, and as the ripples settle, another muskie, like the one before it, takes the bait as the other one did and comes in easier than you kind of hoped it would. Then again. And again. And again. And again. You switch baits. Same thing.

You trudge back up the trail and tell the old gent how you hate to complain, but this isn't quite what you expected heaven to be like. He looks at you over his glasses, checks his book and, in a voice like quiet thunder, says, "My dear boy, this ain't heaven."

the bass also rises

JUNE 23

You have witnessed, as have I, the painfully blind indifference of fate to your needs as bass fishermen. For example, at one time or another, absolutely everything works on bass, and at other times, absolutely nothing does. It is the yin and yang of bass fishing.

At those times when absolutely everything works on bass, life is a hit on an inside straight, three-card limit, nothing wild. Such peaks of prodigy, however, exist in comparative isolation. It is those other times, when absolutely nothing works on bass, when life is like the smell of perspiration on a hot day, that drives so many anglers, worn and haggard, off the water and into the dull and wordy business of drink.

Not all, though. Some fishermen are not so easily done in. They go on catching bass with or without the cooperation of the fish, and here's how they do it. They'll be in weeds hoping to pull a decent fish out of them. They'll hitch a hefty shiner to a hook and ask it to tow a good-sized bobber around and around. They'll use a stout pole, a single hook and monofilament line well into the double digits. They'll go where there's a somewhat sandy bottom and plenty of floating vegetation. They like this as close to deeper water as they can get it. They'll ease close to this stuff, hook the hefty shiner through the lips, fix the good-sized bobber three feet or so above it and cast to the edge of the floating vegetation. The shiner sees the weeds, thinks, "Aha!" and heads for them. But, the bobber holds the hapless minnow right there to struggle in vain against the painfully blind indifference of fate to its minnow existence.

These fishermen give the process time. They are not expecting exactly fish-a-minute action, but every once in a while they are proving that, where bass are concerned, a lot of things work when absolutely nothing does.

keep on dreaming, by golly

JUNE 24

I do not wish to go to Paris, or walk the Champs-Elysées or sit like a hippie on the right or left bank of the river that runs through it. Nor do I wish to go to London to see the changing of the guard or Big Ben. I have a pretty good watch of my own. I want to go to the Barren Grounds in the far North of Canada and shoot me a caribou.

I want to spend a week there studying the vast, treeless tundra without seeing a caribou. I want to walk miles and spend hours inspecting the landscape through weather-beaten binoculars. On the seventh day, I want to come upon a trail full of caribou tracks. I want that trail to lead me over a low mountain, down into a vast river drainage, if there are low mountains and vast river drainages on the Barren Grounds in the far North of Canada. I think there are.

I want my guide to tap me on the shoulder and whisper, "Holy cow, look at that!" He will point, and there I will see my caribou. We will begin a three-hour stalk with the wind in our faces. One hundred fifty yards from my caribou, we will stop behind a big rock. My guide will signal, "Okay, hotshot, let's see if you can get that one," and I do. It's as big as an elephant.

We will spend a day and a half hauling it back to our camp. We will be especially careful with the antlers. We will load it into the floatplane and fly it back here to Lost Lake. I will call my neighbor, the butcher, who will help me cut it up, wrap it and carry it to the freezer in the basement. I will reinforce the wall behind my fireplace and hang the antlers from there. If I can't do that, I want to go to Ketchikan, Alaska, and shoot me a moose, if they have moose near Ketchikan, Alaska. I think they do.

mind your own business

JUNE 25

"Our flyfishing vest," the ad reads, "is more than a piece of clothing. It is a vital part of your equipment — functional, durable, engineered to perform for you no matter the demand." So, I bought one.

"This extra lightweight fishing rod is designed by backpackers for the special needs of the backpacking fisherman," reads another. Since I am, at times, a backpacking fisherman with special needs, I got one of those too.

"Send us a sixteen-dollar check or money order," reads yet another, "and we'll send you six assorted nymphs, a floating four-bin fly box, a colorful jacket patch and our all new forty-page free catalog. Do it today." I did it yesterday.

"The finest trophy fishing anywhere (twelve trophy species). Seven days (all inclusive). Deluxe accommodations." I went.

"Money-back guarantee if not delighted." I was delighted.

"Put yourself in a class with the best." Yesiree, please and thank you.

"Try the finest ... " I tried it.

"Double your pleasure ... " I doubled it.

"Send for more information." By all means.

"Write for free brochure." I need more brochures.

"Buy one, get one free." I bought two.

"Quicker, faster, bigger, better, smoother, best. Dependable, reliable, sure-fire, tough, high-performance, portable, lightweight, insulated, unsinkable, comfortable, leakproof (did I say leak-proof?), durable, long-lasting, rust-proof, powerful, quiet." It's mine.

"As seen on ... " I've got to have it.

Now, if you've read this far, it might appear to you that I place quite a bit of emphasis on acquiring quite a bit of outdoor equipment, but if you think I'm going to close this by suggesting you've got a point there, let me remind you that the trouble with you is you worry too much about things that should be left alone.

natural selection

JUNE 26

It's so easy now to appreciate the whole-souled nobility of dreams coming true. Tadpoles are in the process of becoming something else again, and the antlers of white-tailed deer are velvety and promising. We're launching savage if unconvincing attacks on weeds in the garden, weeds engaged in the playful strangulation of zucchini. Whip-poor-wills are giving us sensational songs at sunset and encores at dawn. Now that robins have finished nesting in them, we're taking down holiday wreaths from the garage door. Growing grouse and pheasant chicks are bathing in warm summer sand, something they have in common with our school-free kids. Junior pine trees are maturing into full-fledged Christmas trees.

Most of us are engaged in the endless struggle of squeezing out a living one way or another, and keeping ahead of the tax man, when we'd rather be fishing. Poison ivy is thriving. Bull moose antlers are about as big as they're going to get this year, which is about big enough. Lemonades are fashionable, as are omelets served on canoe paddles in the middle of nowhere, which is not a bad way to go if you like things perfect. Turtles are making mad dashes over country roads to lay eggs where the grass is greener. Muskies are fat, walleyes quiet, trout secretive.

Honeybees are working themselves to death. Honeysuckles are smelling good and looking nice. At night the kids are lying on their backs, counting fireflies and lucky stars. Cherries are reddish and berries fat. It looks like a good year for tomatoes. We're attending class and family reunions, shooting the breeze and living on gumption. At least that's what's happening here at Lost Lake, and I expect that's about what's happening where you live, too.

affordable elegance

JUNE 27

Love is the force behind miracles and, over time, small miracles add up to big ones, which is why you're so feverishly wrapped up in the philosophy of catch and release. But you've gone and caught a couple of trout, and you're going to eat them. Trout don't enjoy a long freezer life, so you'll not be wrapping them up and tucking them in the droning, food-eating machine in the bowels of your house. You'll eat them now.

There are many ways to prepare trout, but the best have two things in common. They deal only with fish that have been dressed carefully and tended well from streamside to countertop and they don't cover up the taste of such a fish as a trout with strong gunks and goos, but preserve the magic of it, and the goodness of it, and the miracle in the catching of it. So you will brush the stomach cavities of this brace of trout you have caught and kept and gently tended and carefully dressed with melted butter and a little salt and pepper. Not much. You will line each cavity with a row of so-thinly sliced lemons and dill as fresh as you can get it. You'll place these fish, then, in a baking dish, cover them with another layer of thin lemon slices, salt and pepper, not much, and dill as fresh as you can get it. You'll put them in the oven and bake them. During the baking, you'll go to the garden for the makings of a salad. You'll rinse it off with the hose running cold. You'll cut it up. You'll add oil to it like a spendthrift, add vinegar to it like a miser, and stir it up like a madman.

More calmly, you'll mix the juice of another lemon, a quarter-pound of melted butter, a cup of serious cream and a glass of Chablis. You'll heat it ever so slightly, timing it to be warm as the fish are done. You'll pour it over them and serve them with the salad and hot homemade bread and iced Chablis, while you hold tightly to the table, lest you float right out the window and up to the moon.

i hope you're satisfied

JUNE 28

I'm going camping, reluctantly. I've got too much to do around here to go camping, and no vacation days coming, but I have no choice. It's been hot here, real hot, and we haven't seen rain in a long time.

Among the first to ask me to go were a couple of golfers. The fairways were dry, they said. The greens were browns. The water hazards were sand traps. "No," I said, "I've too much to do and no vacation days coming." Besides, I have no interest in golf. Several resort owners complained that their docks no longer reached the water, and valuable tourist dollars were pouring into wetter places. I said, "Nope."

Next was a delegation of foresters. "The woods are tinder dry," they said, "and we're worried about shallow-rooted trees. Do you want to happen again what happened to the birches in '88?" Well, of course I didn't. Woods are among my favorite places to be, and birches are extremely high on my list of trees, but what could I do when I've too much to do and no vacation days coming?

A troop of Boy Scouts showed up at my door. They weren't allowed to light campfires, they said, and were sorely in need of s'mores. Though I am fond of scouts and s'mores, I steeled myself and held to the course. It wasn't easy.

What broke me were the farmers. They know I'm the son, grandson and great-grandson of farmers. "There'll be no hay," they said. "There'll be no oats. Corn will never be knee-high to nothing." They showed me their dried-up kids. They gave me a copy of *The Grapes of Wrath*.

So, I'll pack the tent. I'll pack the Duluth Pack with mosquito dope, matches, rope, duct tape, toilet paper, wieners, bread, oatmeal, peanut butter and coffee. I'll pack the mess kit, the rod and reel and tackle box. I'll load the canoe on the back of the pickup truck and head out for three days and three days only. So dig out your ponchos everybody, hunt up your umbrellas, rain is on the way.

the stuff of heroes

JUNE 29

The Lord giveth, as we know, and the Lord taketh away, and for the kids on that late June Sunday morning, it looked like this was going to be a taketh away day. But let's begin at the beginning.

As June usual, we were out at Grandpa's on a Sunday after church. Right off, the little kids grabbed their fishing poles and trooped down to the dock for some little-kid fishing. These kids know their way around a fishing pole, and were determined to give some bluegills a run for their money. They eat so many bluegills their stomachs rise and fall with the tide. The morning, however, was turning out to be one of industry but not of profit, as they were not having the kind of bluegill luck they have become accustomed to.

This was bringing on an atmosphere of gloom and quenching the joyful spirit kids are famous for. They were using little sponge-rubber spiders considered universal bluegill bait by bluegill authorities. They were tossing them out and snaking them over the top of the water as they'd been taught, but it wasn't working. Not at all. So up they surged to an all-knowing Grandpa. Grandpa, however, had tangled himself up with the Sunday paper and was sleeping it off. Their folks were occupied on the turbulent battlefields of lawn-mowing and garden hoeing and offered little comfort and no help whatsoever.

That left only Grandma. So Grandma, as Grandmas do, herded them back down to the lake and showed them how to crimp a tiny split shot about a dozen inches ahead of the little spiders, and how to work them in with slow, steady pulls, a couple of feet or so below the surface, where the bluegills were playing hide-and-seek hard to get, fooling the kids for a little while, but good old Grandma, who figures a halo's just one more thing to dust, not at all.

villainy afoot

JUNE 30

Today's the last one of June, the fourth or fifth or sixth longest of the year, but shorter than yesterday which was shorter than the day before. Where did the time go? What happened to the campfires? To the fishing? To the canoe trips? The picnics in the park? Somewhere to the farther north of us, Canada geese, snows and white-fronted, barely got there, are soon to be massing for the return trip to the farther south of us. Chipmunks are already smiling smug underground smiles over granaried acorns and sunflower seeds.

The signs are everywhere. Look here, look there, winter is waiting to begin. Ants are standing in line to sneak chicken bones into the cupboards of their dens. Robins' songs are dipping. Snails are scurrying to winter quarters. I noticed that this morning. By lunchtime, rows of monarch butterflies, thumbs out, will be hitchhiking off to Mexico. Honeysuckles have that look to them. They know.

You're thinking I've nothing to do but go looking for trouble. You're thinking, "What the heck," we're still a long ways from that cold nightmare that's coming, but note the sky. It's fading. Local strawberry leaves are turning brown. The flimsy calendar has already shattered the crackling blooms of wild roses. Look here, look there, through parted shrouds of hollyhocks. Snowflakes are poised on the horizon. Who built this place, anyway?

Last night grasshoppers were singing their scrambled songs from out at the woodpile, which has got so low, so low, and must be quickly got up to force before we die of the cold. I told the grasshoppers to shut their mouths, but they knew, too, and they knew that I knew. For now, rain is falling straight down on morning glories disappointed and wilted with the passing of the season, morning glories that pose the inevitable question: If summer is here, can winter, indeed, be far behind?

life's little extras

JULY 1

It's July. A dewy July sunrise is sopping up what's left of a June night and laying a purple tint on the waters of Lost Lake. Retreating stars are skipping in and out like messages rising and falling from a short-wave radio in an old movie, and we're fishing, of course. We're fishing with worms we dug with fork and flashlight from between bean rows in the garden, cheap worms that don't jeopardize the hairline solvency of the family budget.

Many of us, as fishing kids, fished with worms. I can't remember how old I was, or more properly, how young, when I hooked my first fish, but that I hooked it on a worm, I have no doubt. I'll never fully outgrow the habit. As fishing kids, certain that if a little bit of worm was great bait, a whole bunch was better, we gobbed them on big hooks. We skewered them on like roasting weenies on willow sticks. We weighted them down real good and heaved them, kerplunk, into the water. Though well and earnestly intended, we did nothing to advance the reputation of worms as the best fishing bait in all the universe.

With our considerable growing up, we've come to understand that worms should be presented as naturally, as unweenie-looking, as possible. Now that we're older, thicker, and more particular, we hook worms only once, near their middles. The hooks we hook them on are as small as we dare use, and we fish them without drag, without sinkers, or as few as possible.

In streams we cast up and let the worm drift easily down, as if there were no fishing person attached. In still waters, we let it settle, gently wriggling, to the bottom, and leave it there, or at most, we inch it along every half-minute or so, with determined care, unrelenting patience and varying degrees of skill and confidence.

main trails and bypaths

JULY 2

Millions of miles away, poised on the edge of comprehension, a swirling galaxy is dying. The cold fluttering around it is enormous, but this is July, and in this frying-pan heat of July, we here in Lost Lake have other things on our minds. The fish aren't biting. For a while there we had a good thing going with northern pike, but they have since got wrapped up in the world of simple obsessions that is July and have developed lockjaw. Once, walleyes were willing enough participants in this cat-and-mouse game of life, but they've got caught up dead center in planetary systems of their own and have sunk clean out of sight into cool holes of wet silence. Closed-mouthed crappies are floating listlessly in hidden vacuums between hither and yon. Trout have escaped into water thin as air, and bass have melted into orbits only they know.

We're fortunate, though, and we thank our lucky stars for it, that under these July clouds white as divinity, we've still got muskies cruising the outer edges of our universe. It's a key element of our existence. Muskies are such contrary critters this weather doesn't interrupt their regular feeding schedules, but like everything else merely ticks them off. The shallow, warm waters that gave up muskies to us earlier in the year are now weed-choked. So we have to track the great fish to bigger waters, cooler and deeper, riddled with rocky bars and weed beds that grow close to topside. During the day, we fish them deeper, but in the evening we follow them onto the bars and into the edges of weed beds.

Quite often we catch muskies like this and, when we do, we gladly put them back in their places, so as we cling to the earth spinning its way through July, we can try to catch them again if we dare.

shad but true

JULY 3

It's hotter than a bottle rocket here at Lost Lake, but my Uncle Jake is going walleye fishing, anyway. I'm afraid the heat has got to him, and I yell at him from my lawn chair under the shade of a willow tree. "Don't go, Uncle Jake!" I cry. "Come back and sit with me in the shade of this willow tree. Come share the rollicking coolness of a cool drink. Take a nap, Uncle. No walleyes will nibble in the heat of a hot day like this one." But, as is his way, he disregards my pleas, pulls on the starter rope a couple of times, and is gone. Though my blood was beginning to stir, it is lethargy in the end that triumphs, and I succumb to the irresistible, cosmic forces of July and resume my optimistic disregard for duty.

After the passage of an appropriate period of time, Jake, smiling the vague smile of a man who has caught walleyes, putt-putts back to the dock. Down in my belly where reality lurks, I get this feeling, and naturally he gives me the unabridged version of the story. He tells me he knew all along the walleyes would be lying just below this July-deep light penetration over rocks and gravel. So, he takes a medium-sized heavy spoon, the kind that flutters when it drops, and he treats it like a jig. He lets it go all the way to the bottom. Then he reels it up a foot or two. He doesn't jerk it, of course, but lifts it at a reasonable rate and lowers it again just as reasonably. The key, he tells me, is to keep the line tight, because ninety percent of the fish hit on the drop, and if you've got slack, you'll never feel the tip-tap of a light walleye bite.

Hearing all this is a marvelous experience, except for one thing. He's telling it to me with his mouth full of fried-up walleye while he's passing me a plate full of hot dogs and cold beans.

a limit of big ones

It's the Fourth of July, the Holiday of holidays, and this fellow with a day off is heading north. There's a trout stream waiting for him off in that direction, and walleyes in the little lake it feeds into. At a blue line on the map, he hurries off the freeway and speeds down a more heavenly road of lesser lanes. Veering off that at last and onto a dirt road, he hurries as best he can the final four miles to a dead-end turnaround and pulls to a stop in a cloud of dust. Someone has beaten him to this stretch of water. He will not be as free on this day as he hoped he would. Yet, he dresses quickly, gathers his gear and hurries down the trail to the river, praying that no one is fishing where he wants to be.

JULY 4

Someone is. In the fading light, a figure in a floppy hat is facing upstream, having at it with a splendid fish. His fish. There is nothing to do but sit there on a fallen oak tree and watch. After a bit, he feels the wind, which he hasn't noticed before, brush its way through a stand of lightly bearded pines to his cheek. Then a blue jay trumpets, not far off. A kingfisher streaks through the golden air to a sandy beach at his feet. From his place on the fallen oak, he observes a small cloud of tadpoles dancing on dark blue ripples. A sparrow swings from the wire of a willow branch. A slow, gray feather floats down and dissolves before his eyes. A partridge beats its chest in an old John Deere sort of way. As the sun begins to set, eddies of lazy water flow into visions of fire. He sees violets where violets last only a little while. Bats dart up out of cattails and pounce on the developing darkness, claiming it as their own.

It's only then the floppy-hatted fishing woman turns to see him for the first time and asks him the eternal question. "How's fishing?" she asks.

"Oh, just fine," he tells her truthfully. "Thank you."

too much of a good thing

JULY 5

Keeping it inside me like this, it eats at my guts. I know I should talk about it. Get it, somehow, off my chest. I should come right out and say I caught a carp. Three, maybe four pounds. It was two months ago, and I didn't mean it. I was fishing for walleyes. I got a bite. I set the hook. It put up a pretty good fight, better than a walleye, so right away I knew it wasn't a walleye.

I realize some people catch carp on purpose and are quite elated when they do it, but I don't. Nobody here at Lost Lake does. I didn't understand what I had done until I lifted it into the boat. I was so surprised I dropped it, and it flopped all over the place. It upset a beverage I had been working on. It tipped over the minnow bucket. It spilled my tackle box and scared my kid. So I killed it. I had to. I took an oar and hit it over the head as it headed for the sandwiches. I should have let it have the sandwiches. Alive, I could have released it. Dead, I had to eat it. I told the kid it was a trout and snuck it home.

I skinned it and filleted it. I took out the mud vein under the strip of red flesh on the underside of each fillet. That left me with a couple of pounds of fish. I smoked that on the Weber, let it cool, and put it through the grinder with two small onions. It's what I had. I added four drops of Worcestershire sauce and some mayo. I don't remember how much. Some. Then the boys came over. Did I tell you it was my turn for poker? I set the carp out with crackers and chips. The boys went nuts for it and wanted to know what it was.

"Trout," the kid said. Now they want it all the time, so every month or so I sneak out and get me a carp on purpose. Is that really so bad? Anyway, thanks for listening. I feel better.

next of kin

JULY 6

We're a big family, but the only time we get together is at funerals where somebody invariably says, "We should do this more often." Even in the summertime when it's the only summertime we've got, we're scattered-in-the-wind on the go.

The Larsons are taking off for their cabin in the Northwoods to blend in like humus with the great outdoors. The Nelsons are spending two weeks in a cathedral of pines, thousands of pines. The white house of the Weinandts is quiet. They've gone off to the middle of nowhere. On an isolated island, the wind is tiptoeing between birch trees so as not to wake the Marlaises. They're newly married.

The moon is dropping sand into the beautiful eyes of the Khoroosi kids. It's time they get into their sleeping bags to dream of scrambled eggs salted with sunrise, peppered with dew. Between great boulders and sandy beaches, some of the Wilber women (nee and otherwise) are lifting up the lovely shadows of their faces and dipping big toes into the cool waters of loon magic. The Aljet boys are taking their red-headed mother to the prairie, where they'll be pitching tents where the deer and the antelope play. The Skeltons, like royalty in a game of checkers, are boarding canoes to answer the accurate calls of the wild. The Huttons are trading espresso for cups of coffee boiled up in campfired coffee pots. The Bouleys are escaping the city for unspecified lakes and rivers. The Bebeaus are taking the off-ramp, following signs that read: This Way to Heavenly Mountain.

In our gardens, pumpkins lie growing green with no one to weed them. We've all gone camping in this summertime, the only one we'll get, because no matter what else we are, we're the kind of family that can't live without wild places, and I expect your family, no matter what else you are, is like that, too.

on being small in a large cathedral

JULY 7

It being somewhat between seasons, a few folks here heard a sermon last Sunday, the gist of which was there are some things in life worth giving your best shot at if for no other reason than to see what happens. The ceaseless excitement of making a marriage work was one. Pulling out all the stops, diligence and legwork necessary to helping kids turn out the way you want them to was another. It was all the talk Monday morning down at Mom's Cafe over on Main Street, where everybody was adding to and subtracting from the invoice as they saw fit.

Those are fine rules to live by, and I'm sorry I missed it, but had anybody asked me, I'd have added that everybody in camp ought to be as useful as they are ornamental. And that nobody should plant more garden than their spouse can conveniently weed in one day. I'd have added that honor should be bestowed where honor is due, and that people should realize a pair of good parents is worth a thousand teachers, preachers, psychiatrists and policemen.

I'd have recommended fish stories be told so they hang together nicely, and even dry fly purists use a worm now and then for humility's sake. I'd have added that well-meaning anti-hunters should stop eating meat, wearing leather shoes and belts, and depriving wood ticks of their blood. They should also stop dining on lettuce and bean sprouts, since without plants there would be no animals. I'd have had it ground in stone that no child need ever be a child of calamity.

Finally, I'd have added that if we want to live here where angels live and eat what angels eat and drink what angels drink, we'd better take care of our Mother Earth and the plants and animals and precious water on it. Then I'd do my level best to follow my own advice.

suffering

JULY 8

A puddling rain had sent us off the lake and into the Elkhorn Tavern and Wildlife Museum, which serves as a rugged backdrop for this more-or-less true story. After a while, the conversation began to lag, when the Professor perked things up by announcing he was a write-in candidate for governor. No one at Lost Lake had run for governor before, except our old dog-catcher who, because all our dogs come when they're called, needed something to do in his spare time.

The Professor figured he'd be a shoo-in, because he'd run on the Sportsman's ticket, filling his cabinet with fishermen, hunters, campers and a couple of berry pickers. He wouldn't need a National Guard or much of a state patrol, since everybody would be too busy fishing and all that to be mad at anybody. Because he'd not be leaving his cabin on the lake for anything, he'd rent out the governor's mansion and use the money for wetland restoration. Official dinners would be held at Mom's Cafe over on Main Street to take advantage of the daily specials there.

We were getting pretty worked up to the idea when Ol' Gladys, who had been sitting like a drowsy woodchuck, interrupted to inquire if any of us had heard the one about a fellow, during Abe Lincoln's time, who was running for mayor. One day a kid came along and told him he could predict the weather with accuracy, for he owned a jackass that scratched his ears on a fence post and hee-hawed something awful before each and every bout of bad weather. Right away, the candidate hired the animal as his running mate in charge of weather forecasting, which was a terrible mistake. Ever since that day, Gladys said, jackasses have been seeking public office.

We could see the lightbulbs go on and off in the Professor's eyeballs, but we all pitched in and bought him a drink, which seemed to cheer him up.

a splice of life

JULY 9

When nature called, I answered. When the sun of April shone, I pulled the tiller from its cave and changed the oil in it. Under the full moon of May, I planted beans and radishes, carrots and onions, potatoes, tomatoes and cabbages. That garden was to be my legacy and my honor. Then the sun stood still and nearly set it all afire. It got as dry as a bald skull. Yet, anger is unhealthy and unscientific, so, in an absolutely cold-blooded manner, I hooked up the hose, and I watered it. For twenty years I watered it.

"Hot damn!" people said when they came over. "Now there's a real man."

Then, when it got enough water, it started to rain. It rained for two weeks. Someone undeserving, I thought, had made it into heaven, and they put him to work on rain. The strawberries floated one way, raspberries another. The squash died intestate. A pumpkin bobbed by the picture window on its way down the driveway, where it hit the mailbox and knocked it loose. As it went by, however, I noticed something on it — a largish, whitish, mothy-looking thing, recognizable immediately as a giant Hexagenia. In the midst of misfortune, God had sent the Hex Hatch, and trout, wherever there were trout, were feasting. So I said, "Who needs a garden?" and went fishing.

The river was high, yet within minutes I stalked, hooked and landed a twenty-four pound beauty. It was later identified as *Pinus strobus*, more commonly known as white pine. I went on to land many others. There was a five-hundred pound cedar, a freshwater record for these parts, and a rising tire from a '57 Chevy. Later, I hooked the Chevy, a record that will stand for years. There was a washing machine (though not of great size, it put up a spectacular fight), a shoe, a pair of eyeglasses, and a set of false teeth.

I should mention that I returned each of these to the water, unharmed.

an unforgettable occasion

JULY 10

Drifting down the river was both restful and exhilarating. For July, the water was high, and we glided swiftly through ripples and whirlpools and battled our way around giant boulders and fallen-in trees to the mouth of Cripple Creek. It was a logical place to make camp, a smooth spot under a canopy of spruces. As we put up the tent, rolled out the sleeping bags and ate supper — there were two of us, the dog and me — we spoke of the mysterious groaning that seemed to surround us, a series of spine-tingling moans, sometimes low and barely audible, sometimes louder. On closer inspection, we found they came from us ourselves, when we realized we were being stalked by a giant mosquito.

A place that had been a patch of light between the trees was now solid black. Without breathing, we followed the outline of the black spot with our eyes. My arm stole out toward the rifle at my side. Suddenly, it was towering over us, and all hell broke loose. There was a hair-raising snort right in my face. The dog flew into action with loud barks. There was the pounding of heavy feet on the ground, the crashing of brush, savage growling, furious yapping, and the staccato of snapping teeth. Yelling, I fired a few shots in the air. The mosquito bolted.

We stirred up the fire and shared boiled coffee until daylight, when we discovered we had made camp in the center of mosquito country. We decided to make a more thorough investigation. Following the trail, we found his tracks enormous. Suddenly, I jerked my head around and saw the huge, one-eyed mosquito, teeth gleaming in a hideously distorted snarl, breaking cover not five yards away. The dog made a flying leap for its throat. The creature paused just long enough to swing a giant paw and send the gallant dog spinning through the air into a clump of bushes twenty feet away.

To be continued, I hope.

equally unforgettable

JULY 11

Previously ...

My gallant dog had made a flying leap at the throat of a charging mosquito, only to be swept spinning through the air by a giant paw into a clump of bushes twenty feet away. That momentary pause gave me just the time I needed to spring to my feet, grab my rifle, swing it around and fire from the hip with the muzzle inches from the massive insect as it charged full upon me, snorting with rage.

As I fired, I leaped back with the recoil of the gun, and the great hulk hurtled past me to fall in a heap. No more had it crashed to the ground than it was on its feet again, bellowing with defiance. It turned back toward me, and I sent another slug smashing into the massive neck, hoping to break it. The heavy lead ball brought it to the ground a second time, but the great insect refused to die. It scrambled to its feet, roaring in pain and once more braced for a charge. I had one cartridge left. I had to make it count. Spitting blood, it lunged. I aimed low behind the ear and fired my last shot. The brute rumbled to the ground, never to rise again. The curse of Cripple Creek was dead.

I went over to examine the most hideous specimen of animal life I had ever seen. Even in death, it gave me the chills. Looking at its gigantic size, its distorted head and broken teeth, and the point from which it launched its attack, I realized it had been a man-hunter, a killer. It had deliberately stalked us so silently that even the dog hadn't heard it. The close call made me shiver, and with the smell of blood in the air, deep in mosquito country, with no ammunition, I revived the dog and raced down the trail to the river.

We had made it through this one, but there were more mosquitoes out there and, as we furiously paddled away, we knew the next time we might not be so lucky.

it's nothing, really

JULY 12

It's painful to admit it, but I'm only a so-so shooter, maybe less. You should see me. If I were living back in the age of Mountain Men, I'd be dead by now. At our weekend trapshoots, invariably I yell, "Pull!" Then I sit back and let the paranoia set in. "Don't feel so bad," someone says, but I do, and the most disquieting thing about it is it's my fault. I don't practice as often as I'd like to and certainly not as often as I need to. I am, and will be until my far-off retirement days, relegated to the second-class status of a so-so shooter, maybe less. I've learned something, though. When I shoot and miss, in my inexperience I figure it's because I'm pointing the barrel of the gun where the target isn't. While that is a real and definite possibility, the case of the missing shot might as easily be solved at the other end of it.

What the good shooters do when they pull up on a target is push the gun forward and then bring it back to the same spot on their shoulder every time. Given ten or fifteen minutes a day, even in the stifling confines of my bathroom, den and kitchen, I can learn to do that. Standing in front of a mirror with my eyes closed, I can bring the gun up sharply to my shoulder and aim it. With my eyes open, then, I should be looking straight down the barrel, seeing only the sight at the end of it, and maybe a bit of the rib. My head should be straight forward on the stock.

I can do that a dozen times a day from now until hunting season, wearing a hunting coat so the butt won't drag on it in the field or hang up under the armpit. Then, in a couple of months, when I move out into the cleansing quiet of the great outdoors and a partridge happens by, I'll hit it, and people will say, "By golly, lookit that!" which will be an elegant enough elegy for me.

body and soul

JULY 13

It takes the hard work of a thousand ants to open the bud of a peony. How do they do that, do you suppose? Do they punch some kind of ant clock before reporting for peony duty? Do they get briefed, eight o'clock on the dot, with a peony report until one day the thing explodes into blossom, causing ants all over the place to relocate to other peony plants? Do ants measure their lives in the time it takes to pop a peony?

You might ask what the heck this has to do with anything, and I've got to tell you, nothing — but yesterday a child drowned. A little kid was wading and drowned, and what is there to do about it now but watch ants in the garden haggling over peonies?

Tragedy needs no invitation, but comes soon enough on scouting missions of misery on its own. Unwatched for the smallest of moments, a little girl chasing a butterfly falls off a dock. The wind teases a rubber ball on the water too far for a wading boy to find the bottom under it. A fishing partner falls overboard. What do you do then? You keep your wits about you. That's the first thing. You get them out. That's the second. Then you make certain your partner's or your child's mouth is clear of foreign matter. You tilt the head back and arch the neck to open air passages, to give you a straight shot from the mouth to the lungs. You pinch the nostrils closed. You put your mouth over your partner's or your child's mouth and blow twelve times a minute into the adult's, twenty into the child's. You allow them to exhale naturally. If the air passages are blocked, you try holding the mouth closed and blowing through the nose. You stick with it. You stick with it forever.

If, as you make your way through the bean-rows of your days, you get careless or unlucky, and the victim is not your partner and not your child, but you, what in the world do you do then?

supper

JULY 14

Before the sun goes burning down on its wick, mix up the bread dough, the brown bread dough, the way you do. Punch it down in a bread pan. Put it in a warm place with a dish towel on it.

Go down to the river and catch a big catfish, sweating like a swamp. Wrangle it home. Put the bread in the oven. Send the kids out to the garden for potatoes, for tomatoes, for lettuce and onions, for peas. Put a record on the record player — B.B. King. Turn it up. Peel the skin off the catfish. Rinse its naked indigence in cold water. Tell the kids to get the lead out, to shuck the peas, to wash the other stuff with the garden hose, to get the worms off the lettuce. Check the bread. Turn the record over. Put the potatoes on. And the peas.

Fillet the catfish. Cut it into chunks. Dry them off with paper towels. Sprinkle them with salt and black pepper, and red pepper. If you're fond of red pepper, put enough on to curl your nose hairs and make them cry for mercy. If you don't cotton to it so much, pass the box over with the lid shut tight. Coat each piece with cornmeal. Take the bread out. Make one kid set the table. Make another put the salad together. Heat up an inch of cooking oil in your cast-iron skillet. Heat it up enough so the catfish bubbles when you lay it in there, then lay it in there. Go down to the cellar for a jug of rhubarb wine. Pour it in the good jelly glasses like water running clear. Turn the fish. Fry it until it's browned all over. Cut the bread. Mount the catfish on the Christmas platter. Sprinkle it with lemon juice.

There goes the clock. There goes the sun. Call everybody to the table and, while a luna moth picks at the lock on the screen door, give thanks to God and to the catfish, without whom none of this would be possible.

under the weather

JULY 15

There are sixty ways of doing everything right in the great outdoors, and at one time or another every single one of them depends on the weather, the single most important factor in determining what kind of a day we're going to have. It's been lousy here, so lousy this week's had eight or nine days in it, and it's not even half over. We here at Lost Lake like to think of ourselves as weatherproof, but we're not. We went fishing this morning, but it was so rat-gray and rainy we came in and collected like seagulls at Mom's Cafe over on Main Street.

One advantage of bad weather is that it's grist for the mill of conversation. My Uncle Jake started it. He said he knew last night what today would bring when he saw his neighbor's cows huddled together. This, he said, is a very good sign of rain.

"Yes it is," said a dark-haired lady from the other side of the lake. "And early this morning my lazy old cat was frisky as a kitten. Also a very good sign."

"Sure is," said my second cousin Howie, who noted likewise how ants in his driveway had built up dikes around their holes to keep the water out.

"It all adds up," said the English teacher, somewhat out of his field. "And a bee's wing never gets wet, so I knew something was coming down, since I hadn't seen a bee in quite a bit." Ol' Gladys said spiders in her henhouse had vacated their webs and glued themselves to the walls.

"Here's how I know it's going to rain," said Mom, the sails of the tattooed ships on his arms bulging under the weight of platters and coffee pots. "I got me a green tree frog back in the kitchen in a jar half full of water. If it's going to rain, it sits in the water. If not, it's not, up the ladder it goes."

The Professor started to tell us there are scientific explanations as to why all these occurrences are pretty good weather predictors, but I lost track of things about then, because I got to thinking how smiling is the sensation of feeling good all over (even when you'd rather be somewhere else doing something else) and showing it principally in one spot.

thin disguises

JULY 16

Mom's Cafe over on Main Street is many things to many people. The omelets are pretty good there if you're not too fussy about your omelets. The coffee's hot if you don't need your coffee too hot. But Mom's is more than that. It's a place to meet new and interesting people and learn new and interesting things. You hardly ever come away from there without acquiring a specific piece of information to improve the quality of your life. Like this morning.

I had come for coffee. There was a stranger sitting at the counter next to a bucketful of big bluegills. "My, my," I asked him, "however here in late July did you go about obtaining a bucketful of big bluegills like that?"

He looked at me kind of surprised and asked if my heart could stand the truth. I said it could. "Good," he said, and asked me if I had a little boat, and could I row it over to the shady side of a drop-off fringed with vegetation? I said I had and could. He asked me if I had an ultralight spinning outfit rigged with two-pound mono. I said I did.

"Good," he said. "Attach a light-wire, long-shanked number eight hook to it and enough split shot to counter-balance a quill-type bobber that will show off the slightest bluegill bite." I nodded. He asked me if I'd dug a canful of worms from my garden. "I'm not a worm man," I said, "but I have."

"Good," he said. "You'll be fishing six or seven feet down, so anchor your boat on both ends to hold it still. Cast. Point your rod at the bobber and twitch in the line an inch or two at a time. Bluegills often nip at a worm before taking it, so tease them a little and set the hook with a short jolt."

He asked me did I have all that. I said I did. "Good," he said, heading out the door, humming the William Tell Overture to spread light where there had been only darkness.

an element of truth

JULY 17

On a Sunday evening, I am on the screen porch, with Walt Whitman. We hardly get together anymore; we're both so busy. I go to the cellar for a jug of chokecherry. I pour us a glass, and say, "Now, where were we?" "We were speaking of love," says he. Ahh," says I.

"When a conservative man falls in love," says he, "it is a gradual process, and when it happens, it's a dull thud of a surprise to him."

"You know," says I, "it's like that with fishing."

"On the other hand," says he, "when a romantic or a sentimentalist falls in love, he dives right in, often with dire consequences."

"You know," says I, "it's just like that with fishing." I pour us another glass of wine. Walt's like that. "Those bitten by the love bug," says he, coining the phrase, "experience torment and frustration, joy and expectation all at the same time."

"You won't believe this," says I, "but that's how it is with fishing."

"A man in love," says he, "stares out the window, oblivious to his surroundings. His memory fails him. He sighs at the moon."

Says I, "Fishing is like that, too."

"Do you have more wine?" says he. I pour us another round. "Over the years," says Walt, "a person develops an admiration and devotion to his mate that is as endless as the sands and the tides."

"Wow," says I, "that's just how it is with fishing."

"Love," says he, "is a process, an embryonic growth of stages." "What a coincidence," says I.

"Being in love," says he, "is the most exciting, challenging, enjoyable, yet the most exasperating individual experience of a lifetime."

"I agree," says I, "So's fishing."

"The satisfactions and rewards of fishing must be endless," says he.

"It's like being in love," sighs I.

"Well, it's getting late," says he, heading for the screen door. See you, Kiddo." "Anytime," says I.

a point of entry

JULY 18

There's a river not far from here, about three miles east and a little north. A mile up from its mouth, where it empties into the lake, there's a sort of grassy, open place where deer come out of the trees to eat and drink. You can see quite a distance both upstream and down. There seem to be fewer mosquitoes there. On a broad, sandy patch at the head of a sandbar that reaches well into the water is where I set up camp as often as I can, though I'm not crazy about camping in sand. The river has such a nice ripple to it there. The sand is so clean. The bluffs behind it speak so of wilderness. Time is generous when I'm there, so blue, so lucid. The green around there is the deepest green I've ever seen, and the earth is as welcoming as any place I've been. Nowhere are the lights of a settling down sun better to look at. If you're thinking there's no logic to all this, you're right. It's how I feel about all campsites, about all campouts — the overnighters, the three-dayers and the red-blooded, two-fisted three-week ones to the moon.

Lying awake there in my hundred-dollar sleeping bag — a hundred dollars fifteen years ago when a hundred dollars was a hundred dollars — I listen to distant howls. Or I listen to the steady thump of rain on the fly. It sounds like home. I take a deep breath. It smells like home. I touch the side of the tent. It feels like home. No matter how much of it I get, I never get enough.

When I'm to be buried, I'd like to be buried there with my paddle stuck up in the sand to mark the place. Campers coming along will see it and say, "Look, some dead guy's buried there," unaware that, by then, I'll be a piece of driftwood going bony gray, and I'll be sharing their fire on this broad, sandy patch at the head of a sandbar, on the lookout for deer coming out of the trees to eat and drink.

on the other hand ...

JULY 19

When are people going to learn it's a foolish thing to lay down hard-and-fast rules about catching fish? No sooner does a person get lucky and catch something than he arrives at a set of conclusions on how he did it. Then, he tells everybody. And, worse yet, he writes it down, making it a part of the public record. Before you know it, he starts to believe it himself, though fish have since changed the game, upsetting the apple cart of his philosophy. It never fails, unless you expect it to, in which case it always does.

Take yesterday. I was putting my twelve-footer in just as my cousin Georgie was sneaking his out. He looked awful. His hair was heaped on his head. His eyes were bugged out like a walleye's. A tic was working its way up one side of his face. It's hard to chat with a fellow in that condition, but I asked him anyway if everything was okay. It wasn't. Last week he was fishing. Not for anything specific. Just fishing. Casual. Casting a shallow-running crankbait that had once been reddish. Half its lip was gone. The other half jutted sharply to the north. Listening to a ball game on the radio, he hooked a log that swam away with him and his boat. When it cleared the water a couple of times, he saw it was a muskie, so he got careful. An hour later, his line broke, but the fish had had it and went belly up. That's when Georgie became an expert. He told everybody he could find. He got his picture in the newspaper over a headline that read, "Muskie Myth Exploded!"

I looked past Georgie to the lake. It was full of fishermen frantically scraping paint off shallow-running crankbaits missing half a lip and the other half jutting sharply to the north, tuning in to a ball game, casting casual, not having any luck and blaming Georgie. "How silly," I thought to myself, but I got his autograph and hurried out there for a look-see, just in case.

at the heart of the matter

JULY 20

Why do I hunt? I hunt so I can be hunting. I hunt so I can keep time to the drip-dripping and sliding of raindrops off my hat while I wait for ducks to come to my decoys. There are few better things than that.

I hunt so I can bump heads with fire-breathing bucks five, six, seven, eight days in a row. I hunt so I can listen for the trickle of their tracks in the leaves. I sit and sniff the air for them like a poet onto something good. I say "A little closer, a little closer," but it almost always never happens.

I hunt so I can hang with bushy-tailed convicts snitching acorns. I hunt so I can nose in the underbrush like a floppy-eared hound for cottontails, and bark at raccoons in treetops at midnight and chase my tail 'round and 'round in the red dust of sunsets. If that's too much for you, I hunt so I can run with wolves and drum with woodpeckers on hickory stumps and wade in looking-glass pools. If you're not a hunter, that makes no sense. If you are, you know what I'm talking about.

I hunt so I can circle the ghosts of long-forgotten farms where farmers and their wives sat on front porches and talked things over, where ancient apple trees and the wind talk things over. I hunt so I can cool my heels with paddling packs of muskrats in peace and quiet and neither hate nor fear anything. I hunt so I can lean against oak trees and make polite conversations with dogs in the yellow and gold of autumn. I hunt so I can wear a red bandana tied around my neck and a compass stuck in the pocket of an old flannel shirt over the machinery of my heart. I hunt because it's something I can count on.

The explanation is simple, then. When I don't hunt I'm all lonesome and empty inside and nobody's home.

a heart in no hurry

JULY 21

As half-frozen rain fell on rain, hidden under sheaves of ferns and beds of moss as thick as hoar-frost, a tree was born in the dark womb of an acorn. It grew. As the sun streaming with light swept down and gave it strength, it grew. Surrounded by peach leaf willows and alders and chokecherries, it grew so much it's a wonder its body held its weight. It filled the niche of its space beautifully and fit the earth well as a hiding place of years. Edged with the ornaments of life, of birds and bees and moons, it sang into the empty spaces. Then it died. In the dead calm before darkness, it died. Like an old man not knowing what to remember, it died.

A small fire killed it. Born in dry sheaves of ferns and brittle moss, a small fire, offering only a little death, crept close and killed it. Yet, the tree didn't fully kneel to death. Not right away. The green city of its leaves fell soon enough to eternity and didn't come back. Then its smaller branches fell in circling eddies. Then other branches went pale as bones, gave way and followed. Five years, ten, more, and its bark was gone, exposing its nakedness. After three more years, as rainbows came and went, rot began to eat at its heart. Fifteen, twenty years after it died, the oak stood against the night. It held fast against thickening snows and driving clouds. Like a defeated warrior refusing to genuflect in defeat, it stood while woodpeckers bored into its trunk and owls made homes there.

Then, though there were no eyes there to see it, nor were there ears there to hear it (we are poor listeners to the whispering distresses of trees), it fell. Did it sigh? It fell. Now it lies there in sheaves of ferns and beds of moss, turning the color of earth while partridges beat drums on its skeleton and dance on its grave.

thrown for a loss

JULY 22

We here at Lost Lake figure if you haven't got elegance, you haven't got anything. Consequently, we are very fond of catfish. We know people who so love walleyes that if they caught one, they'd take it to bed with them and hug it all night long, and a trout for sure, but wouldn't touch a catfish with a yardstick. We don't know why that is.

The catfish has too long suffered a bum rap as a bewhiskered, lowbrow type. Too many otherwise unuppity people don't appreciate its nature, its appearance, its origin, its character or its habits. They think of catfish, when they think of catfish at all, as a trash fish, a rough fish, simply because it doesn't shave, feeds near the bottom and does some sideline scavenging. They don't know the real fish, the fish beneath that rough exterior, the fish ever so much more dignified than a couple of county commissioners of my acquaintance, and one guy who's running for the House of Representatives. There is no more delectable freshwater fish than the firm, white flesh of catfish.

Any sturdy, inexpensive rod and medium-sized bait casting or spinning reel wound with twelve- to thirty-pound test will handle all the catfish you've a mind to handle. A good-sized hook to start with is a number six. You'll need a leader just above it, and a bell sinker to hold it down to where the bait will float a foot or two off the bottom.

Notwithstanding the iffy stuff of myth and legend, the only thing I can think of that clouds the funky, redemptive beauty of catfish is sitting down on one, as happened once to a friend of mine. You might as well kill a fellow straight out as have him sit down on a catfish and lose his appetite for such a lovely fish forever, though under those circumstances, it's completely understandable.

learning the hard way

JULY 23

"Gesundheit!" he said when I sneezed, and right away I saw what he was up to. He wanted me, a bona fide expert, to share the secrets of the outdoor trade for little or no cash. He wanted me to impart to him some relevant and appropriate information, some useful and instructive data, some advice or words of encouragement to make his life as fulfilling as it ought to be, so I grabbed him by the sleeve before he got away and did what I could.

I told him to pour white vinegar into the compartments of his tackle box, to let it sit there a couple or three hours, and it would effortlessly lift out the rust spots. I told him to soak rusty lures in the same stuff and rinse them off with water, confident there would be no soapy odors to alert the fish of his dreams. He said he did that. Determined to help the poor fellow, I told him to wad up a good-sized chunk of aluminum foil into a good-sized ball and to use it to clean his campfire cooking grill, one, two, three, just like that. He said it was a habit of his.

I reminded him that wind direction is one of the most critical factors in hunting deer, elk and moose, and if he'd tie, as Indian people tied, a little feather to his gun or bow to show how the slightest breeze was blowing, he'd do okay in that area. "Do it all the time," he said. I asked him if he saved space on his camping trips by stuffing extra socks and underwear in toilet paper rolls. "Certainly," he said. I asked him if he always went camping with a big roll of duct tape because it's a handy substitute for rope, wire, string and glue, that what's tied down with it stays down, and that he could use it to mend split canoe paddles, cracked gunstocks, fishing nets and snowshoe webbings. "Always," he said. Then I clipped him on the jaw and taught him a lesson he'll never forget.

an indication of good breeding

JULY 24

It's so hot outside that catching fish is a more or less impossible luxury, but if you have no dream, you're a poor devil indeed, which is why I find myself on the lake fish-wishing for northern pike with my Uncle Jake. Incorrectly, I assume he will aim the boat over to a bay we have fished all season, but is now weed-choked, and I sigh. Jake steers off that course, however. "I don't want none of them hammer handles," he says, and heads for a sunken island that drops sharply to thirty-five feet or more.

The littler northerns of the aforementioned bay are more numerous and more agreeable, but the big, bigger ones my uncle is insisting on are more randomly dispersed in this deep-water, drop-off structure. This is hit or miss fishing; more miss than hit, if you ask me. We're fan casting one-ounce, seven-of-diamonds, chartreuse spoons.

I get bored and get to thinking how so much care goes into the selection of a hunting dog and how little in the naming of it. I get to thinking how a rose by any name may smell as sweet, but what you call your hunting dog takes some concentration. A dog's name should reflect its character, mirror its stoutness, image its intelligence. It should, in short, be a tribute to the dog and to you, its master. Like my dog, Butch. Butch is a Butch — a tattooed, no-nonsense, no-frills hunting dog. Had we named him Fluffy or Pierre, there's no telling how he would have turned out. He carries a can of chew in his back pocket, and if a church lady stops by, pats him on the head and says, "Nice poochy woochy," he crawls under the porch and dies of shame.

I'm about to remind my uncle then that my arm is tired from casting and I want to go home, when he hooks onto something quite impressive, so I keep my mouth shut and reach for the net.

eleven years old and counting

JULY 25

The warm summer sunlight is as thick as butterscotch, and the kids here at Lost Lake are filled with the mild, steady pain of a passing July. Trying to ignore the disquieting symptoms of a summer vacation two-thirds done for, half-a-dozen boys have gathered at the edge of Whatchamacallit Bay to fish for bass. Rather quickly, they pile up a couple of tackle boxes worth of good bass lures — some theirs and some their old man's — in the tangled mess of weeds Whatchamacallit Bay is so famous for. They know, sure as shootin', there are bass out in that impenetrable jungle. But there doesn't seem to be a thing they can do about it, and with each passing moment they're losing ground.

They're holding a gripe session on the subject when they're interrupted by the arrival of a girl. It isn't that girls aren't sacred to them, or soon won't be, it's that at the moment they're busy being eleven-year-olds. "Jeez," the girl says, "you guys are doing it all wrong."

Of course, her being a girl, they pshaw the thought and keep pshawing it until she demonstrates. With an ease that makes their skin crawl, she sticks a pretty big floating plastic worm through the middle onto a pretty small weedless hook. (What else is new?) The boys interrupt her cast to remind her to put some weight on the thing.

But she says uh-uh, and lays it way out there on a lily pad in the middle of the worst of it. She lets it lie there a little bit and then kind of twitches it into a little open spot. She lets it rest the full eternity of a minute there, and then ever so slightly twitches it again. It looks like a snake, maybe, on a casual frog-hunting mission. Her first hit comes just as the boys are saying I told you so, and for supper she eats bass, they eat crow. It's as simple as that.

indeed

JULY 26

Dream in reverse, to the last time you packed your tent, your sleeping bag, your frying pan into the canoe and went away to where there was no measure of time but the beating of your heart. You got rained on, didn't you? You went with the rising of the sun, a seven-foot Frisbee, and before you got two-hundred-and-fifty rods down the river, thunder came like the sinister snores of winos, like rattling bags of coyote bones. This is no exaggeration, as you know. At three miles, there was a hint of lightning in the air, wasn't there? At four, you were caught in a deluge of dismay.

I don't want to sound contradictory, but did that send you to the Yellow Pages for fun of a different color? Did you turn your back on the river with its minor peculiarities, with its multitude of secrets? Did you make an illegal U-turn and sweep like a scythe back to the vacant lot of your living room and sofa? Of course you didn't. With the egg-yolk nucleus of the rising sun, you loaded your canoe. You tied it down good. When the needled, bent branches of piney pine trees called, you rolled up the sleeping bags. You were dream hunting, and you went. There was no holding you back. You rode on the back of the bucking canoe, a dry husk of a thing in need of a drenching. You unparched the paddles. You packed the coffee pot, the beans. You packed the clothes, the kindling, the fishing pole, the rain fly.

From your hayfield, your office, your kitchen, from your subway and elevator cage, you set your heart on the horizon, gave her the gas, laid the pedal to the metal. You put yourself in a time warp of rejuvenation. "Phooey on the rain," you said. "Rain's all right," you said, grinning and bearing it until the worst was over. Slick as a sipping trout you sallied forth, a beauty in baggy clothes, and if anybody needs a lesson, there's a lesson.

for the record

JULY 27

We have come out to the deer shack to clean up around the place, to mow the grass, to dig a new latrine, to cut firewood. But mostly, we're sitting around, reminiscing about this and that.

"I don't understand," says one of the boys, in whose head it is usually snowing, "why it's so bad to be caught up a creek without a paddle. Sooner or later, you'd float down and catch up to it. Now, if you'd be caught down a creek without a paddle, that might be a problem." We agreed.

Another one of the boys — we call him Florida because he's a walking, talking low-pressure system — mentioned how he couldn't comprehend why so many people didn't know they could tell the approximate time by finding the lowest point on the horizon and placing their fingers lengthwise between that spot and the sun. Each finger equals about fifteen minutes. This allows them to get their duck boats off the flowage before dark, on the outside chance they've left their watches at home.

A third fellow, who was once arrested for the intoxicated use of metaphors, (a crime of which I, too, have been accused) shared the following with us from a magazine he was reading: "Nature is in great need of our mercy, understanding and care, but some people's religious instinct to adore and revere it is awfully misguided. The natural rights of animals," he said soberly, "include, among other things, a fair chance for survival, food, reproduction and seclusion. Their rights do not include the right not to be hunted, for such a thing would have no basis in the daily, objective reality of predator and prey in nature. Trying to give human rights to animals is like inviting a wolf and a lamb to tea and asking them to behave themselves."

By then, the chicken on the barbecue was done, and we went to the pump to wash our hands.

burdens and strategies

JULY 28

You drive through the afternoon and into the night. This was last fall, but you think about it all the time. With the windows down, you roll along the highway, stars out and radio heavy with country music. You talk, you and your kid, about school, about life, about nothing. You stop at a fast-food joint for a double cheeseburger.

"There are going to be lots of birds," you tell your kid. "We're going to get lots of birds." She answers with a smile. Later on, you check into a motel and order up a pizza and a jug of milk. You watch a little TV and talk some more. Before the sun's up, you've eaten breakfast, and the two of you are taking the canoe off the pickup, loading it up and paddling it out to the duck blind.

It turns out to be a beautiful day, but there aren't lots of birds around. You don't get lots of birds. You eat your sandwiches. You drink your coffee and cocoa. Your kid gets bored. She reads. She watches a great green bullfrog. A spider drops in. "How you doin', spider?" she says, but spiders have no time for eleven-year-olds. She gets up and moves around. That's when a dozen mallards come scooting by. There's no chance for a shot. That's it. There'll be no ducks today. You pack up and paddle in. Before you begin the drive home, you skip a few stones on the water and chase a butterfly. Along the way, you stop again for cheeseburgers and talk about nothing much.

When you get home, your kid right away falls asleep on the sofa. You pull her boots off and let her stay right there. Her arms are all akimbo, the way kids sleep when they're really tired. There's a half-smile on her face. And you think like you always do of the old saying about if you hunt with your kid, you'll never have to hunt for your kid, and with a lump in your throat, you pray that's how it's going to be.

a dramatic discovery

JULY 29

If there's one thing I can't stand, it's a complainer, but what the heat and bright lights of late July days do is drive walleyes into deep, dark, hard-to-find places. Strangely enough, though, not always.

A bunch of us regulars have come from the Post Office to Mom's Cafe over on Main Street, when in comes my Uncle Jake with a gleam in his eye and a crooked grin up his sleeve. We take an extraordinary interest in this, because when he's not holding a pair of aces in a nickel-dime, nothing-wild poker game, the aforementioned condition indicates he's caught fish and means to keep the details more or less to himself.

Our emotional appeals get us nowhere with the rascal, but a promise of a quarter-pound sugar doughnut (half down and half after the fact) turns him into a regular chatterbox. So, with broken ships of doughnut chunks floating in a sea of coffee, and sugar crumbs clinging to his whiskers, Jake tells us he did, indeed, catch fish. They were walleyes, and he caught them accidently, while fishing for bass. Such forthrightness in a fishing story nearly floors us and speaks highly of Mom's sugar doughnuts.

Bass, as everybody knows, avoid summer by seeking shelter in the shadowy shade of weed beds and, lo and behold, so do some walleyes. Jake says these are big walleyes, too — big enough not to be bullied by co-habitating bass, muskies and northern pike. Eyeing the second half of his bribe, Jake tells us this is a dim, middle-of-the-night business. Still and quiet, he says, he slipped up close to a likely-looking weedy spot next to a drop-off, took a floating lure and cast it as far as he could. Then he sort of twitched it and teased it in, coaxing some real nice summertime walleyes out of hiding and into his twelve-foot aluminum boat that leaks a little and gets your feet wet.

the whole truth and nothing but

JULY 30

You ask me why you're not catching fish, and, committed to taking the truth out of hiding and setting it free, I'll tell you, but if you want the unvarnished gospel, it's time to cut through the double-talk, the dancing around, and right out admit that some of your fishing habits are bad habits, and you got them through apish imitation. Fisherman see, fisherman do, if you'll excuse the expression. You want to be a fisherman who fishes in lonely isolation. But where do you fish? You fish in crowded waters where everybody else who wishes to be fishing alone fishes because you do, too.

You should be more like my friend Joe Smith, who isn't like that. Joe has complete access to his own mind. He's a stream fisherman. Like most stream fishermen, he's a trout fisherman, but he's a northern pike, walleye and bass fisherman, too, and almost always on streams with plenty of fish but few fishermen. There are streams like this all over the place. Many are fordable with a Captain-May-I giant step. In them are unfished-for fish. On warm summer days, Joe wades in his tenners and cut-off blue jeans, as casual as a beer can. He carries his gear in a fishing vest. Parking his pick-up at backroad bridges, he moves quietly into the water, casting upstream, retrieving with the current, using either a fly rod or spinning outfit. His favorite baits are slow-settling 1/16-ounce jigs and featherweight 1/32s. He tries to keep them on the bottom, but doesn't want them to drop like a rock when he hesitates to shoo a mosquito. Nobody manages these streams, so Joe takes on the job himself, almost always putting back what he takes out.

I know what you're thinking. You're thinking, how do I know so much about Joe's fishing secrets? Is Joe his real name? And where exactly are these streams, anyway? And as a writer committed to the truth, I can tell you they're all good questions.

mirror, mirror on the wall

JULY 31

In my mailbox today, I found a stack of hunting-clothes catalogs. This is good. As we head into the hunting seasons, smart hunters need clothing adequate not only for the warm and extremely cold conditions ahead, but also clothing that makes us look good. We don't have to bag a deer or shoot a duck to have a successful hunt, so long as we look good not doing it.

Cold is a critical condition to prepare for when hunting in the autumnal out-of-doors. Fortunately, the new catalogs appear to offer the finest in cold-weather and social faux pas protection. There's stuff here that's wool-lined, durable, handsome, roomy, built with meticulous attention to detail, pre-washed for softness and a broken-in look, in denim, red, olive, stone, saddle and blaze orange, in regular sizes and tall. It's soft and plush in teal heather, red heather and indigo heather. What's heather? What's indigo? And over here, just right for all occasions, are double seats, double elbows, adjustable waists, pocket handwarmers, large cargo pockets, leg pockets and knit cuffs in fourteen perfect shades of camouflage. And here. Here is totally windproof, exceptionally warm, lightweight, head-to-toe protection in magenta, spruce and navy.

Original. Double-stitched. Thickly-napped. One hundred percent cotton flannel. Two-button pockets. Long, round tails. Machine washable. Slate blue. Rose. Burgundy. It's all here. Brushed on both sides. Made in the U.S.A. And other places. Murl. Forest green. What's murl? Plaid. Insulated. Technologically advanced. Blister-proof. Guaranteed. Best-selling. Unique. In classic fits, natural fits and relaxed fits.

This is all so important, because a thorough knowledge of hunting techniques and animal behavior can make a hunt productive, but only a handsome outfit can make it truly pleasant.

august and all

AUGUST 1

August. August. August. A is for August, the month of the Sturgeon Moon, the Blueberry Moon and the Moon of Green Corn. In August, spring-born raccoons, squirrels, porcupines, skunks, beavers and muskrats carve out cubbyholes of living spaces where they can, while our kids, with plenty of troubles of their own, wade through the month as cautiously as herons in a frog pond. They're too, too aware life is passing them by, that where goes August, there goes summer. They're running out of fishing time, and they know it, so before the iron gates of pencils, books and dirty looks click shut behind them, they're trying to get in as much as they can, though they have to be careful. August waters are basically low waters and clear waters, and the veteran fish of August are on to the tricks of kids.

In August, our kids don't (we hope they never do) roar up to a honey of a fishing hole. Instead, they use discreet, sometimes roundabout approaches. They take long, circling routes, much as they do on the way to school. They fish as noiselessly as kids can. They go as slowly as they can with time running out and cut their motor to drift or pole where they need to be. Much as they'd like to, they don't rev the motor, vroom-vroom, but keep it purring softly at constant speeds. They don't drop their anchor kerplunk overboard, nor do they beat on the bottom of their boat. They do their fishing at sunrise and sundown, when they can, when fish move into shadowy shallows. They do all this, as you can imagine, with one eye out for school buses coming down the road.

They do pretty well, too, these kids of ours, with their fishing, which prompts their dads to yell, "Hey, kids! You catch 'em, you clean 'em," which has a tendency to curb the hyperactivity of kids in August. At least it does here at Lost Lake, so I suppose it does where you live, too.

barking up the wrong tree

AUGUST 2

We two-leggeds are inclined to view ourselves as vastly superior to animals. Yet, the longer you look at it, the more aware you become of the similarities. For instance, there was an old guy who lived around here. We called him the Colonel. He was an auctioneer. For years and years, he owned an Irish setter, though it could have been the other way around. The two had been together so long they got to looking alike. When one came down the street, we were never sure which one we were tipping our hat to. And when the dog died, we must have buried the old man by mistake. It wasn't until three years later, at a bake sale in the basement of the Methodist church, when the setter slipped in and ate Mrs. Peterson's brownies during a spirited debate over the growing political influence of the religious right, that we realized what we'd done. The Colonel never would have eaten Mrs. Peterson's brownies without permission. He was Baptist.

I've got relatives who growl like grizzly bears until they've had their morning coffee, who eat pizza with the enthusiasm of piglets, who drink tea with the daintiness of sipping trout. I know people with the ears of cocker spaniels, the eyes of walleyes and the giggles of hyenas.

As a matter of fact, the more people I see, the more I'd rather not be compared to, but there's a muskie out there, an elk, a moose, an eagle, a loon, a wolf, that I could be thicker than yogurt with. So just because we walk on two legs and come from storks instead of eggs, we ought to be careful who we call a dog, a mouse, a silly goose, an old cow, a nag or a snake in the grass. When comparing them to our fellow humans, we could be giving innocent animals a nasty inferiority complex.

pull!!!

AUGUST 3

You remember the Professor. He's a fellow here at Lost Lake who's such an expert on so many things, you hardly ever come away from a visit with him without having acquired knowledge of a character flaw you didn't know you had and information on how to correct it.

A bunch of us regulars were sitting around in Mom's Cafe over on Main Street, discussing the upcoming bird seasons and how, during the last few weeks, we'd seen more birds than we had in all the days of the year past, and the one before that. "That's so," said the Professor, "and the situation is that come opening day, you'll hardly hit one of them. You will, in fact," he went on, somewhat unnecessarily, I thought, "suffer more misses during the first few days of the season than any of you thought possible. And the reason for those multiple misses is that during those opening days you'll be practicing, boys, practicing on the real McCoys. Those birds that should be falling to your guns will be disappearing over the horizon." He did of course, as is his way, hit the nail on the head. We therefore and consequently decided to get out and do some practice shooting as often as we could.

So, as the black-eyed Susans droop with August and purple martins gather to discuss departure schedules, we'll retrain ourselves in the handling of our shotguns. We'll reacquaint ourselves with the shooting techniques that proved okay a year ago, so when those first fabulous days of bird season bust upon us, and the first birds explode from cover like rockets on the Fourth of July, we'll meet them with calm confidence, disproving the theory that there's no connection between effort and result, and between what you need and what you get. And don't blame me, by the way, for that last sentence. It's the Professor's.

pin curls and pipe dreams

AUGUST 4

What is fishing, exactly? Is it the art of fishing, or is it the actual catching of fish? I don't know. Tonight, we're dreaming big bass dreams, my Uncle Jake and me, here in the early days of August. And since bass, the big ones of our dreams, tend to be somewhat less cautious after dark, we're out on Lost Lake as the ten o'clock news unfolds back at the house. Though a medium chunk of a moon and a handful of stars are lighting things up a bit, it's dark out here. We can see hardly anything, but we've got everything organized and in its place, so there won't be any fumbling around. We're in the shallows, too, so we're being cat-on-the-prowl quiet. We have no intentions of scaring off the fish of our dreams. We're loaded up with heavier-than-usual line, so when a fish accepts our invitation to a late-night snack, we can get it more quickly to the boat without spooking the whole herd of them, and so we can pull loose from the weeds we're getting caught up in. We're using longer, stiffer-action rods for the same reasons.

As I said, it's dark, and we're going mostly with darker lures, weedless and single-hooked, but you've probably figured that out by now. They're big bass, these bass of our dreams, and it's basically big baits we've got on — swimming worms that twist and turn, bladed, buzzing spinnerbaits and jitterbugs. We're throwing them quite a ways out there, listening for the satisfying splat of their landing, giving them a long five-count, bringing them in slow and come-and-get-me steady.

So, is fishing the art of fishing or the catching of fish? I wish I knew. Uncle Jake and I have a bet, two bucks and supper dishes for a week with a couple ladies we're married to, doing the same thing on the other side of the lake. So, just in case, I'd like to know.

in one door and out

AUGUST 5

Old age doesn't come when you get to be sixty or seventy, or eighty, even. It comes to you in August. It couldn't come in June. In June, spring was springing with the sparkle of Ferris wheels. It couldn't come in July, either, because in July, summer was spreading before us like a picnic in the park. It comes in August, in August like dust riding in on crows' wings. It's in August when it hits us that a hundred years of hard labor lie ahead of us, and we're nothing but weekend fishermen and always will be. And not all weekends, either. Only those not sponged up with lawn mowing and bicycle fixing.

I think of this as I grab a quick cup of coffee before heading off to work. I pause to look out the kitchen window, past the peony bushes in faded flower hats, past the wilted roses, to where a mother mallard tends her nearly grown chicks. Mallards. Greenheads. How that mother mallard and her mate waltzed down the cool streets of early spring! Stubborn snowbanks still clutched at winter. It was she who chose the nesting site a long rifle shot from the lake in a muddy stubble field. The nest, hardly a nest at all, was a mere depression, hidden as deeply as possible within the sparse, gray cover. There, she laid her eggs, one a day for two weeks. Her mate watched out for skunks, foxes, raccoons, ravens and raiding house cats while the warmth of her body gave life to the eggs. For twenty-eight days and nights she sat there. The tiny puffballs in the here and now are nearly the size of their mother.

Which brings me to old age and August and the TV screen of my kitchen window. In a month, maybe less, they'll be gathering into flocks to leave us, and our lake. It makes a person wonder where time leaks away to, and how so many precious moments slip out the holes in the screen door and down the path of no return.

pigeon feathers

AUGUST 6

A gentleman writes, in a tight, rigid script, that he has caught me more than once writing on the same subject in a surprisingly similar manner. This, he says, upsets him, and he wishes I'd quit it, or else.

Well, my dear sir, answer me this if you can. How many times have you heard the Kingston Trio sing, "Hang Down Your Head Tom Dooley" and not enjoyed it as much as or more than the time before? And how many times have you seen the *Nutcracker* (that's a ballet) in which your little girl was a snowflake, and not had a lump in your throat at each and every closing of the curtain?

And tell me this, Mr. Quick-to-criticize, no matter how many times you've heard Kate Smith sing "God Bless America," don't you bust your buttons with pride? And that DU print, my good sir. I'll bet you look at that a hundred times a day and don't complain. Do you not hunt the same woodcock woods year after year? Do you not walk the same bean fields for pheasants in a "surprisingly similar" manner? Do you not fish the same trout streams day after day after day? How many times since Christmas have you eaten spaghetti and loved it? Three dozen? Four? How many times have you worn that swell necktie that looks like a muskie? Whenever your wife's been out of town, that's how many. And how many times have you watched reruns of M*A*S*H* and been darned glad to do it?

Yet, you hold it against me because I take a shortcut when the bullheads are biting on Frog Creek. Let us be consistent, sir. What this country needs is a little consistency. Say hi to Mom.

Your son,
Jerry

the awakening

AUGUST 7

Four of us were fishing in a regular regulation fourteen-foot fishing boat. That was two, possibly three, too many. Each was casting his usual lay-her back, swing-her forward and let-her-rip overhand casts. Consequently, we had a lot of line blowing around out there. We had hooks on the loose and no fish. It reminded me of a string of fishing people I'd once seen doing likewise, shoulder to shoulder, elbow to elbow, hip to hip, on a fishing pier. It was mayhem. It was chaos.

But while I was in that crowded fishing boat, wishing I were somewhere else, I stumbled upon a piece of philosophy, which is, *it's not enough merely to wish; one must also do*. So, I drove to the Elkhorn Tavern and Wildlife Museum, where I spoke at length of the situation from which I had recently fled.

It's sometimes painful to acknowledge large debts, but a guy there to whom I, and subsequently you, now owe an obligation of gratitude stepped forward and showed me how to cast what he called a loop cast. It's an underhand maneuver that squirts a lure safely and surely — in a crowd or not — straight out, and with a soft sploosh, too, rather than the usual splat. He retrieved a rod from the back of his pickup and held it straight out with both hands on the butt. He rolled those hands over, bringing a gorgeous little loop to the tip of the rod, and centrifugal force. At an opportune millisecond, he loosed the line, setting it free and sending the lure out like a shot past the ladies' bathroom, out the door and into the parking lot. It was beautiful.

This takes practice. The first time I tried it in the backyard, I hit the bird feeder; on the second, the kid's swing set; and on the third the dog on her rear end, and the sensitive thing hasn't spoken to me since.

in retrospect

AUGUST 8

Looking back, I think I know how it happened. I woke up early as usual, put the coffee pot on and headed outside to fix a leak in the boat, because I was going fishing with my Uncle Jake. As I opened the front door, it squeaked, so I went to the garage for a can of WD-40.

When I got to the garage, I saw a mouse in the bird seed and went back to the house for a trap. Passing the bird feeder, I saw it was empty and headed back to the garage. In the meantime, the dogs were raising all sorts of Cain to be let out, so I stopped to do that and noticed the youngest one had worked his collar off again. I went to fetch the leather punch and a rivet to make it smaller. He stopped me with a stick to throw, which I did, too high up on the roof of the woodshed. Hunting for the ladder, I remembered the kindling box was empty. I looked all over for the ax to split some of that, tripping over the shovel as I did. That reminded me I needed fishing worms, so I went to the garden to dig some. The garden was awful weedy, and I thought I'd seen the hoe up by the rosebushes, or what was left of them, and went there to get it. Naturally, it wasn't there, though the rake was, and I raked a little pile of last year's leaves into another little pile.

By then the pup had found another stick for me to throw, which I did, though he couldn't find it, and I had to help him. The stick had landed under my pickup, which reminded me it needed an oil change. I didn't have any oil, but my wife always has plenty in the trunk of her car. I went to the house for the keys. By then I figured it was too late to pick up my Uncle Jake, so I hooked the boat up to the pickup, drove to the lake, backed it in the water, and it sank.

all in the family

AUGUST 9

I've read that if orangutans are taken from their environment, they'll die out of lonesomeness. If that's so, then I'm more closely related to orangutans than I thought, because if I can't get out to a piece of woods to explore, or a mountain meadow, or the bend of a lazy river, if I can't sleep out in the open air snuggled deep into a warm sleeping bag, or in a small tent just big enough for me and a dream or two, if I can't treat myself to a falling star between the branches of sheltering pine trees, or step off a well-traveled trail once in a while with a pack on my back to travel light and free, or take a canoe loaded down with good luck even deeper into the wilderness …

If I can't strap on a pair of snowshoes and hike away from the trampled slush of city streets to hills where my own tracks are the first to land on new snow, if I can't ride a high, wild river or wade a brook or pitch a tent in the shade of an oak tree and stay awhile, or climb a cool mountain and dance with wildflowers …

If I can't head for the hills when I need to, keeping my eyes wide open for rattlesnakes and grizzly bears and poison ivy, if I can't curl up around a rough-and-tumble summer storm and swat mosquitoes all night long and listen to the zip, zip, zipping of tent doors, bubbling coffee pots and sizzling frying pans on camp fires …

If I can't go barefoot and eat beans and bacon day after day, paddle my own canoe, propel myself with the speed of a turtle, hit the trail, dress for the occasion, pick myself up and put myself down, get lost, fall through the ice, suffer frostbite and quicksand, follow wild animal tracks and zodiac signs to who knows where, catch a falling star, dodge an avalanche of moonbeams, stalk mushrooms and collect night sounds I've never heard before, I'm going to hunt me up an orangutan and say, "Move over, cousin, I'm with you."

the night watch

AUGUST 10

It's the tenth of August, almost the eleventh, and the sky is enormous with the absoluteness of a full moon we have longed for. It reflects up from the lake, over thin, feathery ripples breaking lightly against the shore. We scattered residents of Lost Lake, and you too, I think, because you have the same full moons as we, have waited for it at south side windows and patio doors after the ten o'clock news. When it finally comes, there it is.

August full moons are magical enough full moons in the usual full-moon sense. Like all full moons, they're moons of exclamation points. So we stand illuminated before our windows and patio doors, appreciating this one, but extending ourselves beyond the farthest bloom of it, and counting the sleeps to the next one and the one after that, to the full moons of September and October. We're not wishing any of our lives away, but those are the full, full moons that bring woodcocks down from farther north than we are. During those full moons of September and October, those extraordinary, glowing full moons when woodcocks come, we question whether or not, in the commonplace sense of our lives, we ever experience any times more noble and wonderful.

Woodcocks are comical-looking birds, I suppose, compared to other birds. Their bills are too long, though they look just right on woodcocks. Their eyes bulge, but they're quite good-looking eyes on woodcocks. Their twittering flight patterns are perfect for woodcocks. And they ride in on the full moons of September and October, in gradual trickles at first, under the cover of the glowing darkness of full moons. And we, on this August night, under this August full moon, at our south side windows and patio doors, come apart at the seams with the anticipation of it.

camping chronicles

AUGUST 11

We're packing for a canoe trip to the Boundary Waters Canoe Area Wilderness, Georgie, Howie and me. Going camping with them is okay, but has its drawbacks, as the man said whose mother-in-law died, and they came to him for the funeral expenses. For one thing, they insist on taking a couple of great big bath towels along, when space and weight are such precious commodities.

They're not alone. People always make gigantic arrangements for bathing when they're going anywhere near the water, but don't bathe much when they're there. It's the same with these two. They claim they'll get up every morning and go for a dip before breakfast and religiously pack the big towels. But, once we're there, they somehow feel they don't want that early morning swim so much as they did when they were back in town. Once or twice, virtue has triumphed, and they got up at six, took their towels and stumbled off for the water.

There's always an especially cutting east wind when they go bathing in the river in the morning. And they pick out the sharpest stones to walk on. And they have to hop and shiver two miles through six inches of water before they get deep enough to douse themselves. And when they do, invariably a huge wave comes along and knocks them down into a sitting position on the sharp rocks. And then another comes and carries them out to the middle, where they frantically swim for shore and wonder if they'll ever see home again. Just when they've given up all hope, the wave retires and leaves them sprawling like clams on the sand, and they look back to find they've been swimming for their lives in two feet of water. Then they hop and shiver back to the tent. They also claim a refreshing swim in the morning gives them a good appetite for breakfast.

To tell you the truth, it's hard enough feeding them as it is.

a little patience, please

AUGUST 12

The first lesson the Book of Job teaches is that Satan invented fly-fishing. Satan boasts he can win Job over to his side by making his life miserable. God says to try it, so Satan invents fly-fishing. Job was prosperous; his domestic relations were harmonious; he was, in short, a success. And Job was a high liver. God didn't object. "If you've got it, spend it" was His motto back then. It's only when Satan interferes and invents fly-fishing, and Job gets caught up in it, that his life becomes one of anguish. What I can't figure out is why Job gets all the publicity, since it's like that for me, too.

The first hint we get that all isn't right with Job is an apprehension of evil early on in the story. I also experience apprehensions of evil — worries about leaking waders and being caught baiting up worms. The poet implies Job might merely have imagined his troubles — ah, hallucinations of someone wrapped up in sinking-tip lines and Latin words for June bug. What's new? Equally tormenting to Job is a skin condition the translators of the Old Testament call boils. I've been there. It was poison ivy. The poet further tells us Job lapses into melancholia — that's exactly what I lapse into when I miss a hatch or can't match one. At one point, Job casts aside his rich raiments (so who needs 'em) and shuns the society of his fellow man. I, too, am something of a lone fisherman. Job laments his wretched lot, which is what I also do when I lose a nice fish. "My sighing cometh before I eat," laments Job. Are not all of us occasional victims of campfire beans and weenies? And on and on.

This clearly shows the severest of all miseries come from Satan, for Satan believes, as I do, that the surest way to a person's heart is through an eight-foot fly rod for a five-weight line. Wherefore should you all hate Satan and eschew things wherein it is suspected this most odious spirit delights. Rather spend your time in prayer and good works on behalf of those of us in Satan's grip, and don't complain about it.

georgie's close encounter

AUGUST 13

Rounding a sharp bend in the river, Georgie almost collided with a sow grizzly bear and two nearly grown cubs. For an instant, he thought they were large floating logs but, remembering there were no trees of any size on the north slope of Alaska, he quickly realized his mistake. He stopped paddling and drifted toward the unsuspecting animals until he got so close he could hear their heavy breathing.

Take out the garbage, Dear. One of the cubs saw him first, and woofed and lunged for shore. The sow, more surprised than the cub, surged toward the gravel bar in frantic leaps. Once on land, she didn't hesitate, and small stones and sand filled the air behind her as she plowed across the shore and crashed into the alders with the cubs close behind. Georgie smiled.

Georgie, please take out the garbage. Suddenly, the current caught him. He shot downstream, flashing by boulders and cutbacks. The valley began to close in on him, and the river bulged into long, narrow pools. Georgie savored the countryside. He passed a cow moose and her calf lying on a sandbar. Three caribou bulls paused to drink at the water's edge. A pair of whistling swans took off at his approach and, high overhead, a gyrfalcon spun and dived through the rat-gray sky.

Georgie! Jolted from his reverie by the rough water, Georgie broke through a set of rapids and entered a stretch where the waves were less violent and the channel more negotiable. But, no sooner had he caught his breath than he was back on the roller coaster. Chest-high breakers beat into his canoe, sending icy rivulets down his neck and up his sleeves. The river became a furious blend of white-capped froth and plunging troughs. Finally, physically and mentally drained, he found a gentle eddy and pulled in for the night. Lifting his dripping pack from the kitchen table, he headed confidently for the garbage can.

a remedy for optimism

AUGUST 14

Of all the silly, irritating foolishness we're plagued with, this weather forecasting fraud is about the most aggravating. Before a camping trip, I stayed up to watch the forecast on the ten o'clock news. It predicted precisely what had happened yesterday and the day before. For the following day, it predicted cold temperatures, thunderstorms and east winds strong enough to blow your socks off. I gave up thoughts of camping and stayed indoors all day, waiting for the rain. People, jolly as can be, stopped by on their way to picnics and fishing, on their way to fix up duck blinds and tree stands, as the sun was shining and there wasn't a cloud in sight .

"Ah," I said to myself as they left, "won't they come home soaked through and through." I chuckled to think how wet they were going to get and put a log on the fire and got out a good book and rearranged the contents of my tackle box.

By twelve o'clock, with the sun pouring in through the windows, the heat in the house was unbearable, and I wondered when the heavy rains and cold winds would start. "Ah!" I smiled. "They'll come this afternoon, and won't those son-of-a-guns get wet then." At one o'clock my kid asked if she could go outside to play because it was such a nice day. "No, no!" I said with a knowing look. "You don't want to get wet, do you?"

When the afternoon was nearly gone, and still there was no sign of rain, I tried to cheer us all up with the idea that it would come down all at once just as the others started for home and were well out of reach of shelter, and that they'd get more drenched than ever. Not a drop fell.

That night, the forecast for the next day was hot and dry, so we dressed in our flimsiest clothes and set out. Half an hour later, it commenced to rain, and a bitterly cold wind sprang up. It kept up for the whole day, and we came back with coughs and runny noses and went to bed.

a parable

AUGUST 15

The Professor, my Uncle Jake and I were planning a two-day float trip downriver to scout out a new bowhunting area. We made up a list of things to take along, but had to tear it up and throw it away. The upper reaches of the river wouldn't allow us to navigate a canoe big enough to carry us and the things we had written down. The Professor said, "You know, we shouldn't be thinking of things we can make do with, but only what we can't do without." That's real wisdom, not merely as it pertained to that situation, but regarding our trip down the river of life.

How many people on the voyage of life load up their canoes until they're in danger of swamping with a pile of things they think are essential to the trip, but which are not? How many pile the poor little boat with fancy clothes and big homes and cars, with friends they don't care two cents for and who don't care two cents for them, with entertainment nobody enjoys, and with — oh, the heaviest load of all! — what the neighbors think, with luxuries that cloy, with pleasures that bore, with empty show? It makes the canoe so heavy they can't paddle it. It makes it too cumbersome and dangerous to manage. They never know a minute's freedom from anxiety and care. There's no time for dreamy laziness, no time for ducks skimming lightly over shallows, no time for sunbeams flitting on the ripples of trout streams, no time for climbing trees and looking down on bucks with humongous antlers.

Let your canoe on the river of life be packed with only what you need — a homey home and simple pleasures, one or two worthy friends, someone to love and someone to love you, a kid or two, a dog, enough to eat, enough to wear, a little more than enough to drink because thirst is a dangerous thing, five guns and six fishing rods, and that's all.

positively speaking

AUGUST 16

There's nothing quite like the feel of a big brown trout slashing wildly across the surface, its tail throwing water to the wind, or the sight of a muskie's immense, heart-stopping swirl under the torpedo of a crankbait. I'm uncertain about a lot of things, but not that it's a blast to hook onto a lunker, a hawg, a whopper. Pitting my jungle experiences and the electronic gadgets of the scientific community against the wiles of the big ones, there's no doubt about it, is a gas and a real pleasure. I mean, most of the time it is. Almost all the time it is, but not always.

Sometimes it feels better to fish the flash and thunder of the big little ones, as in bluegills, with a couple of kids. In the summertime with a couple of kids, we don't overdo it. We adjust our fishing habits to the late-summer habits of bluegills. We take our time, but we go to a small, shallow lake on a quiet, mosquito-humming evening. We might use fly-fishing gear with surface bugs and poppers along its shorelines and around and about the heavy vegetation. If we think of it, we might switch to wet flies tipped with maggots or worm pieces to bolster our luck. At other times of the day, if we care to, we follow the fish into the deeper waters of bigger lakes, drift-fishing more put-together worms or crickets or grasshoppers, covering quite a bit of the lake and getting down to where overgrown bluegills cool their heels. Once we find them, we might anchor close by and pounce on them good. Or not.

If the catching of these summertime bluegills with a couple of kids doesn't increase your pulse, if it doesn't make your heart hammer with a little excitement, it will provide it at least with a more-or-less consistent flutter. I am fairly certain of that.

puppy love

AUGUST 17

Except for some emotional scars, Butch and I — Butch is my dog — have recovered from our trip into canoe country and the attack of a giant mosquito, which we were eventually able to overcome, but it makes you think, about dogs I mean.

Butch and I are preparing for our next adventure, which is bird hunting. We agree there aren't enough numbers to count the joys of bird hunting, and not nearly enough to count those of hunting over a good dog. But that's the rub. The road from pup to dog to hunting dog to great hunting dog can be painful and potholed, because there are as many theories about raising and training pups as there are about raising and training kids, with one distinct difference. Kids show up one morning at the breakfast table, read us their rights, say they live here, and that's that. But we get to pick out the pups.

It's this picking-out business that offers the great challenge, the very real responsibility. Before choosing a pup, people should determine, no ifs, ands or buts, just what exactly they'll be expecting from the dog this pup will become. Some dogs point, some set and some retrieve. Some are swimmers and some aren't. Some will fetch your sneakers, light your pipe and set the supper table. Some won't. Butch maintains — and he ought to know — that people should decide precisely what the dog's duties and chores will be, and then choose a pup from a breed with those potentials; that while people would like a dog that does it all, with the exception of himself, such an animal probably doesn't exist. He insists they've got to specialize, and though sometimes mutts make the best of hunting dogs — here again, he uses himself as an example — it's wise for people to check a pup's credentials, its pedigree, its heritage, before buying it. And, he adds, they should be thankful it can't do the same with them.

behind the scenes I

AUGUST 18

Bass are biting on the I Don't Remember River and its feeder streams, though you can't prove it by me, but what else is happening out there, anyway? Well, for one thing, bobolinks are molting from the brightness of their summer jackets into the heavier dullness of winter coats. I hate to mention this, but the newspapers are full of back-to-school sales, in case your kids have outgrown their clothes. And the last wild rose blossoms of summer are gone, and in their stead have come good jelly-making hips loaded with vitamin C. Queen Anne's lace — wild carrot — is growing thick along the roadsides.

Some of us are listening pretty closely for the first calls of katydids scratching itches in the night. The first frost will come six weeks to the day after the little critters sound off. (I only bring that up in case you want to cover your flowers when the time comes.) Young-of-the-year ruffed grouse are looking almost like their mothers. We like that. Dripping velvet is camouflaging the antlers of white-tailed deer. It's hard to count the points that way, but our imaginations take care of any misconceptions. And high-climbing wild grapes are ripening at the edge of the woods. It's good, good stuff, these wild grapes. And where it's cool and wet, touch-me-nots are blossoming. So are pearly everlastings and joe-pye weeds where it's dry.

Goldfinches are eating what they've been waiting for — ripe thistle seeds. This is the only decent reason for the existence of thistles. And bears are dissecting old logs for grubs and ants in the rotting wood, and gobbling them up if they can find them, and fattening up on roots, berries, mushrooms and insects if they can't. And wild plums are ripe for the picking, which we do, and that's not all …

and II

AUGUST 19

Because they're among the most obvious of weeds blooming now at the height of hay fever season, goldenrods are taking the heat for this seasonal malady. But goldenrod pollen is basically too heavy to blow around. Blame ragweeds. And on these dew-heavy mornings, early sunlight, though not as early as it was, sets aglow the silken strands of spiders' homes. The round, delicate webs are those of orb spiders. And wild raspberries keep coming and coming, and we can live with that. And in the quiet, well-oiled perfection of August, muskie fishermen are gearing up for the red-hot action of cooler days and nights. And sugar maples and box elders are letting go their seeds, which flip and flutter to the ground ahead of the comforting, nurturing cover of fallen leaves. And moonlight is shining on dying fires and sleeping campers, and hummingbirds are hovering over feeders at two-hundred wing beats a second. And hazelnuts are getting ripe. And Jupiter's a just-before-dawn shiner.

And yellow jackets are late-summer tough and pushy. And cottontails are having new families, as usual. And algae is scumming over ponds, and shining semi-brightly tonight is the Dog Star in Canis Major, companion to the great Orion, and blamed for this weather that poisons the water with the above-mentioned algae, causing animals — two-legged and four — to run amuck. The dog days. And adolescent muskrats and beavers are poking about for homesteads of their own. They've not been taught to look both ways before crossing the street.

And if you're the type who listens to the evening news, you'll swear the world's gone to pot, but you step outside, look around, and you see it's gone to seed. At least it has here at Lost Lake, and dollars to doughnuts that's how it is where you live, too.

make mine sunny side up

AUGUST 20

You know how it is. You pack your packs. You pack the pots and pans, the skillet, the hot pads, the turners, cups, bowls, plates, forks, knives and spoons. You pack the toilet paper, the stove, fuel, funnel, matches, foil, grill, socks and plastic bags. You pack the underwear, the pants and t-shirts. Maybe you throw in an extra roll of toilet paper. You pack a sweater and, what the heck, more matches and another pair of socks. You pack your hat, your rain gear. Your towel and washcloth. Your bandana, rain fly, tent, ground cloth, sleeping bag, toothbrush, wool shirt, soap, first-aid kit, aspirin, shovel, ax and rope. You always run out of rope, so you pack more rope. And just in case, more toilet paper and matches. You never know. You pack the candle, rod, reel, map, flashlight, compass and tackle box.

You need food. You pack wieners, bread, beans, ketchup, marshmallows, chocolate bars, graham crackers and a big bag of gorp. You put it all in your pickup truck, tie down the canoe, throw in the paddles and drive five hundred miles to the landing. You paddle two days, set up camp, eat supper and go to bed. Then it starts to thunder, and there's nothing between you and it but the thin thickness of your tent. There are various kinds of thunder. There's the deep, rumbling roar, the sharp crackle, the loud crash traveling at 1,100 feet a second, which is plenty fast. Primitive people attributed thunder to the sound of gods angry with them. I think that's right.

I suppose I should have saved some space here for a discussion of lightning, as well, but lightning doesn't affect me, since by the time it happens, I'm huddled at the foot of my sleeping bag with my eyes closed.

making a run for it

AUGUST 21

Yesterday, summer was blooming like a lanky lad, glowing like a pretty girl. But that was then. We were brave in the face of danger, liberal, courteous in dealings with our enemies, protectors of the oppressed, the adored of the opposite sex. That was then, but summer's almost gone, and this is now. We look back at what could have been, shake our heads at trout we could have caught but never did, at rivers we could have paddled and camps we could have made. Oh, the Odysseys and ecstasies that were to have been ours. The Iliads. The vast stretches of gardens we had wanted to hoe. But here we are.

Yet, we forge ahead. We pick the two or three tomatoes plucky enough to have made it. We make a little sauerkraut and turn misshapen cucumbers into pickles. We can peaches bought from farmers' markets. We eat suppers of fried-up catfish, and baking powder biscuits with blueberries in them. Though it was a lousy year for blueberries, we splurge now and then. At sundown, we sit on the porch swing and wait for the circles of Saturn and the moons of Jupiter. We think maybe next year. Then someone calls, an old friend, to ask if, six or eight weeks into the future, we'd join him and his decoys on a trip he's planning, to where ducks fly thick as grass.

And we think, omigosh, here comes September, forty feet wide and running deep. We've got to clean up the deer camp, shoot some clay pigeons, fire practice arrows at the hay bales stacked three high out behind the woodshed, rev up the canoe paddles for missions into jungle stands of wild rice. We've time to catch a bass or two, right now, to sharpen the hooks on muskie plugs, to take a moonlight stroll with whoever will have us, and to take a final summer fling, a one-on-one campout, with our kids before the school bus comes down the road and carries them away forever.

clearing the air

AUGUST 22

This is how they tell it down at the Elkhorn Tavern and Wildlife Museum. The English teacher over at the high school came home, looking cheerful and happy. His wife took one look at him and said, "Absolutely not! You are not going to get another gun! Not one! Not now! Not ever!"

"Why do you speak in riddles," he said, "and who said anything about a gun?"

"It's bad enough," she wailed, "that you have five or six guns now, and the kids need shoes and the muffler on the car is shot."

"Don't beat around the bush, my Little Chicken," he said, "and if I've said anything about guns, I should drop dead."

"You came out of your mother's belly without that gun," she said. "You've lived this long without that gun. And, by God, you'll be carried to your grave without it."

"What gun?" he said.

"I've seen you casting sheep eyes at that sweet little .20-gauge side-by-side in the window of the hardware store," she said. "And I know what you're going to say. You're going to quote someone who said, 'He who will not when he may, when he will, he shall have nay.' Or you're going to say, 'When good luck is knocking at my door, is it right to shut it out?' Or 'Let's make hay while the sun shines,' and 'He who hesitates is lost.' The refrigerator is kaput, the roof leaks, and you without even a cost-of-living increase. You have no more sense than a cuckoo."

Then, as they tell it down at the Elkhorn Tavern and Wildlife Museum, she started to cry as if the world were ending and said, "Oh, what's the use. Go get the gun." Whereupon, he shook his head sadly and said, "You wound me." Then he went out to his pickup truck and got it.

stranded

AUGUST 23

Migration! If you want to talk migration, here's migration! It's the twenty-third of August, and red-eyed vireos are setting down plans to leave the thick thickets of their summer homes for far-away winter ones in South America! Big flocks of purple martins are saying adios and heading for Brazil! They say they've got to get out before the bug supply goes! Wood thrushes are disappearing! Ring-billed gulls are about to skedaddle! Sandpipers and yellowlegs are almost kaput! Red-orange and black redstarts are vacating wood lots and swamps and shrubs in the suburbs for South America!

Warblers — all kinds of them — are edging southward! Swallows are considering the same kinds of moves to that end of the map! Robins, some of them, are gathering in premature premigration get-togethers! Bobolinks are ready to leave our fields and meadows, farms and marshes! Red-winged blackbirds are coming out of a molt-induced semi-retirement just in time to head out! Plovers are moving through! Monarch butterflies are heading down to somewhere in and around Mexico! Ovenbirds and their "teacher teacher teacher teacher" calls are doing the same thing! Great and I mean great flocks of nighthawks, sometimes numbering in the thousands, are grouping in bouncing flights to follow retreating insects to the south! South! South! South! From early evening until after the ten o'clock news, we watch them go! Hummingbirds are definitely on the way out! Arctic terns are soon to be Antarctic terns!

By day! By night! They're streaming over river valleys, seacoasts, prairie potholes, cornfields and mountain ranges, traveling in short hops or thousands of miles at a crack! What guides them so surely! What makes them go! What brings them back! I don't know! Do you?

a many splendored thing

AUGUST 24

Somebody said I am often a child masquerading as an adult. I think it's because I chase rainbows. When you're a chaser of rainbows, you wind up in the weirdest places, and you almost always have a good time. Sometimes you wind up in fog, very thick fog, the mother lode of fog, when you're chasing rainbows, and you don't know how that happened. And sometimes you wind up with the wind rumbling down a mountain, and sometimes with bear cubs born entombed in snow. You never know.

Sometimes you find yourself where hope awaits just a couple of bends downstream, and sometimes in the cool eddies of faraway rivers. Sometimes you find yourself breathing air scented with willow and spruce until you're fit to be tied. But you keep trying. What could possibly keep you from trying? Sometimes you get a glimpse of heaven. You play hide-and-seek with flocks of geese, and once you've had a glimpse of heaven, you look at the world with a fresh pair of eyes. Sometimes you end up on a cloud-shrouded island, and you haven't the slightest idea how you got there. It doesn't matter. It's worth the trip, even if you don't get a nibble.

Experience counts when you're a chaser of rainbows, but it's not necessary. Anybody who's willing to masquerade as a child for a while can do it. Anybody who's willing to cruise the rocky pinnacles of ecstasy and beat the odds where the leaves of trees rustle. And drift downstream amid rough rapids, and brave a little rip in your waders when a rainbow leaps clear of the water and dives deep and swims hard and fights as only a rainbow can. And your rod feels alive as it twists and turns and splashes, flashing in the morning sunlight, all fifteen inches of it, fat and silvery and full of spots, with faint, reddish streaks down its sides. You can do worse, I think, than be a chaser of rainbows.

if you can't say something nice …

AUGUST 25

People who aren't very good-looking often find some measure of satisfaction when those who are start to sag. Imagine our disappointment, then, with those who don't. Howie doesn't. He's my second cousin, the dry-fly purist, as good-looking now as he's ever been, and he gets on my nerves. He's the one who taught me how to make this. You laugh, but maybe you've never tried it.

We were at the deer shack at the time, and it was Howie's turn to cook. There were about ten of us, and we were hungry. Howie took down the big skillet, heated it up and browned five pounds of breakfast sausage in it. He had made the sausage from a deer somebody got last year. I forget who. Maybe he did. He drained the excess grease off the sausage and added two twelve-ounce cans of evaporated milk. Stirring constantly, he added about half a gallon of whole milk and let it simmer for ten minutes or so. (This sounds like a lot of gravy. Maybe there were fifteen of us. We get so many visitors during deer season, you'd think there's nobody left in town. Howie'd know. He's got a terrific memory.)

He brought it to a boil, a slow boil, thickened it with half a cup of a flour-and-water paste, and salt and peppered it. He winked at me — he winks at everybody, but I hate it when he does it to me — and asked if I'd whip up some baking powder biscuits, which I did, from a mix.

Anyway, he served the gravy over the hot biscuits. It was good. He said it's even better as leftovers if you reheat it with a little more milk to thin it out. I don't know. There weren't any. But enough about Howie. It's high time I quit anthropomorphizing him, and don't think I don't know it.

unidentified floating objects

AUGUST 26

You've heard, I believe, of the boy who cried wolf. That was me, and it wasn't wolf but *yikes*! A friend had asked me to go canoeing on Such-and-Such a River with him. I said yes. Whereas I live to go canoeing, it's almost a religion with me that I sit in the back of the canoe. On this day, however, I was a guest, and it wouldn't be remotely possible to be sitting where I wanted to be sitting. *Yikes*, I said. Then when we got to the river, I was somewhat amazed at its turbulence. *Yikes*, I said again. I would like to have had additional information on that river.

The water was high, the color of wet cement. It churned impressively, and the speed with which we began our descent was breathtaking. *Yikes*, I said, and grabbed hold of my hat with both hands. The powerful current gripped the canoe, and we swooped through boulder-choked gorges. We rode on the back of a writhing serpent beset with narrow channels and scattered rocks stirring the water into jolting back curls. Then it got bad. The river squeezed into a twisting canyon and around and around sheer rock walls. The driving current exploded against them, turning under and rising again as treacherous boils. It was touch and go. Draw stroke, draw stroke, I cried, and *yikes*. A quarter-mile later, the river took a sharp bend and dropped out of sight into a maze of waves, boulders and holes. There were monumental rocks all over the place protruding from the water. Thump! Thumpthumpthump, we went, and *yikes*. Those rocks were the size of Volkswagens.

Then there was a tree spanning the river, and it was all over. Angry currents swirled through the submerged branches. This is called a strainer. It's a death trap. *Yikes*, I said again from the front seat in which I sat. I'm glad it wasn't my canoe, the poor thing.

the last word

AUGUST 27

Usually when people tell me they're going to make a long story short, I bless the ground they walk on and offer up prayers for the salvation of their souls. Usually, but not always. Sometimes their attempts at brevity leave me hanging.

Once a fellow said to me, "I caught a muskie yesterday. To make a long story short, there it is on the wall." And there's a thirty-pound fish there, the Moby Dick of muskies. I hate that. I need to know more about this. I need to know what kind of line was he using? How heavy? What kind of bait? What time of day? Where? What did he have for supper? What's his favorite color? Were there witnesses? Does he need a new best friend? I need to share in the excitement, feel the pull of the fish, experience the thrill.

Another once said, "Gee! I saw a nice buck this morning. To make a long story short, it broke a Pope and Young record." I hate that. I need to know more. What kind of bow did he use? What kind of arrow? What time of day? Where? What did he have for supper? What's his favorite color? Were there witnesses? Is he in the market for a new best friend?

It happens all the time. "There was this old tom turkey with a foot-long beard hanging out in Peterson's back forty, and to make a long story short …"

"You'd never guess what I did yesterday, and to make a long story short, we're darn near tired of moose meat …"

"To make a long story short, I was out of shells when he charged …"

Even I do it. Like last week, a scratched-up fellow dressed in tattered camouflage came busting into the Elkhorn Tavern and Wildlife Museum with a five-hundred pound she-bear hot on his heels. I knew there was a story there somewhere, but to make a long one short, I didn't stick around long enough to find it.

a different drummer

AUGUST 28

I'm a hunter. I've made up my mind to kill long before the smoke of autumn is on us all, long before the hunt begins, before the pheasant flies above the corn rows, before the partridge leaps for pine tree protection, before the shadow of a deer looms across my path, before the mallard sets his wings to my decoys. I'm fully aware that I'm about to take the life of a beautiful wild creature, a creature I care deeply about, and I do it anyway.

Why? Why do I skulk through brush and wetland and forest with death on my brain? Is it to feed an empty belly? It's not that for me. My freezer's full of strawberries and porkchops. Is it to satisfy leftover animal instincts of tooth and claw? I don't know. I'm born and bred no differently from those good people who choose not to hunt, nor from those who rant and rave and plot and cry, "Shame" at me and what I do. It's not that, though I admit to what may be an aboriginal feeling of satisfaction when I hunt. Am I, then, a demented fellow who finds pleasure in pain? I hope not. I've seen enough pain in my life. I don't need more. Do I need the space, then? How could I? I like sharing my life and land with wild things.

I'm by no means alone. There are other hunters of wildlife. There are diseases, blizzards and automobiles. There are my brothers, the wolves and coyotes. There's time. I claim "Hunter" as an honorable title. I'm proud of being a good hunter, a law-abiding hunter, and hunting gives me pleasure. That's all I know, and all I need to know.

clearing the air

AUGUST 29

"C'mon down," my friend said long distance.

"I can't," I said. "I'm too busy."

"But you're a writer," he said. "You have nothing to do."

Little did he know. I had a tire to change on my wife's car and a screen door to fix. I had to stop by Mom's Cafe over on Main Street to see if the fish were biting. I had to stop by the Post Office to verify it. I had to shoot hoops with my kid and chase a frog. There were tomatoes to pick, flies to tie, shells to reload, firewood to split, a hole to dig and a kite to fly. I had to work the dog.

They had told me over at Mom's, and said it was so at the Post Office, that muskies were biting on Whatchamacallit Bay, so I launched my twelve-footer to check it out. That took awhile. Before I knew it, it was time for a coffee break, and back to Mom's I went. Then I cleaned the camp stove, changed a mantle on the lantern, fixed a zipper on the tent, caught some bluegills, and ate lunch. A bear had visited my neighbor the night before, so I went over to calm his nerves (the bear's, I mean). Then I had to shoot some arrows. I figured my duck blind would be in terrible shape, so I paddled out there for a look-see. Sure enough, it was. I hiked on over to my tree stand. It, too, could use some shoring up.

I got an idea for a story while I was out there, but forgot it before I found a pencil. I spent a little time dreaming about a big fish I am going to catch, and then switched over to a buck with humongous antlers. I read a story about the secrets of jigging walleyes, and another about the secrets of calling turkeys. That really gets me going. I played catch with my kid and got my wife and climbed a hill out back to watch the sun set. Nothing to do, indeed!

lasting impressions

AUGUST 30

You can see it in the jumbled mass of roadside weeds, in the jumbled mass of roadside grass. In the anxiety of hummingbirds. In butterflies sucking the sanctity out of wildflowers. In the apprehension of unpicked tomatoes. In the meager flow of footprints in the sand of lonely beaches. In the trickle of time running out for wooly berry-spending bears. In the velvet-dripping antlers of white-tailed deer. In the amorous adventures of moose.

You can feel it in the incessant, whispering breeze. In the growing carpet of leaves. In the glow of sinking suns. In the picture-book mountains you climb. In the unmistakable footprints of disappearing days. In the hurried drone of honeybees. In the growing gold of hills and valleys and plains. In the reds and yellows and browns. In spongy bogs and marshes. In the orderly progression of Orion and the Great Bear. In the lingering opportunities of bullfrogs. In the promises of apple trees. In dew doing wonders with spiders' webs. In the efforts of mergansers.

You can smell it in stampeding herds of buffalo masquerading as clouds. In the colors of dipsy-doodle trout. In ring-necked pheasants, partridges and grouse. In the solicitations of elks. In the welcome solitude. In the rugged climb of night and the ghostly gardens of June, July and much of August. In the calls of geese. Of owls. Of wolves. In the business of mice. Of squirrels. Of flat-tailed beavers.

You can sense it in the gathering of firewood. In the pickle making. In the growing anticipation of pumpkins. In the smell of spent shotgun shells. In the raking up of maple leaves. In the trophy set of circumstances we're given when summer's almost gone and breaking up is hard to do.

a lucky shot

AUGUST 31

There was a fellow here at Lost Lake who's gone now, and nobody misses him. It's because he made a lucky shot once and got his deer. We don't like that, though as hunting season draws near, we remember.

He saw the flicker of a tail and blasted away, regardless of the odds. He wasn't hunting. He was using his privilege to hunt as a license for thoughtless abandon. Every person back of a gun knows pretty well what his chances are. This guy's chances were nil, and he knew it. He shouldn't have fired because he didn't know if this deer was a buck or a doe or a fawn. He didn't know if one of his partners was standing behind it or sitting on a stump. He didn't know. He didn't care. He claimed to be an experienced hunter, yet an experienced hunter has formed the habit of squeezing the trigger only when his sights are dead on the target. He was lucky, he said; he got his deer. And I guess he was lucky. He might have only wounded it.

A quickly dispatched animal is brought to a merciful end, but a crippled one is condemned to a lingering death. It will bleed to death or slowly starve to death or stand in helpless wonder as coyotes tear it apart, or it will freeze to death months later — done in by the callousness of a single man without honor. He had a buck-only license. Had his lucky shot claimed a doe or a fawn, what would he have done then? He would have sneered at the animal, cursed his fate, and left it there to rot. He would have stolen away like a thief in the night, like the thief he was.

Hunters are bound by moral obligations. We may not always hunt under ideal conditions, but we must always wait for the ideal shot.

MACIEJ

great expectations

SEPTEMBER 1

A cricket sings down at the woodpile, and with the first light of its first dawn, September rears back, throws open its arms and calls to its children. "Come," says September, and we do.

Milkweed pods bust open, shooting parachuting milkweed seeds into September's lovely afternoons. Jupiter checks in as the evening star. We put half-a-dozen .20-gauge shotgun shells into the pockets of our old hunting vests and go hunting partridges. White oaks drop acorns to feed nearly every living thing out there, and to sow the seeds of their own tomorrows. Full moons beckon flights of woodcocks from the north. Rafts of coots blow in, and dry leaves of wood lot trees send monarch butterflies gossip-drifting south.

September calls. We'll need to build our tree stands. Limb by limb, we'll set our eyes climbing up stout-limbed pine trees. In those stands, we'll wait for white-tailed deer, whose summer coats are changing to the thicker, grayer ones that will shield them some from the icy bark and bite of what's to come. Jumping mice say "Uh-uh," and settle down for an eight-month winter's nap.

September calls. We'll paddle canoes and flattish johnboats loaded with chicken wire, cattails, hammers and two-by-fours to mend duck blinds. We'll watch cornfields for pheasant potential. We'll hunt our waters for solitary bands of muskies. We'll scout for Halloween-promising pumpkins in the garden.

September calls. It might sound like a turkey calling, a Canada goose, an elk. It might sound like a bobwhite quail, a chattering gray squirrel, a whirr of teals' wings, a cricket down at the woodpile, but it's September, all right, and when it calls we say, "Oops, by golly, that's September, and I gotta go." At least that's how it is here at Lost Lake where I live, and I suppose that's about how it is where you live, too.

sic transit gloria mundi

SEPTEMBER 2

Somewhere out there, under a mouse-eared willow tree (or maybe the tree's a pine or cottonwood, or maybe there's no tree at all), there's a nice river (though this river may be a lake or pond or stream). Under this tree (which may be no tree) in this water, there's a trout, growing as a rose grows in a garden, seeing itself mirrored in the jewelled galaxy of an empty sky. (This trout, by the way, could be a bass or walleye or bullhead.)

And this trout might have stayed there forever. But it looks hard one morning with dew and sees a meal approaching, a buggy-looking thing with a buggy tail and spent wings, and it seems like this wouldn't be too much of a labor (a piece of cake, really) to fetch it, so it does.

For the trout, it is great fun being a trout, but then it ends. It inhales the spent-wing looking thing, only this piece of cake isn't. It tastes of hair and feathers, of feathers and hair, and it won't go down. It pulls, rather sharply, on this trout, and it takes this trout, against its will and better judgment, away with it.

A trout is equipped with no bitterness, but this one throws its weight into the responsibility of staying put. This trout (remember, this could be another fish) throws its weight to the task with wild running, but there is no letting go. Across pastures of water, the fish, reflecting the blue-green of the water and sky-blue of the sky, rises to shake off its chains. In the tumbling foam, within the water-roots of the mouse-eared willow, this trout fights to be one with its water until it is lifted into the endless, suffocating air of eagles, where even the grass has its song, though only the wind hears it.

a child of calamity

SEPTEMBER 3

Son of a gun. I failed one of those brutal "How Do You Measure Up" tests that so frequently sour the pages of ladies' magazines. I failed it.

Consequently, I launched upon a vigorous campaign to become a man of the nineties. Hip. Hot. Sensitive. In. To tell you the truth, however, I'm a little disappointed with myself. To become a man of the nineties, I must first, I am told, get in touch with my innermost self, and I can't quite get the hang of it.

Every time I lie back and close my eyes to dig deep into my innermost self, the only picture I get is the one of pheasant country — cornfields, thickets and fence rows. I smell pheasant country. I hear it. I do. But that's not the half of it. When I try even harder, I find myself in whitetail country. Right in the middle of it. I hear the songs of forests and inhale whole flowering meadows. I breathe the same tingling air whitetails breathe and walk the same trails. I've gotten drunk with them a couple of times on the sheer beauty of the place.

Though I fight it, I drift into trout country and the living, singing waters of it, and the silences and stillnesses of it, and the shining wet stones and leaf-brown pools of it. There are times I end up in lakes, or big, sluggish rivers or marshes with mallards or two dozen honkers. I find myself up in oak trees, eyeball to eyeball with squirrels. Hell, I even race eagles from cloud to cloud and perch with them for dinner, family-style.

When it really gets out of control, I ride wild horses after buffaloes. I muck with moose. I arm-wrestle elk. I lead three thousand caribou in the Hallelujah Chorus. I dance with wolves. Maybe I should just give it up and accept that I'm a man of a lesser era. Forever unhip. Cool. Insensitive. And out.

a reluctant departure

SEPTEMBER 4

I am trying to sleep in this tent dipped in darkness. The dim polestar is riding on the starboard wing, Orion is frozen in the southwest sky, and I am besieged by mosquitoes. Smack.

While hunting for a misplaced thought, I come instead on this one, which is that mosquitoes have a very important role in maintaining the ecological balance. Smack. Each of the billions of mosquitoes outside this tent, some of which are inside it, has an indispensable function in the natural scheme of things. The fate of the universe, as we know it, hangs upon the survival of mosquitoes. Smack. That piece of information is easily overlooked when they come determined to preserve their species at the cost of mine.

If you are not so dumb as to offer a sandwich to a bear, the bear will not generally chew off your arm. No matter how ferocious they might appear, wildcats, when meeting you on the trail, will run helter-skelter in the opposite direction. Wolves are aloof and harmless in the backwoods. Porcupines are no fun, but can be deterred with a stout stick. If you don't poke at beehives, bees will give you room to maneuver. Caution in snake country will get you by anything that crawls. Smack. But not mosquitoes. You can't throw scraps of meat at mosquitoes to quiet their nerves. You can't pet them to quell an attack. You can't form a business relationship with mosquitoes. Smack. You can't deal commonsensibly or kid around with them. They think they've got the right of way wherever they go.

Those are the facts. There are billions of important mosquitoes out there and in here; their bites, I suppose, are small prices to pay for quality time in the great out-of-doors, yet I think I'll forsake the tent tonight and sleep in the house.

blood is thicker than water, but not by much

SEPTEMBER 5

Life, it is said, is a journey, and the kind of journey it turns out to be depends upon the person who makes it. Take my Uncle Jake. He has a son who grew up, moved away to the big city, and does hardly any fishing at all anymore, which makes him the black sheep of the family. But that's not half the story. The son has a couple of little kids of his own who don't, in fact, know the difference between bobbers and bluegills or Panther Martins and purple finches. As you can imagine, the depravity is unbearable to my uncle.

Then, one day, when he and I are out in his boat hunting for muskies, he shrieks, "Eureka!" sounding like an old screen door slamming shut, and demonstrates the genius in his bloodstream. Jake's plan is this. I (meaning me) will take my brand new movie camera and make propaganda fishing films of him, the expert fisherman of Lost Lake and the Universe, doing all kinds of fishing, starting with the basics.

He'll do trout and bass. He'll do northern pike and walleye. He'll go into catfish and sunfish. He'll cast. He'll troll. He'll wade. He'll dig worms, tie flies and seine minnows. He'll clean, fillet and fry. He'll do all this to the background music of appropriate sounds.

He'll be a Grandpa, attending to the spiritual needs of his fallen-away grandchildren. And, he said in a tone of voice I'm used to, if I (meaning me) will give up sleeping, eating and bird hunting this fall and leave off going to church, we'll have the thing done by Christmas, which is one of the mixed blessings of being his nephew. But enough about me and my problems. How's everything going with you these days?

a question of survival

SEPTEMBER 6

If you take prairie potholes away from mallard ducks, you've got no more mallard ducks. You take popple trees away from partridges, and you've got no more partridges. If you don't give hip-hoppety toads room to maneuver, you don't have any more hip-hoppety toads. It is the way of all things. They cannot be without habitat necessary to their being. I'm not so wild any more, myself, but there's habitat I need to ensure the survival of me.

I could not exist, for example, without the unbroken forests, the lakes and rivers of canoe country. I couldn't. I'd die without ridges of, say, two or three thousand feet, laced with deer trails. You could cross me off, mark me null and void, if I couldn't look in on small farms, once in a while, where crabapple trees grow wild and untamed grapes smother hillsides.

Like zooed grizzly bears, I'd suffocate without the companionship of little trout streams squirming in all directions, and thick, thorny growths and oaks, and stands of serviceberries. I must have swamp cover to live, and muskeg bogs, where appropriate, and inaccessible valleys crammed with long distances. I'd starve to death without blueberries. You might as well wrap me up in a bad cold and fever as expect me to live without the essential life-giving ingredients of sagebrush or white pines. I'd dig my own grave. I'd dig it deeper if I could never hear the sounds of geese or breaking waves. I'd be as useless as blooming Christmas cactuses in July.

For my winter habitat, and I freely admit it, I must have snow country. So, when you go to drain off a wetland or pave over a piece of prairie, will you stop and think of me? Is that too much to ask?

metaphorically speaking

SEPTEMBER 7

It sounds uppity, but some of us, as we have aged, have mellowed even as the year has mellowed into September. As we have climbed the mountains of our days, we have grown at last to appreciate the finer things in life — good books, food, music and turkey hunting. We are especially fond of turkey hunting, because that's the way we are, and because it's the most gol-darned fun thing you've ever heard of.

But this is fall now, autumn; the sun is in the seventh heaven, and the moon is up there, too, and there's a big, big difference between hunting turkeys in spring and hunting turkeys in fall — roughly the difference between sunrise and sunset. Spring turkeys are lone birds, solitary, looking for romance and taking unkindly to company and competition. Fall turkeys, on the other hand, are get-together gadabouts, ganged up like junior high school boys at a sock hop. Spring birds do their talking mostly early in the day, and basically they do quite a bit of it — busybody meddlings, poetry readings and the like. But, come fall, they find they haven't much to say anymore, and don't say it. Gobblers in the spring are on a hormonal bungee jump and are liable to be a bit careless. Those in fall, however, are as cautious as penguins on the Fourth of July.

So, basically, what we turkey hunters have to do now is take what we've learned about hunting turkeys in spring and chuck it, or most of it, anyway. It's sort of like a kiss with the morning sun being every bit as pleasant as a kiss with the setting of same, but each is given and taken under an entirely different set of circumstances, the expectations of the one contrary to those of the other, if you hear what I'm saying.

it's a jungle out there

SEPTEMBER 8

There are days, and we all have them, when nothing goes right. It's like I get up, and there's a lion crouched and waiting for me, a lion that rises from its sleep and sniffs the air for me, and roars and leaps just out of sight. Then it creeps up and watches me wherever I go. Waiting.

I could be walking down a dimly lit partridge trail and heading straight for quicksand. I could be climbing up a tree for a look-see and missing a rung on the ladder. But on this day, when nothing's to go right, I am in my canoe going helter-skelter down a moving-right-along river. The water's cold and I'm out of control. Before I know it, the lion steps out, and I wash up broadside against a fallen-down tree. I'm convinced the meek shall inherit the earth, but I put the thought aside and take immediate, though ill-advised, action. I sharply lean away from that fallen-down tree. When I do that, I dip the upstream side of my canoe into the moving-right-along water. My canoe fills up. I go overboard. The bottom of my canoe now becomes the top. When I come bobbing to the bubbly surface, gulping for air, it is I now washing up broadside against the fallen-down tree. On a day truly gone bad, I get trapped under the tree, or caught between the canoe and the tree, and I get bashed and battered, if not drowned. I need a better defense.

Next time, I will stifle the natural inclination to lean away from what's stemming my downstream progress. I will lean, rather, toward it. I will let the moving-right-along water glide and gather between me and it, ultimately freeing me from the lion's grisly grasp. Then I will press on with nothing between me and my dress code but the lion's second cousin, two bends down and to the right.

adjusting the heart

SEPTEMBER 9

So much of what we go about doing, we go about doing backwards. According to my tattered dictionary it's *Mettre la charrette avant les boeufs* to the French. To the Germans it's *Die Pferde hinter den Wagen spannen*. To the Italians it's *Metter il carro innanzi ai buoi*. No matter how you put it though, it's *Putting the cart before the horse*.

When our kids tell us they wish to become hunters like us, the first thing we do is a double flip for the gratefulness of it. Then we hurry out to get them a gun or bequeath them one we have outgrown, if it is possible to outgrow a gun. The gun should come much later.

Long before the gun comes, the kids should be taught to hunt fiddlehead ferns and morel mushrooms, and shown how well they fry up with trout. Then they should be taught to hunt trout. They should learn which animals are making which tracks, and why.

They should learn of the young of the wild and of the old, and learn of wildflowers. They should become intimate with beaver ponds. They should learn to build campfires and hang stewpots over them, and taste changing weather on their tongues. They should learn this slowly and be allowed their mistakes. If one trips or tips over a coffeepot, or causes you to lose a nice fish, what difference does it make? They should learn to move noiselessly, to sit endlessly, to listen and to see what there is to see. They should learn their place in the natural order of things, and how when they go hunting, they must go humbly and with honor.

Then and only then will their love and respect for all living things grow. Then will they understand the difference between the awfulness of killing and the uncompromising joy of hunting. Then, and only then, comes the gun.

true blue

SEPTEMBER 10

We're not friends in the classical sense. Achilles and Patroclus, Damon and Pythias, those were friends in the classical sense. Today, we do not have such friendships. I used to have best friends, but then I got married and my wife became my best friend, and my former best friends positioned themselves, if at all, a few rungs down the friendship ladder. Then I had a kid who became my second best friend, and my former best friends went out the window.

What I have are buddies. Bowlers have bowling buddies. Pool players have pool-playing buddies. I have outdoors buddies, one of whom is a turkey hunter. He is your average turkey hunter, I think, with above average intelligence and a fair share of courage, though he has his faults. He's generally late for work, late for supper and late with the payment on his pickup truck, but during turkey-hunting season he's up every day before dawn. He wakes his family with his early rising, with his dressing, gear-gathering and breakfast-making, but in the woods, he moves like a ghost. He fidgets during a fifteen-minute sermon, but in his hunting blind he sits for hours, still as a mouse. He doesn't care what he looks like at church or on the job, but he'll spend an hour applying makeup that makes him look like a tree.

He doesn't own one stock, not one bond. His money's tied up in shotguns and turkey calls. He can't walk to the mailbox, but enjoys the two-mile hike into turkey country. He can't locate a pair of socks in his sock drawer, though through tangled brush on foggy days he can pick out a tom's beard at sixty yards. He can't remember to take out the garbage, he can't remember birthdays or anniversaries, but he never forgets an opening day. That's about it. He's no Achilles, but I'm no Patroclus, either. For better or for worse, we're a couple of hunting buddies, and we do the best we can.

cultural affairs

SEPTEMBER 11

The intricate eccentricities of its inhabitants is one of the things that makes Lost Lake such a nice place to live. Just about everybody points that out to visiting relatives. There's this gentleman, for example, who, among other things, is an absolute whiz with plastic garbage bags. We call him the Professor.

Last night at the Lost Lake Fish, Game and Cribbage Club meeting, it was his turn to give the presentation, so naturally the subject was garbage bags. He started out by reminding us never to venture into the out-of-doors without a batch of garbage bags, and he showed us how a dozen of them fit just right in the hip pocket, opposite our wallets.

He showed us how putting two around our cameras, clothes and food, one tight and one loose, sealing air pockets between them, keeps our goods afloat when we capsize our canoes. He demonstrated how lining a cardboard box with one turns it into a handy-dandy minnow bucket, live well, ice chest or wash basin. He stuffed a big one with leaves for a mattress and a little one wrapped in a T-shirt for a pillow. He cut one down the sides for a ground cloth and a tarp. He turned one upside down and snipped out head and arm holes for a raincoat. He dropped sticks, a piece of birch bark and a couple of matches in one and tied it tight to ensure the dry makings of a dewy dawn's campfire. He tucked the bottom half of his sleeping bag into one to keep his toes warm and dry.

He showed us how to catch rainwater in one, how to use one for shade, for a fish trap and for hauling out our trash. He had even more to tell us about garbage bags, but the lunch committee was getting anxious, so we gave him a standing ovation and dug in.

oh, brother

SEPTEMBER 12

The day had started out with flying colors and all the promises you could hope for, but then, after supper, everything basically went to hell. We had come out to spruce up the deer shack for the soon-to-be season, and we did that. Then, during a resting-up session, everybody got to telling stories, and one thing led to another.

One old guy started it when he told us mosquitoes were so big when he was a boy, a pair of them knocked him down one day while he was squirrel hunting and stole his lunch. Someone else claimed the wind blew so hard in '41 it caught his yawning partner by the mouth and turned him completely wrong-side out. Another old-timer swore that in the '30s there was a terrible dry spell. On his way to the lake, he met two walleyes swimming up a dusty road out of habit. His buddy said he struck a match that same year to light a campfire and accidentally set the lake on fire.

Somebody's brother-in-law said that once he had a contrary horse he'd ride up to the mountains elk hunting. One day, he said, the horse went to kick at another one and kicked itself plumb in two. He said he never saw a critter look so surprised as that one did when its hind end came off. He had to shoot both ends to put them out of their misery, and hasn't gone elk hunting since.

I know you're thinking that no matter how thick you slice this stuff, it's still baloney. I can tell you my own sense of ethical conduct was sorely tested, too, and I would have hesitated to believe any more than 25 percent of it if I hadn't remembered that a couple of the boys were 32nd Degree Masons, and the rest were high up in the Elks Club and the Knights of Columbus.

satisfaction guaranteed

SEPTEMBER 13

With September come some of the most special seasons of the year: partridge, woodcock, turkey, bow and arrow, squirrel and Christmas. I know what you're thinking. You're thinking, baloney and bah humbug. You're thinking anyone who mentions September and Christmas in the same breath is playing with a pocketful of small change. You're thinking the Christmas season comes during the latter half of the late middle of December and ceases the next day. My friend, you are wrong, especially if you have kids, and during the Christmas season everybody has kids. Reality being what it is, if you don't start shopping now, to the distant sounds of sleigh bells, you'll wind up stuck with the plastic, picked-over stuff.

By getting the jump on the season, you can give the kids the gift of drifting a dry fly through the tricky currents of a nearby river before it freezes up. If your pocketbook can take it, teach them to tie and then to bounce deer hair bugs into gaps of water lilies for bass. Teach them to lob red-and-white striped spoons for big northern pike before the rush begins. Such things take time. Teach the younger ones to skip flat little stones, six, seven, eight times, on sunlit bays.

By shopping now, you can give them trees to climb before they outgrow the habit, and canoes to paddle. Show them where half-buried agates lie, a million years old. Before they're gone, give them tents to pitch and tools to scramble eggs with over half-a-dozen hot coals. Teach them to be good partners, but to travel lonely paths by themselves, too. Give them something that will last, like how to carry a tune the way loons do, and to follow deer tracks through swirling clouds.

If that's too much, give them an eye for wildflowers, an ear for birds' songs and a pocket knife to sharpen. The pocket knife's for carving whistles out of willow sticks. Merry Christmas.

here's the thing

SEPTEMBER 14

There is nothing that makes you ponder the mystery of your existence quite as much as sitting down upon a gathering of poison ivy plants. At such times, you use up all the prayers you know. Yet, when you are hunting, fishing, camping, hiking in poison ivy country, and you do not fully appreciate the attitude of poison ivy toward trespassers, you should expect to make sacrifices to short-tempered bunches of the stuff.

You are educated. You have spent hours on a computer. You know about poison ivy. I don't have to tell you it has three shiny green leaves that turn red and orange in the fall, leaves notched at the edges, small greenish flowers growing in bunches, and later, clusters of dirty yellowish white and waxy berries. I don't have to tell you poison ivy grows all over the place, usually twining on tree trunks, but crouching on the ground if necessary as little bushes.

I may have to tell you, however, that too often you approach the great out-of-doors with too open a heart, trusting that no harm will befall you. Too often you forget that poison ivy will attack to defend itself, its territory and its young. Too often you forget that once poison ivy has tasted human flesh, it loses its fear of humans and hungers after them. "Ha! ha!" it thinks when it sees you coming carelessly, full of supper and savoir-faire.

Too often you forget that when you are in poison ivy country, you must make plenty of noise to give warning of your coming, give it a wide berth and be content with enjoying mere glimpses of it in its native habitat. In other words, as you live out the long stream of your life, familiarize yourself to the ways of wild things before sitting down on them.

general conclusions

SEPTEMBER 15

With grouse there are no guarantees. They fly when you expect them to sit. They sit when you figure them to run. They run when you're betting the baby's milk money they'll explode with eye-popping urgency into the thick air of September and disappear into the purple haze. Though sometimes they don't. Sometimes they slip off to the side, and you don't even know they're there.

You are a grouse hunter in need of grouse, though you can't find any. So you set yourself down under a little clump of a willow tree to ponder, to use your think tank, your sky piece, as God intended you to use it. You decide that grouse have to eat, and what they eat are berries, apples, buds, acorns and grapes, and you go to where there are such things. You conclude that they take their meals in brushy brush, secondary growths of popples, alders and willows like the one you're sitting under, and you go there too. You determine that grouse need cover, cover that tears at your shirt, that tears long, gaping tears in your pants. This is the cover of stream beds, fields and forest edges, so thick great horned owls can't sweep through on outstretched wings and too-big-around hunters can't squeeze through, though you try. You understand that on sunshiny days grouse carry on more in the open, but then they hunker down under balsam boughs when the foul fall stuff moves in.

So, what does it all mean? To tell you the truth, I don't know. All I've got for all my thinking is a torn shirt, long, gaping tears in my pants, a trembling ticker and tuna-noodle hot dish for supper, because, like I said, with grouse there are no guarantees.

it was a dark and stormy night ...

SEPTEMBER 16

Do you duly appreciate the good fortune that comes your way every once in a while? Do you bask in the glow of the good times you have had in the great out-of-doors? I think not, and I think I know why. I think it's because, over the years, the fine points of what you have to be thankful for have blurred. I think it's because you don't keep a journal. Had you kept a journal, you might be flabbergasted to find how much merriment you have amassed as you made your way through your outdoor adventures.

Do you remember when you forgot your compass and spent the night in a swamp with a million mosquitoes? Had you logged the joy you felt when the sun rose so rosily in the west, that memory would be as fresh now as it was then. Do you remember when you neglected to set the brake on your pickup, and it rolled into the lake? Do you recall how happy you were when it missed running over your new graphite fishing rod, which you dropped in your haste to get out of the way? Had you noted the incident, included the time of day, the weather conditions, the flora and fauna, you could relive that feeling each time you leafed through your journal.

Even the briefest of field notes become valuable memory aids for how much you have to be grateful for. Like when you fell from your tree stand and pulled yourself together in no time at all. And when you stumbled into quicksand and lost nothing but your new waders. You were happy about that. From a universe so vast you cannot conceive its magnitude, you are thankful that some little molecules of mud have been gathered and molded into the body and soul that is you. You are glad to be alive because, from time to time, you have tasted the good life and found it sweet. Write it down.

crime and punishment

SEPTEMBER 17

I should start by telling you the terrible thing that happened, because it's what this story is all about, but I'll begin at the beginning. I must admit I wasn't always so particular, but now I'm a fanatic about game laws. If the book reads shooting starts at 7:15, I might wait until 7:25. If it says the limit's five partridges, I might quit at four, if I could ever get four. I won't shoot an illegal anything or take unfair advantage anywhere. It's gotten so I feel smug about it, which is good when you don't have much to feel smug about.

It's a long time between sunup and when the opening of duck season dawns at high noon. I was ready long before that. It was raining cats and dogs, but that's good duck-hunting weather, and I was going duck hunting. I had all my gear laid out by 4:30. Then, when I was into my third cup of coffee, I got to thinking, "I bet those city guys will try to beat me out of my blind again." They always do.

Then, like an omen, the rain let up, and I threw everything in the back of the pickup and took off. It was about ten o'clock. I drove the five miles or so to the put-in point, paddled the couple of miles to the blind, tossed out the decoys and dozed off. A noise woke me, and when I peeked through a wall of cattails, I saw two guys pull up in a rowboat. I didn't even poke my head up, I was laughing so hard.

Then they said they were game wardens. Without being asked, I showed my license and stamp. I pointed out my cased and unloaded shotgun, the steel shot, the picture of my wife and kid, and a half-dozen Ducks Unlimited membership cards. "Hope you get your man," I said.

"We will," they said. "You put out your decoys twenty minutes too soon." They were nice about it, even righting a bellied-up old decoy on the way out. The citation was for illegal use of decoys. $92.50. I tried to punish myself further by not using decoys at all this year, but it didn't help much. This duck we're having for supper tastes like crow.

we ain't amused

SEPTEMBER 18

Throughout the long, proud history of Lost Lake's Fish and Game Club, there has run like a steel core the annual tradition of saving your deer heart from the previous year and then preparing and sharing it at the September meeting to give us a jump start into the hunting seasons coming up. Not Wally, though. Oh no, not Wally.

Last Saturday night at the Elkhorn Tavern and Wildlife Museum, he gave us the low-down. The truth came out, clunkety-clunk. Right away last November, he pickled his heart, hid it in a dark corner of his refrigerator and helped himself to it whenever he felt he had to.

You're thinking that's not fair, and I'm agreeing with you. But he looked so pitiful and appeared so contrite that we voted to form a support group and forgive him if he'd fork over the leftovers and the recipe. There were no leftovers, as you can imagine, but here's the recipe. He took his heart, put it in a saucepan, covered it with water, added salt and pepper and two bay leaves, brought it to a boil and simmered it there for two or three hours. It was a nice heart from a fat little forkhorn. Then he drained it, cooled it, sliced it poker-chip thin, put the heart slices, and the slices of a pair of medium-sized onions, and more salt and pepper, into a nonmetallic container. He covered it with a mixture of three parts water to one part vinegar. He put a lid on it and put it in the dark corner of his refrigerator. It was ready, he said, the next day, so he took a couple of slices, laid them out between two pieces of bread, and dabbed some nice mustard on it, and on and on.

According to Wally, this should serve ten people, which seems about right if half don't want any, but with his reputation sagging the way it is, it's hard to know what to believe.

need i say more

SEPTEMBER 19

Out where concrete gives out, where pavement and airplanes pass only in the night, there is where you find bowhunters. There is where they hold sun-dappled woods in their wide-open arms. There is where they find a direct connection between the beatings of their hearts and the absolutions of moonlight. You should be out there, too.

You should be out there where the world's so big, so wide, so wild. Nowhere is less hurried, nowhere is less crowded than the bowhunter's world. There's where hawks hang without motion, high in the enormous sky.

Ah, the interesting things I, a stranger, can tell you about turning your life into a work of art. You could become (as bowhunters become) a piece of the woods. You could wrap yourself (as bowhunters do) in ballads of birds' songs as ancient as the sea. You could smell (as bowhunters smell) the sweet spices of pine boughs. You could sing with the gladness of being alive (as bowhunters do, but to yourself, since bowhunters must be very quiet).

I remember this one time. I was sitting in an oak tree (as bowhunters sometimes do) with more pretty leaves about me than April has roses, and this chickadee came up and offered me a cup of tea. Being offered cups of tea by chickadees is a benefit bowhunters often enjoy. Once an old, clean-shaven gray squirrel offered me a puff of his pipe. Another benefit. Once a mosquito, looking very like a Chicago gangster, bit me, but not too bad. I just sat there (as bowhunters do) passing myself off as a lump on the skyline, brown as a bag of Necco Wafers.

What more can I say, except to end this by reminding you that immortality is not impossible and the rest is up to you.

first rate

SEPTEMBER 20

You have licked clean the wounds of the day. Stars are sailing in old shipping lanes across the sky. Owls are hoot-hooting from a stand of pines across the way, and in the woodbox a cricket is cussing out the coming cold in a futile attempt to keep it at bay. And for maybe the five thousandth time, on your way to bed, you pause at the doorway of your sleeping child's room. For maybe the five thousandth time, your heart lodges in your throat at the moonbeam beauty of that face, but there is something different about this night of nights.

It has come to pass that this child of yours has finally come of an age, has finally grown old enough, strong enough, mature enough, to join you, with the near rising of the sun, in the field, fully armed, as a hunter. And what about that?

You have taught this child well what it means to be a hunter. You have taught this child that to be a hunter is to apply the Golden Rule to the hunt. You have taught this child that a true hunter is quick to do a fair share and more. You have taught this child that a true hunter is willing, sometimes, to travel long, hard trails without complaint. You have taught this child a love of wild things, and that a hunter does not try for every shot, nor claim a shot someone else has made.

A true hunter is generous to that which is being hunted, never cheats on an animal or on a partner, or on his or her mother, the earth. A true hunter shoots cleanly, kills cleanly and makes every effort to retrieve fallen game. A true hunter is, above all else, a sportsman, a gentleman, a lady. And you have taught this child with your own good example. The evidence is in. Go to bed, old one. Go to sleep. You and this child of yours are ready.

a silver lining

SEPTEMBER 21

A guy down at the Elkhorn Tavern and Wildlife Museum is relating how once, when it was raining, he pulled up the hood on his camouflage coat. It was full of water. "Don't tell me about that one, Buddy," I said. "I've been there."

Then he whined how one time he paddled his canoe up to a campsite and unloaded it, whereupon the canoe continued downriver without him. "Done it," I said. He went on to tell how a bear, that very same night, stole his bacon, beans and schnapps. "Three times," I said. "Maybe four."

It's true. I don't have any big fish mounted on my walls, or deer antlers or taxidermied birds, but I've got a trophy case of hard-luck stories. If it's happened to you, friend, it's happened to me in aces. Forget to put the plug in your boat before you backed it into the lake? That's old hat to me, kid. Run out of gas? Of course. Leave home without a rod and reel? Absolutely. Neglect to secure a nice stringer of fish to the side of the boat before you plopped it in the water? Naturally.

Fire three times at the most beautiful buck you've ever seen without releasing the safety on your rifle? Do it again without shells? Drop an arrow from a tree stand just as a buck makes his way toward you? Drop your glasses down an ice-fishing hole? Rip your rear end open on a barbed-wire fence? Bring .20 gauge shells for the .12 gauge gun? Leave your hunting license on the dresser? The out-of-state one? Drop an anchor overboard without first tying it to the boat? So have I.

You say a couple of mallards floated nice and easy over your decoys? Then they circled back and did it again? And you were setting the decoys out at the time? Amigo, that's small potatoes to me. No, don't come to me with your tales of woe, boy. I've got plenty of my own, though when you see my glass is empty like this, you might offer to fill it.

greased lightning

SEPTEMBER 22

There are some here at Lost Lake who maintain that anybody who does not sweat at his job is probably not making an honest living. I appreciate the theory, but writers, as you can imagine, are suspect. Teachers, preachers and county road workers are also in the iffy category. I mention this as a roundabout way of getting to the point, which is that some deer hunters maintain likewise about other deer hunters. Within their chests there beat the hearts of galloping globetrotters. They accept misery and measure it by the mile, convinced that hunters not covering a hundred paces a minute, not tromping over a dozen square miles a day through woods and fields and swamps, getting all tuckered out, are not hunting at all and will never stumble onto a buck with humongous antlers.

This is okay with the rest of us, though we are intensely sympathetic towards them. You see, if it is so, as bass fishermen claim, that 25 percent of a given body of water holds 90 percent of the fish, then it can be believed that only a smallish chunk of the woods, fields and swamps is inhabited by deer, and only a wee piece of that is an integral part of their daily routines.

Thinking whitetail hunters, then, hunt only these simmering hotspots, with their heads as much as their feet, concentrating on picking this cover apart, sifting through the evidence for precise locations. They search for sign and weigh it against potential, quite unlike a helter-skelter hunter who, with no clear trail between his mind and his heart, proceeds willy-nilly, having no idea where he's going, no idea where he's been and no idea why.

a plan of attack

SEPTEMBER 23

A while ago I had so much summer, I thought I'd never run out of it. I had so much summer, I spent every last bit of it and don't have a thing to show. The long days are gone now. Bats that dizzied the moon are gone. Fireflies are gone. It's been two weeks since I've seen an active wildflower. I should have banked some of it, stashed it in the Peoples' National Republic State Bank of Commerce and Checking Accounts but, like a dope, I didn't.

Suddenly I'm looking into the open muzzle of autumn, and I'm turning over a new leaf, so to speak. I'm going pheasant hunting. I'm heading for the covers of Grandpa's cornfields, for timber-choked river bottoms, for weedy railroad rights-of-way, for postage-stamp-sized patches of grass too skimpy to hide a mouse but with plenty of elbow room for pheasants. Then I'm going after partridge on every logging road around, along every creek and pothole. I'm going to find some woodcock, lots of them, Canada geese and mallard ducks. I'm going to try pass-shooting at dipping, rising, zig-zag-flying doves.

After that, I'm going fishing for feisty brown trout. I'm going to cast substantial streamers upstream and across and make them resemble limping minnows coming down. I might use weighted nymphs instead. I'm going to get in on some red-hot muskie action, too.

I'm going to find me some wild rice, and I'm going to press me five gallons of apple cider. Later, I'm going deer hunting, so when the coagulating days of winter come, I'll have no need to shrug my shoulders, stare back into the raw wounds of my immediate past, and wonder what happened to the thousand-dollar bills, the hard cash, of autumn.

the greatest show on earth

SEPTEMBER 24

It's been quite some time since you've written on the white pages of winter with your footprints and tire tracks and left your shovel marks on snowbanks, but you don't know what tomorrow will bring, so you have come trout fishing before it's too late. You have come to your favorite stream, though stream is too big a word for it. In places it has the whitewater of a trout stream, the living, singing whitewater. In that it is like all trout streams, yet it is unlike any other. Like all trout streams, it is never the same for very long. Around each bend, it has a different look, a different feel.

It is as easy spending words as it is spending pennies talking about it, but this stream, this narrow stream, is a secret in the hearts of you who fish it. Its fame with you lies in its privacy. You celebrate its privacy. The water in your stream is pure and clean, bedded with sand and gravel and stones, the way trout must have it. No pollution comes in to steal the sweet oxygen so necessary for trout. Its temperature does not rise above sixty-five degrees. Its water leaps over falls and dances down riffles. It tumbles pell-mell like pent-up children busting out of school. It gurgles in whirlpools. It chuckles, pretending to ignore you, or it whispers confidentially of stout trout under its banks, aristocrats in an aristocratic society. They rise to kiss its surface, to nibble on the toes of fallen mayflies. It is more than you can bear.

It is easy to forget that you have come here in a great rush to fish in no great hurry with funny-looking flies you have tied yourself. It is easy to forget (there I go, spending words like pennies again) that you have come here in a great rush to fish in no great hurry, with the bright promissory note of your fishing license, on a stream, a lively stream, good for nothing but the finest things in life.

as cunning as solomon

SEPTEMBER 25

Theoretically, the score is tied. Day and night are about equal today and tonight, but we've seen this game before. Night will win, and a bunch of us locals are taking a break here in the Elkhorn Tavern and Wildlife Museum. We're basically bemoaning our fate as duck hunters. Each of us has come in from redecorating our duck blinds with cattails and tall grass, and we're up to our waders in woe. According to our calculations, ducks are not as down, down and out as they have been; they're up, in fact, but so are hunters, crowding into our lake. Most of them are from someplace else. They'll be sky busters. They'll shoot at ducks heading into our decoys, and they won't be too fussy where their BBs land. We're feeling undercut by futility.

Then a stranger slumped in a corner butts in. "I hate to toot my own horn," he says, lying through his teeth, "but where I hunt ducks, I hardly ever see another hunter. I take my time, work my dog, and get plenty of action."

We here at Lost Lake are leery of levity, especially from strangers telling jokes on duck hunters, so in a minute we have him by the throat and going under for the third time before he coughs up the lowdown. He says he and his pup pussyfoot along all the creeks that feed into and empty out of Lost Lake, where the rest of us are elbow-to-elbowing each other. He gets the ducks, he confesses, where the ducks go when we chase them out from where they want to go. Elementary.

I'm not giving up on my duck blind, not at all, but the next time you see somebody hunting along the river, say hello; it'll probably be me. In the meantime, goldenrods are keeping bees in business, and asters, those stars that grow from stems, are shining as neatly as do those that dangle from the moon.

a critical afternoon in september

SEPTEMBER 26

I went fishing Sunday and didn't get a bite. I came home and shot at clay pigeons, but couldn't hit a thing. Looking to play a little catch, I hunted all over for the kids, but couldn't find them, so I went over to my second cousin Gilbert's. He's organized and an inspiration to me. He is, as the saying goes, the captain of his soul. His lawn is mowed. His oil is changed. There's never a weed in his garden for very long. There is a place for everything he owns, and everything he owns is in its place. Actually, he's married to my second cousin on my mother's side. Another second cousin, Petie, who had also been fishing and hadn't caught anything, was there, too, looking for his kids and a game of work-up.

In the garage, Gilbert showed us his latest project. He said he had been worried about his new little outboard motor, which like all of them was hard to handle off the boat, cumbersome to carry and impossible to prop safely in its proper place. The possibility of scratching its newness kept him awake at night.

Then he hit upon a plan, as he always does. He went over and retrieved a two-wheeled dolly from Petie, who had borrowed it from him in June to move a refrigerator. Across the upper uprights of the dolly, high enough to hold the motor off the ground, he bolted on a length of two-by-six. Then, so the dolly would stay standing with the motor on it, he drilled some holes in the undercarriage and bolted on a 12-inch-square piece of plywood and a couple of triangle braces.

He said if I'd return the ladder he lent me back in July, he'd make each of us one, so we'd have no need to use his. We were so impressed we placed him on a clean, five-gallon grease pail and crowned him king. Then we borrowed his kids for a little game of keep-away.

butch

SEPTEMBER 27

The wind coming off the lake smells of ice. Only yesterday, it smelled of fish and wet grasses and gasoline from fishing boats. Today, it smells of ice, and it drives drifting sheets of Sunday papers across the water. Butch has died. In the way of dogs, he did not live as long as we who locked him in the kennel and let him out again when we remembered.

People should not write about dogs that die, nor about how they did this or that, nor about their last days, nor about long sequences of things. It's nobody's business, and nobody cares. Everybody has dogs of their own, growing old. We inherited Butch from a country boy exiled to a city with no room for dogs.

Butch rode solidly in a canoe and in the back of our pickup, with his head over the side, though that is not a good habit. He kicked up pheasants and fetched ducks. He let a little girl use him as a pony, a doll and a pillow. That's about all. Once he wandered too far and got beat up by a raccoon that tore off his ear. It took him three days to come home. I think it was a raccoon. He was smart enough, but at least once a year he'd get a snoot full of porcupine quills. He shed something terrible. It is still not possible to shake out a rug or mop a floor around here without coming across that hair.

We must have disappointed him with our cruelty. It took us a year, maybe more, to stop the cataracts from clouding his eyes, to stop the arthritis from hurting him. Now he lies by the garden, and the wind coming off the lake smells of ice and drives drifting sheets of Sunday papers over the water, and his hair in the carpet still won't come out.

a transmigration

SEPTEMBER 28

I'm a fairly firm believer in life after death. What's got me worried is life before death. I don't know how it is with others, but I've got to write when I can and where I can, at a stop light, in the bathroom, perched up a deer stand and … Shhh, there goes a mallard … in a duck blind. Since I've got a day job, a family, two dogs, and an old house with a leaky roof and a big yard, I've got no choice … *Darn it, there goes another one* … I'll bet Hemingway didn't have to do it like this. Or Jack London. Or Gordon … *Jeepers, three more just went over and almost took my hat off* … Mac Quarrie. Or Aldo Leopold or Sigurd Olson. I always thought outdoor writers wrote in book-lined studies or dens with fireplaces lit, and old dogs lying at their feet … *Oops, those were wood ducks, I think* … The walls would be filled with outdoor art and mooseheads. Maybe Pavarotti … *Good Lord, look at that* … plays real low on the record player and a bear rug's on the floor. It's not fair. I keep hoping to hit it big someday, but it doesn't look like it's going to happen.

Well, maybe I can't … *Holy cow!* … have it like those other guys, but at least I've got enough sense to know when … *Excuse me* … enough is enough.

i can't help it

SEPTEMBER 29

There's been loose talk about me lately and, after kicking it around a few days, it's my intention to be straightforward about it, to come right out and put the rumors to rest, to admit that I'm a tent man. I'm obsessed with tents and tentage. When I'm not sleeping in a tent under a starry, dream catcher of a night, I'm thinking about it.

I'm thinking about it this very minute. Does that make you edgy? It's at its worst right around sundown. It's then, no matter the weather, no matter the season, that I have this need, this yearning, to set up a tent. Don't laugh. I'll set up a tent when new leaves are sprouting from fresh trees, and when old ones cut themselves loose and float in great drifts to the earth. I pounce on the opportunity, if no one's looking, to set up a tent in snow when the only night sounds are owls chipping hoots from a full moon.

You who have got a first look at the miracle of twilight rising like Lazarus, from an unzipped tent flap, know what I'm up against. If I can't be sleeping in a tent, I need to be folding one and nestling it in a Duluth pack alongside a sleeping bag and coffee pot. Or I need to be cuddling one between the thwarts of my canoe, securing it safely with ribbons of yellow nylon rope. I need to take one and drift with it down random rivers, any rivers. I need to carry one on my back to wolves trafficking in loneliness, or down to loons or over to moose. At the end of a perplexing day, I want to curl up in a tent, surrounded by stakes and poles and mosquito screen.

I've joined a support group, but it's not working out. Tonight we're camping out in the tall pines on the other side of the lake.

serious matters

SEPTEMBER 30

There are no more pathetic creatures in the world than people who think they know trout. They do not understand that trout are trout and trout fishing is trout fishing and let it go at that. Even Jonah, who knew fish inside and out, would have been baffled by the behavior of trout. Perhaps he was. Yet few can resist peeping and prying into the trout psyche in weary attempts to get some nice rhyme and consistency into something not fundamentally expressible in ordinary terms. One is inevitably reminded of dunderheads trying to understand astronomy in Euclidean principles, not realizing that in astronomy, as in trout fishing, the shortest distance between two points is not a straight line.

Trout fishing is not a science. It is a malady, feline in its cruelty. It pounces upon its victims. It cripples them, it plays with them, and it revels in their misery. Sometimes it steals away and hides, and people think they've freed themselves from it. They flatter themselves that they are no longer its slaves. Wretched creatures they are, for in a minute the sun breaks through and the river has its talons around their throats again, and brook trout have beaks in their vitals.

"What a stylish thing to do," people think. "How essentially simple." They soon discover the essentials to successful careers as trout fishermen are wallets and waders, both of them big. And those who marry trout fishermen may be sick of anything, but a short ways into the marriage, they find they are sick of nothing but trout fishing. And, oh, what a falling out there is.

The cruelest irony is that this affliction seldom destroys its victims outright. It incapacitates them and sometimes extinguishes fires of ambition within them and gone are their hours of tranquil bliss. But it is the diabolical nature of trout fishing not to deprive its miserable prey altogether of life. And so we see them crawling aimlessly about the world, too sick to live as they ought to live, yet not sick enough to die.

bound for glory

OCTOBER 1

Here's October. Get your ticket now. Throw a saddle on it. Ride it into the glowing glow of pumpkin patches and far-off woods of campfire smoke and quiet places. Climb aboard and go choo-choo-chooing all over the place. Squeeze it like a grape until it spurts.

Here's October. Crouch at a creek-side and catch a fistful of maple drip-dripping leaves floating by. Snatch a fistful of October's stars rotating in the flared black nostrils of night. Promenade through October's brown, bright-as-brass grass. Observe the ripe chipmunks. Beware whiskered oak trees erupting with lava-flows of leaves. Hear October's winds crooning, "Baby, oh baby." Pay attention. Somewhere under the lengthening shadows, pretty brook trout are hanging steady, heads against the current. Explain to the children, groping down dark schoolhouse hallways candle-lit with brief recesses, about the discrepancies of October's mountains rising later and later each morning. Explain why it wasn't so in June or July, though a canker was in the cabbage already at the end of August.

Here's October. Taste the uncooked bouillon of its gorgeous gold ambiance (excuse my French). Dig potatoes. Pick apples. Hang onions up to dry. Tell, and swear to it, how once you saw a naked rose shivering in October's moonlight. It's worth mentioning. Meditate on the messages preached by Canada geese assembled across October's wild blue yonders.

Here's October. Oh, mercy. Moan with pleasure as this miracle month with the Harvest Moon unfolds before your eyes. Listen. October is knocking at the gate. Throw a saddle on it, take the off-ramp and go choo-choo-chooing all over the place.

a misspent youth

OCTOBER 2

I am good at some things, but great at nothing. I blame it on my youth. When I was young, a notion would hit me, and no matter how tiny it was, I leaped into action without sizing up the situation or waiting to cool myself off to rational thought. That's how I got into calling ducks instead of studying algebra. To this day, I have no idea what the relationship between x and y is, or how it came to be.

There was this old guy who used to live around here. I got him to teach me about calling ducks. He quarterbacked the whole thing, and I couldn't have asked for more. He never quacked into his call, and he never blew into it like a whistle. He sort of coughed into it, more or less muttering, *q-u-i-t-t*, using the muscles in his belly to supply the ooomph. Also, he tried to bounce the sound off the water so as to make it seem his decoys were making the music. That always brought a ripple of applause from passing ducks.

To get the attention of birds quite a ways off, he'd give them a series, loud and long — about eight notes long — of these *q-u-i-t-ts*, beginning with the loudest and longest and tapering off at the end. He'd keep it up, too, like a kid having a conniption, until they took notice of him. Then he'd switch to a kind of confidential, welcoming-home spiel to encourage their continued progress in our direction by singing the same tune, only toning it down to a sugar-coated, "C'mon in." When the ducks got real close, he'd send out a contented, pull-up-a-chair-stay-for-supper *tooka-tooka* call, about five times per, with a pause in between until they set their wings.

It almost always worked for him. It almost always works for me, too, though when it doesn't, it's a terrible thing to endure, not rating, of course, as bad as inflation on the scale of my problems, but running neck and neck with unemployment.

confident as angels

OCTOBER 3

Ax songs of woodchoppers are splitting the air in after-work, pre-supper ceremonies, and bluebills, buffleheads and goldeneyes are flocking to bigger bodies of water to rest from migrating labors. We're so far into October we couldn't get out if we wanted to, though we don't. My Uncle Jake and I have come to one of his secret muskie lakes. It's about twenty miles south of town and a couple east, which is about as far as the road goes into reality.

From the vantage point of his experience, Jake is on to the common knowledge that muskies are setting in plenty of provisions now, filling their root cellars and chest freezers. A river both feeds and empties this lake, as rivers do to so many. Its current, as it meanders in and out, cuts a ditch along the lake's floor. The edges of this ditch make a nicely defined hangout for suckers and perch, of which muskies come in and easily make mincemeat. That's where we go in Jake's boat, a sturdy thing with an idiot's love for muskie fishing, near the mouth opposite Watchout Point.

It's a muskie-ideal, pesky October day, and Jake opts for a perchy floating lure. He makes a long, low, line-drive cast. I follow suit, naturally. As soon as our lures hit the water, we bring them in a foot or two. Then we let them bob to the surface, pause for ten seconds, and use the tips of our rods to make six short, sharp twitches. I make seven because I'm an individual. Then we reel in very slowly, maybe ten feet (eleven for me), pause again, let the lure pop to the top like before, and on and on and on in an activity that is very appealing to October muskies.

a kind of surrender

OCTOBER 4

The air smells of grapes, though grapes don't grow here. I am no grape expert, but grapes don't grow in a marshy flowage like this one where, all alone in my blind, I wait for ducks. Off to the west, a blue jay is sawing at the silence with a jagged cry.

Bored, I peek through the cattailed curtain that hides me. One of my decoys, a lecherous old scarecrow of a thing, has slipped from its anchor rope and taken up a split end position across the bay. Another, a BB-dimpled mallard of considerable experience, has taken the snap from a gimpy wooden one and is fading back to pass. These decoys should better spend their time luring ducks to me.

Like all duck hunters, I have a habit of looking into the limitless sky. This soft October afternoon is within chucking distance of being over and done with. Pink clouds, the color of chrysanthemums, are folded gently against a pale sky, pink clouds that draw the line where man ends and God and ducks begin. I suppose I should have stayed home and worked in the garden. I remember stories about ducks, so many ducks, so long ago, but, like everybody else, I couldn't pick out the century to be born in and must make do with the time slot my miscalculating mother dropped me off in.

Once I read that everything is something it isn't, and everybody is always somewhere else. I like the sound of that, but I have no idea what it means. There it goes. The sun is belly up to the moon, the evening star is cut in half by a cattail, and I am faced with the touchy task of herding decoys into my canoe. That's fine by me. I've had enough hopefulness for one day.

now he knows

OCTOBER 5

A few days ago, a terrible thing happened to the Professor. He almost lost his Top Dog status as Master of Information and Storehouse of Knowledge on and about white-tailed deer and the hunting thereof. Here's how it happened. Usually, we are in a constant state of surprise that one head can carry all that his does on the subject, but then a couple of bowhunting youngsters reported some success with rattling. You know that rattling is the calling up close of deer with the knocking of antlers together. This shocked the Professor, who is not basically open to new theories. "For crying out loud," he thought to himself emotionally. "Is this possible?"

Suddenly, he found himself out in the left field of ignorance and felt his life grow thin, and worse, he was speechless. A red-hot lump began to grow in his belly, and he couldn't stand it. So, with a determination that is bifocal, he set out on a fearless and independent study to correct this intellectual deficiency, if indeed there was one.

From the outhouse door at our deer camp, he embezzled a pair of ancient antlers. Stepping as high as a rooster in mud, he climbed to his perch of a tree stand, resolved not merely to live but to learn, and began the experiment. He banged the antlers together. He clinked them. He hit and he smacked them in the way, he imagined, of disputing bucks. He made a terrible ruckus with, as he fully expected, no results.

It was when he was on his way down that he saw the animal coming. His eyes registered twelve points, though his imagination added some. And as his heart leaped to his throat, his foot missed a rung on the ladder, and he basically slid the fifteen feet to the forest floor, becoming, on the way down, a battered but immediate expert on the rattling in of white-tailed deer.

circumambulation

OCTOBER 6

We can go on and on about October, about how times change and styles change, how the in becomes the out, the out becomes the in, but up here at Lost Lake, historical developments go in pretty much the same cycles, year after year. Woodcocks are coming through again, taking their time, as always. Tiny web-riding spiders are floating in on silken strands, as usual. Streams are running heavy with fallen leaves, and wooly bear caterpillars are forecasting this winter's weather, as they always do. Some foretell of snow up to here; some about half that.

We can go on and on about Taurus the bull wading through the nighttime skies on schedule. About how cedar waxwings, the here-today-gone-tomorrow birds, are gone today. Like a wound up Walt Whitman, we can go on and on about maple leaves catching fire in the morning light. About sunsets settling on ash-blue lakes, and lights appearing like magic, a great stir of lights, up and down the shoreline. About valleys gauzy with fog.

We can go on and on about birds hanging up, far out over fields. About the special illumination of the moon lighting a peaceful path across the lake, as if it were part of a song. About the Northern Lights, Aurora Borealis, tossing a football back and forth in October's skies. About campfires set between parentheses of pine trees and tents. About how October catches us off guard and breaks down our defenses like a ten dollar bill blowing our way across a downtown parking lot.

We can go on and on about how you can never paint a picture of a goose's cry because it would float up off the canvas anyway as soon as your back was turned. At least that's pretty much how it goes up here at Lost Lake where I live, and I suppose that's pretty much how it goes over there where you live, too.

confusing the issue

OCTOBER 7

Fred, my pheasant-hunting friend, stops by my house to pick up the shovel I borrowed from him last week. I tell him I lent it to someone else and ask him if he needs it real bad. He says he doesn't, but the guy he borrowed it from claims the owner does. Right away I see neither one of us is doing any digging for a while, so I ask him if he wants to go pheasant hunting. "What do you say, Fred?" I ask him, "Want to go pheasant hunting?"

Fred has a sharp and pleasantly cynical wit, but is somewhat excitable. "What do you mean go pheasant hunting?" he howls. "Are ya nuts? Every time we go pheasant hunting, those danged birds make fools of us. As soon as we get them figured out, they figure out something new. We hunt for hours and hours and if we're lucky we get to shoot maybe two and a half seconds. If we hit one, it disappears, and we can't find it. If we're ready for them to get up in the middle of a field, they don't do it until the very end, and vice versa. They drive our poor dogs to neurotic distractions. And when they thunderball up in front of me, I lose control of a couple of internal organs, and you know it."

I have two philosophies of life. One is that once you're a pheasant hunter, you're always a pheasant hunter. The other is that sometime during the course of each day, every person ought to make at least one sensible remark. So, I ask him if he can understand why when people had to cook outside on an open fire, they longed for an inside kitchen, and when they got one, they started wishing for an outdoor barbecue pit. Fred sees that I have him on that one, and how absurd it is to let the hopelessness of the world situation creep into our private lives, so he shrugs his shoulders like an unstrung puppet and says, "What the heck. We've still got two hours of daylight." See?

a sober account of passion and intrigue

OCTOBER 8

These stars in my eyes are reflections of an October's night-lighted sky. Through the patio door on this sleepless night, I see the lights of the star-studded, club-swinging Orion, like me a hunter and a dreamer. I am a reader as well as a dreamer, and I know Orion. Of the stories I have read about him and half believe, I like this one, though it lacks the degree of accuracy required of encyclopedias. If I get carried away, blame it on Hemingway.

Orion was out in the woods. He was bear hunting. Clouds were clotting the sky. Down the path ahead of him came seven girls from the college in town. They were picking berries and dancing and prancing around in the way of college girls. They were beautiful. Orion, who was still in his chest-thumping period, though somewhat on the lonely side of things, cried, "Ho lysmo kes lo okith at!" the translation of which has been lost. He forgot about bear hunting, as you can imagine.

Now the story gets iffy. Orion was thunderstruck. He felt the need for romance and violin concertos. With the love-swift eye of a hunter, he scouted the situation and slithered up to the girls. In a voice dripping like honey from a basswood tree, he asked if they didn't want to critique the wildlife prints in his apartment. These were college girls, nice kids, so they nixed the notion and scooted back up from whence they came, with Orion close behind. By and by, they ran into a game warden who favored a bucks-only season. She turned them into doves and shooed them off.

And as the years roll on, every once in a while, on a sleepless October night, I look out my patio window and there they are, the Pleiades, just out of the old hunter's reach, and Orion, as passionate as candlelight, still firmly committed to the spirit of the chase, and the hope of a mildly successful season.

a handful of aces

OCTOBER 9

Tonight is one of those nights where the stars are silver speckles dueling in a dream of black skies. A slipper of a moon is illuminating the outside with a flawless light, and inside the old wood stove is spitting up an occasional puff of pine smoke to keep the place smelling good. A bunch of us are scattered around here in the hunting shack for no particular reason.

Three guys are playing smear in one corner. Another is up in his bunk pouring a funky country western tune out of his harmonica. One whose heart is a laughing gland is telling an old story to a couple of little kids, who giggle every time they hear it to keep from being sent to bed long past their usual time. It's something about a worm dropping out of a tree onto the neck of the third grade teacher during the Labor Day picnic, how she fainted dead away and became the life of the party.

One fellow is reading Shakespeare, and I'm sorting it all out on paper as best I can. Two are dropping ice cubes into old-fashioned glasses, debating whether or not there's a God, and if so, why is there poverty and baldness. Someone's making coffee. In the magnificent half-minute of this night, we're poised on a rainbow rising full circle.

Coming out here was the Professor's idea, the flagship of his pickup truck leading the flotilla of ours. He's the standard-bearer of whitetail wisdom and, in his endless quest to lift the damp veil of ignorance, he's telling a college roommate of one of our boys how unnecessary it is to cut the throat of a deer you've shot, and how it's equally uncalled for to cut out the tarsal glands, and unless it's really hot out, to leave the hide on a deer as long as possible to keep the meat clean and moist.

Then the stove spits up another puff of pine smoke, and I get to thinking how a person can follow all the rules of a religion and miss entirely the glory of it, but he can't do it on a night like this.

speculation

OCTOBER 10

Today is my anniversary; at least I think it is. When Columbus Day fell on Columbus Day, I would know if it was and approach the day with confidence. Now that they have moved it around, I'm never quite sure, and I hate to ask. Today is Columbus Day, and I think it's my anniversary. It used to be.

It gets me to thinking about my mother-in-law. This is a story she loves to tell. Not long ago, she was digging around in her freezer and excavated a roast left over from a fat little buck that filled my father-in-law's tag last season. "Aha," she thought, and since the tribal chairman's wife and her husband were coming to supper, she fixed it up for them. The tribal chairman's wife is an interesting person. She respects old age, but she's approaching it herself with extreme caution, which is, I know, beside the point.

"My, my," she beamed after the meal, "that was positively the best roast beef I have ever eaten."

"Why, thank you," said my mother-in-law, with a twinkle in her mashed potatoes, "but that was deer meat."

"Impossible!" cried Her Honor, "You know I hate that stuff." It's a good story.

Fortunately for my kid and me, who like venison any way we can get it, my mother-in-law taught the recipe to her daughter, who told it to me. She puts four teaspoons of beef bouillon and a cup of water into a big roasting pan and adds a good-sized chunk of venison, alongside it a three-pound or so piece of pork roast. She peppers them and salts them with garlic salt. We add onions. She puts the lid on the pan and puts it in a 350-degree oven for about four hours. She turns the meat every hour, more or less.

And that's about it, except for something else my mother-in-law taught her daughter, which was how to select such a splendid fellow as me to marry and how to have such a wonderful kid as Katie.

to be loved is to be understood

OCTOBER 11

For duck hunters to be content, we must have duck-hunting weather, which is lousy weather, weather that bawls like sick cows. Good duck hunting demands it. The problem for duck hunters, then, is that October sometimes supplies that kind of weather, and sometimes it doesn't. Sometimes, as far as duck hunters are concerned, October is so crooked you can't tell by its tracks which way it's headed.

When October comes with a blighted bluebird sun, duck hunters stagnate like rotting squash, unable to scratch where it itches. When, on the other hand, October delivers the good stuff, the cold, wet, frigid, squally stuff, duck hunters scurry to duck blinds and shiver with anticipation. Freezing rain, sleet and snow amuse us. Winds that churn frizzled waters into tumbling, whitecapped seas make us smile. We tweak the cheek of sleet. Freezing to death? We love it. Who knows, black dots of ducks might struggle in through the leaden, low-lying, low-flying clouds to lonely companies of decoys, ice-coated and straining at their anchors. They might even come in too fast for trembling, popsicle-stiff trigger fingers to do what they were made to do. It doesn't matter to duck hunters, for we are hunting ducks in duck-hunting weather.

And when the day is done at last, when the feeble sun quits altogether, and we are faced with the inevitable collision of day and night, we only reluctantly wade through hip-deep, cattail-tangled mud and muck to scoop up tuckered-out decoys. And after supper, hot-showered and fluffy-robed, as we sit before friendly fireplace fires to tally up the day's wreckage, as surely as four is the double of two, we lay out purple plans for the next day's hunt, October willing. It is the way of duck hunters.

getting by

OCTOBER 12

You can just about feel the start of a good joke in the air when painters paint and writers write of grouse hunts where grouse hunters hunt against a background of birch trees, flanked by pointing dogs pretty enough to be movie stars. This makes for fine pictures and wonderful stories. I want to be one of those hunters in that picture, in that story, with the dogs and the background, but it's just not like that for me because I'm a victim of indecent circumstances. I do my best, however, and one of the ways I cope with limitless limitations placed on me by the uncompromising way of things is to hunt along railroad tracks. It's there that I can dwell in a kind of heavenly glory.

The railroad tracks around here weave through hollows, run along hillsides and slide beside twisted ropes of rivers, which is perfect. When I'm alone, I hunt left of the tracks, going slow, taking it easy, dipping often into my fanny pack of possibilities for food and drink and chewing gum. Then I cross over to the other side of hope and hunt that similarly, back to the pickup. Occasionally, I get my wife to drop me off where the tracks criss-cross a country road and pick me up a dozen miles later, where they bumpety-bump over another one. When I hunt with a pal, one of us walks the tracks proper and the other bird-dogs the cover on a zig-zag course, ten and twenty feet out. Being sensible people with our priorities in place, we take turns. It works sometimes, and now and then, back in the truck, under a tide-sucking moon, we end up complimenting each other all the way home.

By way of parenthesis, I might add that it's been a pleasure to share this with you, and if it does you any good, send twenty bucks and don't mention it to anybody else.

a flow of minor peculiarities

OCTOBER 13

To tell you the truth, it worries me sometimes — to tell you the truth, everything worries me sometimes — that so many of today's kids aren't staying home at night because they're afraid to stay home alone. To tell you the truth, I've been feeling a little guilty myself, what with all this talk of family values and family togetherness and the humongous lack thereof, so I decide to bring the subject up to everybody as we partake in our after-supper stroll.

"Gang," I begin in my most fatherly, here-it-comes-again voice before the screen door hits the last one on the behind, "we've got to talk." Did I mention to you that this is one of those splendid, middle-of-October evenings where the outside sounds and smells are so fine and the air that touches your face is so soft? And the birches are still so buttery yellow and dogwoods so ketchupy red?

As we walk along the trail, our sneakers rustle through cornflake leaves melted from their trees. "Look at that!" yells a little girl, her face as bright and welcome as an October sunrise. A grouse curves upward in its flight and disappears into tall pines. Little girls and grouse are about the nicest things that can happen to people. A pup holds point on a grasshopper, and the boy it owns creeps forward with a double-barreled walking stick. This boy was born under a lucky star and thinks nothing can stop him. I think he's right. We study a steady line of deer tracks. Grandma, usually as terse as algebra, gets into it and gives us the guided tour. We splash across a stream that puts a semicolon in our path.

"Now what did you want to talk about?" asks my wife as we come back to the house under a twice-waxed moon that hangs over the place. "I forget," I say. To tell you the truth, this memory of mine worries me sometimes.

fighting words and hot flashes

OCTOBER 14

The morning has been a free fall of disappointment, so I come off my deer stand early and stop at Mom's Cafe over on Main Street. I order coffee and pie. I don't like the pie and query Mom as to whether it's apple or peach. "What's it taste like?" he asks. "Like glue," I tell him. "Well, then it's apple," he says. "The peach tastes like putty."

It's then a guy next to me asks if I'm a bowhunter. My camo clothes and made-up face give me away. I tell him to go to hell, but he keeps at me. "Sooner or later," he says, "every bowhunter, if he is wise, discovers that the experience of bowhunting is a mixture of good days and bad, victory and defeat, give and take." I blow him a razzberry, which doesn't slow him down.

"It doesn't pay for bowhunters to be sensitive souls or to get easily discouraged," he goes on. I take the hat off his head and sail it toward the bathrooms.

"The keys to being a successful bowhunter are hard work and cleverness," he continues as I scrape my pie plate into his coat pocket. "Too many bowhunters erect a proper stand and then sit in it for days on end without observing a deer. This is a mistake." I poke him in the eye.

"One whiff of human odor, one clank of your bow, the unavoidable commotion as you enter and leave the woods, alert deer to your constant presence." I pull up his pant leg and pour coffee down his sock.

"Therefore you should never hunt from the same stand more than a couple of days in a row." I clip him on the jaw.

"The best bet is to find a number of high-use deer areas and erect several stands for alternate days."

A fly comes by then and drops into my coffee, which is okay because I've got to get out and put up some extra tree stands, anyway. "Well, thanks for the info," I tell the stranger on my way out.

"Any time," he says.

lost and found

OCTOBER 15

I am a partridge hunter, and as long as soft country roads twist and squirm through October like wrinkles in an old man's face, I'll be a partridge hunter. As long as stone fences, mortared with the sweat of farmers long gone, farmers like my hunting grandfathers, wander over the washed-out browns and yellows of harvested fields, I'll be a quail hunter, too. And as long as there's a high, wide-open sky, I'll be an elk hunter. As long as there are marshes lost and hidden in the woods, marshes that draw moose and me, I'll hunt moose. As long as there are bear tracks etched along the slimy edges of marshes, I'll likewise be a bear hunter.

As long as there's a world of drifting, shallow waters with lily pads rootlessly floating, with reeds and cattails and bulrushes and wild rice, I'll be, of course, a duck hunter. As long as there's an arc of sky not bound by dreams, unmarked by city smoke, with a line or two of geese calling down about what a fine fellow I am, I'll be a goose hunter. I can live two months on a compliment.

As long as there's a piece of elegant, wildish countryside, as fine as ever flown over by a crow, stretching away and away to God knows where, I'll naturally be a deer hunter. As long as there are cities too full of everything but common sense and courtesy, I'll go hunting pheasants where pheasants call, each with a different voice, and rabbits and squirrels.

As long as there is life in the wild, as long as there are animals, free and elusive, as long as game laws hold and hunting men and women obey them, as long as I'm able, I'll be a hunter. And when I can no longer go into the wild, I'll toss my heart out there and follow it with my soul, because when I go hunting, it is me that I hunt, and it is me that I find.

minor skirmishes and philosophical reflections

OCTOBER 16

What I admire about people here at Lost Lake is their generous warmth, their enviable patience and their natural fortitude and grace, though none of that was present this morning at Mom's Cafe over on Main Street, when the topic became, "to grunt or not to grunt?" Grunting, as you know, is puffing into a device that is supposed to bring deer in close. The discussion quickly turned messy, and in the ensuing pandemonium, someone said, "I don't know if one of them things really will do something like that." Someone else said, "Well, maybe," and someone else said, "Heck no," and "Don't be silly." As you see, it heated up fast.

Someone snorted, "Wait a minute! Bucks grunt most when they're with does in heat, right? So then a grunting hunter might be able to call in a doe, right? Which might bring in a buck, a buck looking for a doe, or a buck looking to cut in on the action of another buck, right?"

Mom tries to cool things off with a round of hot coffee, but he might as well have saved his breath. "Aha!" someone said. "Nose-to-the-ground, doe-trailing bucks making like a locomotive in a rush would ignore the noise. And over-grunting would shoo them all away."

"Aha!" said someone else. "If a bedded buck or a feeding buck or an otherwise unengaged buck heard a grunt followed by a few quite contented grunts, then those bucks would circle in for a landing."

I, myself, figured the practice might be okay, but just in case, I'd put up in good deer country, anyway and keep getting out early, staying late, watching the wind and not counting my chickens. Of course, I didn't say anything, since being a gentleman is all well and good enough, but an awful handicap in an argument.

a backward glance

OCTOBER 17

One of the great pains to human nature is the pain of a new idea, so we're okay here. We're in old, old territory.

Within the hearts of all hunters, there is a golden commandment that charges all of us to recover, at all costs, an animal we have wounded. Not one of us can disagree with that, and all of us condemn any who do otherwise. We are especially strong on this point when we sit astride the high horse of an easy chair in the dry, warm comfort of our living rooms.

Far off, however, in the soggy, dotted far off, in cold, deep woods when it's raining or snowing, when the black mast of night falls thick and heavy all over the place, when we've been on the trail a long, long time, in a frenzied rush, groping empty air, surely long enough, when the trail vanishes like smoke, then a strange thing begins to happen, and a profound change comes over us. We modify our standards. Maintaining a proper dignity, we convince ourselves that we have satisfied our responsibilities, that we have done our best, and we can retreat to the crackling fires of home, though we have to step over our souls to do it, and whispers of nagging doubts dog our steps.

Every trail starts somewhere with a set of tracks, some clearer than others, and blood, and every trail ends with an animal. No deer can move from one of these points to the other without leaving sign of its moving. No animal disappears. Nothing vanishes but hope. Nothing dissolves but time. Nothing fades but resolve. Though the deer be dead out there somewhere, its soul survives and must be honored. If we fail to do that, then nothing remains to us but sleep without peace and with speculations of our own unworthiness.

grounded

OCTOBER 18

Darkness has faded into the hills, so open your eyes, my slumbering boy. It's time we went hunting. See the rose-flushed sky in the east? Morning calls. Stand alert, nephew, there are coyote tracks in the garden.

Owls have hooted the crossword-puzzled moon into hiding. Crows sing down by the mailbox. Open the windows of your eyes and see white clouds skitter westward. Where were you last night? Flies climb the windowpanes, buzzing. Oaks in the woods have gathered in their places, waiting for us. Get up. Lines of pines behind the house plunge and toss like antelope on the prairie. Tracking snows descend from divine and crippled clouds, for crying out loud. What time did you get in?

Throw off your blankets, boy. Lo, antlered deer come from their coverts. Mallards in the marsh take wing. Awake and hear partridge drum. Hear squirrels chat. Hear moose shake the earth. Your aunt was sick with worry. Hit the deck. Woodcock fly into the tag alders by the swamp, pheasants into the cornfield. I am down in the dumps. Is the gas tank empty? Roll out lest the day escape us. Geese are overhead and heading south. The woods shimmer through and through with little noises. Must I go alone and lonely into the vigorous substance of the great outdoors?

Alas. It is too late. The heavy night has marched again upon us. Now you make the flimsy glow of the TV your evening star. Take your place, indeed, in the world, junior, but from this day forward, leave the keys to the pickup on the hook by the door.

no regrets

OCTOBER 19

It is almost November again, and November's winds, like murky love songs, are almost upon us, and winter, coming in on great ghost-dancing clouds, is almost upon us, too. I see this. I feel it. I sense it, for I do not think, I cannot reason. What I have is instinct, instinct to calculate the murmuring mysteries of survival. And I am blessed with a nose and eyes and ears that cannot fail me, and speed.

I plunged softly into the world when melting snows still threatened newly hatched flowers in a rippling up of spring. With me was born a twin, a doe, much too fragile to withstand a she-bear starving with the long fast of winter, a sharp-eared she-bear with babies to feed. There is a time when it is infinitely desirable to be silent.

If a she-bear does not come for me, nor a coyote stumble upon me, if food is plentiful, and if this winter that is coming, blowing in on great, ghost-dancing clouds, does not grip too tightly, then I will live to be a year old. If farmers' dogs do not find me, I will grow to two. And if wolves do not catch my scent before I am ready, I will reach three. If arrows fall short, into chattering aisles of oak leaves, I will be four, and my antlers, silhouetted firmly against a pure wall of sunset, will grow many branches. If bullets fly wide, I will become five and six and seven.

Then the day will come when a winter, blowing in on great, ghost-dancing clouds, blots out the sky, and I will no longer have strength to fill my empty belly. I must lie down, trembling with cold and emptiness, as ravens come, insistent, and my silent cries become only the throbbing songs of winter, blown away by winter's winds. What the ravens leave of me, then, under a rotting log, will feed a flower just in time for the rippling up of another spring.

you and me, kid

OCTOBER 20

It's been a long week. It's been a long, hard week that sucked up your time with greedy, jutting teeth and, like a tornado, leveled your strength. Then, at last, like an unlocked light beam, the weekend comes, and with it the freedom to run, with rods and reels and guns and tents and canoes, into the hinterlands and, where appropriate, the muskegs.

But, oops. Wait a minute. Slow down. In a whisper, "What about the kids?" Even now, as you round the corner of a late Friday afternoon, their gorgeous laughter sweeps up the driveway to greet you. Cripes. Those kids have lost (in my case) their papa all week to his job and lawn mower and rototiller and leaky hose on the washing machine. Will they lose him now, for heaven's sake, to a duck blind, too, or a deer stand or trout stream?

You are snagged on the antlers of a dilemma. Will it be the "I'm outa here, kid" thing or the "I'm with you, kid" thing? Will you save the sun, and in doing so lose the moon, and stuff a mangled piece of yourself in some faraway corner of a flat planet?

It's a tough one. Yet, though it's not nearly the same as holding them on your lap, there is a way to stay close, in touch, with your kids when you're off somewhere knee-deep in glory. Write letters and notes to them for each day or part of one you're away. Include pictures, games and puzzles. Pin them to their pillows. Send them via the U.S. Mail. Have them hand-delivered by their mamas, who might even read them into the hearts of little ones biding time until the grand reunion union, complete with papas (in my case) and peanut butter hugs and jelly kisses. At least that's how we try to do it here at Lost Lake, and you might want to give it a try over there where you live, too.

hell and damnations theory

21 OCTOBER

The crowded conditions of deer hunting season were downright disappointing for a couple of the boys last fall. Their despair was substantial; their melancholy thick as smoke. They spend 99.9 percent of their lives in the city, doing time, working for the Man, so deer hunting for them is supposed to be a get-away-from-it-all deal, a time rich in stillness, lavish in loneliness. But no, and after a day or two — it was sad — their souls were posted with no trespassing signs, which is not how things on this earth should be.

It was the Professor, engaging the wheels of his imagination, who put those disillusioned youth on a therapeutic path of renewed faith. If it's alone in deer country they wanted to be, it's alone in deer country he'd lead them. With a sense of urgency, he dug out a county map and studied a river, not too big and not too creekish, down the road somewhat. He studied it hard and took a nap while the boys gathered their camping stuff, grub, portable tree stands, clean socks and underwear. Then they piled a canoe atop the Professor's station wagon and woke the old fellow, who drove them to where a dirt road fords the river and dropped them off. Three days later, he retrieved them downstream a ways.

Waterways like this are coated on both sides by some of the richest habitat within a week's drive. The lads easily maneuvered themselves smack-dab into the middle of it, silent and unruffled by unwanted company. It was another world altogether, and there they found a pair of nice bucks that dangled antlers from the back of a proud Professor's station wagon. The rest of us aren't so pleased about it, though. Since then, they've been suffering terribly and without remorse with the sin of arrogance, enough probably to send them straight to hell, though it worries me some that envy can get you there, too.

a pretty firm resolution

OCTOBER 22

When I was born, when I made that awkward landing into this world, I was thrown for a loss from which I have never recovered. Consequently, I have gone about my affairs in an atmosphere of isolation and mystery, never knowing for certain where I was headed and never quite sure where I'd been. No more. While my soul is attached to my body, I am going to draw a hard bead on becoming a trifle more shiftless.

I am going to seize every opportunity to follow my fishing pole into daily miracles of twilight for trout and walleyes, for bullheads and muskies. I am going fishing, and I am going tomorrow, or the next day or the day after that.

Up to now, a dog has never had it like I've had it, so I am going to relax my vigilance. I am going to start living it up in the customary quietude of the great outdoors. I am going hunting. I am, and I am going tomorrow or the next day or the day after that. I am going to book passage on the precious train of passing time and climb aboard the engaging prospects of a duck blind. I am riding out to where the sun sets to the lee side of mountains and look for an elk. I am going to follow the tracks of the moon, stretched out like a path across the water, and find me a moose. I am going to put the hot stuff of memories into active accounts of rowboats and shotguns. I am.

Then, when that final bell tolls and handkerchiefs flutter at my grave like the flutter of oak leaves, the tolling — and I intend to earn it — will be a tribute to a life well used rather than the jingling of a too-late alarm clock. And I am going to start that tomorrow or the next day or the day after that.

enough already

OCTOBER 23

Have you noticed that so often it's the little things that count the most? A little kid's smile dissolves a scowl of iron. A single rose reaching for the sky melts the hardest heart. A puny tune on the radio sends a grouch off on a sentimental journey a thousand miles long. A sliver of a moon restores a person's peace of mind just when dreams of glory are floating away. A ray of sun shining through the clouds penetrates even the most tangled web of trouble.

It goes even further than that. Have you noticed how it's the little boats that lift you with wonder-waiting hopes into the little out-of-the-way honey holes of lakes? Have you noted how it's the little putt-putt motors that set you quiet as a cloud over feeding schools of fish? Have you observed how often the most minuscule baits hook the biggest fish, and how pencil-thin bobbers reveal the most interesting goings on? Have you seen narrow streams, flowing with the ordinary flow of life, deliver up the most fantastic surprises? How do you explain that?

But there's more. A lot more. Have you noticed how the dabbing of a wee bit of oil on a shotgun keeps it as almost new as the sundown song of a whip-poor-will? Have you noted how a droplet of planning makes a campout supper an avalanche of delight? Have you observed how a crumb of care keeps a fine reel reeling and a good tent tentable?

Have you seen how a pinch of practice fairly often turns plain, old-clothes fishermen into anglers and fair shots into marksmen and arrow shooters into archers? Do you see what I'm saying? Do you get all that? Or have I overdone it again?

here's to the moon and here's to you

OCTOBER 24

A dog is barking in the night. Though there is nothing to bark at, you get up and turn on the yard light to draw the garden, the kids' swings and sandbox and basketball hoop, the woodpile and the apple trees back into the tiny universe of your care. You know this place as the ancient mariners knew the sea. You heat up old coffee, settle back and let your thoughts take a walk in the moonlight.

At such times, at such alone times, your thoughts take you to lump-in-the-throat fields where pheasants jump up at your feet, scaring you half to death, and tonight is no exception. You go there to remember. You wander to abandoned farms overgrown with lilac bushes and quail. You hunker down in your duck blind where time melts in its own sweet way. You smell the smoky smells of autumn. You roam hills overlooking rivers of trout. You listen for the high cries of geese, of elk.

You are brought back home by the sound of a cricket, and you think that one can never locate a cricket by its sound. Where the chirp is, the cricket isn't. Your thoughts come back to you then and walk you down the hallway to the darkened bedrooms of your sleeping children. These kids of yours, will they have what you have had? You sit there with your ear to your heart, hearing voices telling you that the majority of people are not hunters, that non-hunters tend to view hunters as curiosities, as unnecessary primitives, as heartless, needless killers of doe-eyed imitations of human beings. And you walk again through lump-in-the-throat pheasant fields, through quail country, under skies full of crying geese and moonbeams.

With the quieting of the dog out there, you lift the chalice of your coffee cup, toast those kids of yours, and make a promise: Sleep well, little ones. Daddy's here. Mother's here. Then you shut off the light, and though you won't sleep, you go back to bed.

solemn promises and mixed blessings

OCTOBER 25

Life is mud. Today I am wanting to be bird hunting with you, but my Uncle Jake says, "Hooey on that noise." He ties hand and foot and gags me with a promise I made last week. He throws me and the fishing tackle into the back of his pickup truck and high-tails it to the river. I can almost see you with your little side-by-side .20-gauge, promenading through those golden, birdy popple leaves. *Ach du lieber.*

When we get to the river, my uncle whispers, "Look at the water," like he was in church. "Would you look at that water?" I cop a peek and have to admit it looks okay. Uncle Jake's a fisherman, as you know, and ordinarily so am I. Today he's a walleye fisherman, a river walleye fisherman, and I'll tell you why. First, the customarily accelerated currents of this river are now at an obliging October minimum, making navigation easy as pie. Second, walleyes are getting more industrious, sensing the necessity, I suppose, of stocking up for the lean, mean months ahead. And third, we pretty much have the place to ourselves, which I must admit is kind of nice, since the rest of you are bird hunting. I'll bet that pup of yours is excited to be out on such a day as this.

River walleyes are staging in the deeper stretches of water now, in pools and drop-offs, in pockets behind bends, elbows and islands. Jake goes light, and so do I — four-pound test and one-eighth ounce jigs tipped with minnows. That's the way to do it. He goes slow, as I do, with the flow, and we go low, near the bottom.

So. We're walleye fishing while you're taking pot-shots at partridge, and I am somewhat in the frame of mind of the fellow who, on being asked, "Wilt thou have this woman to be thy wedded wife?" said, "Yes, I will, but I would rather have her sister."

once upon a time

OCTOBER 26

I don't know who invented the fishing jig, but I think I know how it happened. One day some fellow was sitting in his boat in the middle of the lake. The lake could easily have been a river. He was fishing for crappies, for perch, for walleyes. He was fishing for northern pike. And bass. He wasn't catching anything, not a nibble. A great cloud of woe hung hungrily about his head and shoulders, along with a bunch of mosquitoes.

He was out there as casual as could be when, lo and behold, in the corner of his mind's eye, he got this vision. It was a goodly vision of mystery and wonder, though not too fancy. It was a metal head attached to a hook. With the gleam of hope flaring from his nostrils, and with some diligence and legwork, he went home and he made one. He decorated it with feathers. He made another and decorated that one with hair. He thought it over, and then he decorated one with nylon and plastic. With pork rind. He tied one to his fishing line. He dropped it into the water, and it became a thing alive. It glided. It danced. It waltzed Matilda. It yo-yoed directly off the noses of crappies, of perch, of walleyes. Of northern pike. And bass. He made it weedless and cast it into weeds. He bounced it. He twitched it. While he was wading, while he was drifting. While he was sitting in his boat. And trolling. He hung it suspended. He dropped it fast. He dropped it slow.

On a roll, he dressed one in bucktails, one in long hackles, in marabou feathers, in crinkly artificial hair, in rubber skirts and vinyl skirts. In plastic curly tails. He trimmed one with a minnow and one with a leech. And a nightcrawler. And with this invention of his, which he called the jig, he caught crappies and perch and walleyes. He caught northern pike. And bass.

a logical conclusion

OCTOBER 27

You reach a certain age when you think you've got things figured out, but you don't. What I'm getting at here are tree stands, or more precisely, bowhunting from them. There's been altogether too much ballyhooing over the use of tree stands by bowhunters, some of it spread by me, and I apologize for it.

I know what you're thinking. You're thinking, "Whoa there! There is adequate, and documented proof of bowhunters taking deer while perched up in trees." On that point, you are correct, but other than that, the whole philosophy of the thing is Swiss-cheese full of holes, because the single most important element in hunting from trees is silence. Yours. Which anyone who's tried it can tell you is impossible to maintain.

Here's my point. How many times in the past year have you felt the urgent need to blow your nose, not counting the two weeks in February when you had the flu? Not hardly ever. But put yourself in a tree stand, and it's sniffle-sniffle-sniffle and blow-blow-blow. Even being quiet about it, it's noisy. In the last twelve months, outside of February, did you cough? Very infrequently. But settle yourself up in a tree stand, and it's cough-cough-cough. Also noisy. In a tree stand, you could die of leg cramps, though you never get them at any other time. Shaking cramps from a leg is not a silent business, even if you do it slow and careful.

Though you've got nerves of steel, let a deer try to sneak by you through the pines, and your heart beats as loud and irregular as a drunken drummer in a country band. With the clattering of your heart you tell every deer around, "Hey, deer! Here I am. You can go home now." So, as I say, bowhunting from tree stands is so much hooey, unless, of course, you get your deer that way, and then I guess it's okay.

all in the family

OCTOBER 28

This hunter who sits here, this hunter who is me, is not the hunter that he was. Nor is he the hunter he will be. Sitting in the middle of the family that gathers at my mother's house, I see myself as the once and future me.

I see myself, so long ago, in my second-grader nephew, a slingshot hanging from the back pocket of his jeans. His ammunition is a pocketful of stones. His fields are frog ponds and grasshopper meadows. And I see myself in my oldest sister's boy. A high school senior. To him, the catch and the kill are everything. His sole objective is to fill the game bag with the most of everything and return as the triumphant hunter. Fortunately, he is not, as I was not at that age, very good at it.

Across the room sits my much younger brother, where I sat once. His is the age of acquisition — the best guns, the finest, new-fangled equipment, all the gadgety gear of window displays and catalogs. And over there is a brother-in-law, settled solidly on the couch of early middle age. He and I have learned that patience and knowledge of the ways of wildlife are the keys to successful hunts. We're finally getting good.

There's my youngest uncle over there. He has become a trophy hunter. He pursues only the exceptional animal and measures his skill in points and pounds. There's my dad, who rejoices as much in the sound of flocks of geese as in the pulling of a trigger at the sight of them. I am, I think, beginning to understand that.

And finally, there's Grandpa, who sits warm near the fire as surely as I must in my turn. His hunts are now memories of sunsets and old guns and the sweet smells of woodsmoke and quiet places.

a spider, miss muffet and me

OCTOBER 29

Let me explain how I lost the biggest buck I ever saw in my life. It was late last Saturday afternoon. I was bowhunting. Are you familiar with the story of the little girl who, while sitting on a tuffet eating curds and whey, was frightened by a spider which came along and sat down beside her? It wasn't until late last Saturday afternoon that I grasped the significance of the kid's reaction and felt compassion for her at the loss of her lunch, though any of us would have lost that lunch without the spider incentive.

Some of you, when you lose the biggest buck you ever saw, blame fate or the lay of the stars or a lousy karma, and I understand that, for they have cost me deer on other occasions, too. But this year it was a spider, a big spider, a hairy one, a poisonous one. A black widow or tarantula.

The sad truth is that I had passed up lesser- and no-pointed deer, aiming instead for a six-pointer that had been cutting cabbage from our garden, pilfering pumpkins. I was up in my tree stand in the waning hours of last Saturday afternoon, kind of numb and sleepy. Imagine the jolt I experienced then when I opened one eye at the sound of a snapping twig to see this enormous spider dangling dangerously, looking to use my nose as a landing strip. This life-threatening creature was strung out between my eyes. Naturally, I yelled, "Hey!" and took a swing at it, causing quite a stir. Midway through the swing, I looked down at the biggest buck I ever saw, which ever so briefly looked back at me.

Since then, I don't care much for spiders. I have, in fact, hunted down the spiders around my place, and if you have spiders around your place in need of getting rid of, feel free to call on Miss Muffet or me.

overall growth and lack thereof

OCTOBER 30

A tourist took a wrong turn and ended up here at Lost Lake. We get excited when that happens because, as everyone knows, where tourists go, economic prosperity is sure to follow. This one stopped at Mom's Cafe over on Main Street and was on his second cup of coffee, which proves the point. I was there, too, and couldn't help but notice how, as he read the morning paper, he shook his head and sighed at what he found. I caught Mom's eye and signaled for a refill and scooted a couple of stools over to the stranger.

"Pick up a newspaper," I said to him, "and you find dissension. Turn on the radio, and there's discord. Plug in the TV, and you've got strife. Everywhere you go, people are groaning over hard times, and I'll tell you why. It's because they haven't in quite a while stepped into a pair of cross-country skis and schussed out to where the sap in maple syrup trees has slid down to the root of things. It's because they haven't lately strapped on a pair of snowshoes and gone dancing with moonbeams. It's because they haven't lately sat up in a pine tree waiting on the whims of an eight-pointer that will probably never show up, though you never know. It's because it's been too long since they've visited with the Northern Lights and watched the Big Dipper somersault across the sky."

"People who figure the world has gone to hell," I tell him, "haven't recently heard the laughter of little children bluegill-catching or observed beavers dam-fixing or paddled into a picnic lit by fireflies."

He looked at me with an oddball look, picked up his economy enhancing money and got the heck out of town. Maybe he was right. There's probably more to it than that; but I know what I know.

good intentions

OCTOBER 31

Like a great bird in a flurry of wings, flapping and settling down with a fuss, like a Nor'wester crying for the warmth of a good wood fire, there goes October. If you haven't put up your storm windows yet or tacked plastic over the sun porch screens, you'd better get at it quick. Have you noticed how the last of the leaves on weeping willows are drifting down in diligent, yellow showers? If you haven't sighted in your deer rifle, get at that, too. Orion is up in the east and on the go, and hurry-up redheads and canvasbacks are nodding hello and good-by in nearly the same wing flap.

Have you checked the anti-freeze? Do it now. Snowshoe hares are almost white, and weasels are just about ermines, and tamaracks are dusting off the last of their needles. Have you noticed how there's nowhere a more golden gold than the gold of October's tamaracks? You might as well be wearing your deer-hunting boots to break them in while you're attending to these chores. Whitetails are rising to the rut, or will be soon, and fifteen or twenty loons are gathered on the lake, resting up before shoving off to the Atlantic coast. Isn't that something?

Have you changed the oil in your snow blower and aimed it pointing out? Remember the Halloween blizzard of a couple of years ago? Whew! The Big Dipper, the Great Bear, is riding low on the horizon, stooping to wash its paws before freeze-up in lakes farther north than ours. Have you been helping the kids with their homework and listening to their prayers?

Brook trout are still moving into spawning beds. Witches are gliding across the moon tonight, and ghosts and goblins are having a ball in the pumpkin patch. Do you remember where you put your skinning knife last fall? Have you filled the bird feeder? Well then, I guess that puts you and me more or less in the same boat. Have you put the boat away?

MACIEJ

the prologue

NOVEMBER 1

What sounds like wind rattling windows and reeds down by the river is November creeping in, sending shivers through the glass. In the bay, what sounds like a wailing heron with water coagulating around its ankles is November, too, slipping across the border after dark. What appears to be snow dripping from cloudy bellies is likewise November, and everybody's acting weird — buying antifreeze and oatmeal.

Yesterday, two old turkeys were smoking morning pipes under a crippled oak tree. When I sneaked in for a look-see, there was nothing there but the heady afterglow of cheap tobacco, the unmistakable smell of November. On the way home, I giant-stepped across a meandering stream of apprehension. Sure enough, down there between my legs, half-hidden under a palace of smooth blue boulders, was a brook trout spreading cold, whispering wrinkles on the water. I did a double take and looked again, but there was nothing there but the shadows of November. When I bent down to investigate, a balsam bough reached over and knocked off the treasure of my cap. Ice thistles pricked at my ears. November. Whose idea was it to abandon the delicious, damp-green and rotting-wood smells of October? Who let the wind pile up so high, so deep and tight like a violin string? Who left the door open? And why is everybody acting weird, all shawled and wearily peering sideways up and to the north?

Even me. Why did I go squirrel hunting this morning in the teeth of a Nor'wester without my wool pants and snow boots? And why did I kid you about the trout? It wasn't spreading cold whispering wrinkles on the water. It was nibbling on a chocolate candy bar, drinking cut-rate wine and knitting warm woolen stockings to shield its varicose veins from November knocking on the door.

give it a rest

NOVEMBER 2

It has been difficult to do so before, but now, as snow falls upon the snow that fell yesterday and last night, it is easier.

Summer died as it had wanted to, in its own home. Its death came as no surprise. We had known of its failing health for some time, and during its last days it had grown increasingly restless and ornery, complaining that its coffin had not been built yet and that we didn't care enough to prepare a proper burial. Without one, it was summer's belief, its soul could not ride upon a crane's back to Paradise and would be forced instead into an eternity of wandering, purgatorial loneliness.

After some debate, nearly everyone agreed to bury summer as it desired, in the park on the west end of the lake on Labor Day. Those of us particularly close to summer remained uncertain and divided over how best to meet our obligations. Water skiers, swimmers and suntanners wailed at their loss; school children wept with such vigor that they moved some onlookers (not their mothers) to tears. It was difficult to determine if some of the grief was genuine or perfunctory. Anglers quietly fought to control themselves, as did campers and canoers. It was a profound and sacred moment. Everyone who witnessed it was moved.

In the end, of course, we accepted the passing of summer's earthly existence, accepted its soul leaving the sphere of our daily concerns. We will henceforth periodically recognize and honor its memory as an esteemed guest, but not expect it to participate in our lives. The post-funeral feast included potato salad, hot dogs and watermelons. Afterward, most reconciled their grief and wandered home. Me? I went pa'tridge hunting.

at the mercy of the wind

NOVEMBER 3

Here at Lost Lake, the winds of November blow straight up for a while, then they turn around and blow straight down. Or they stand still and blow in one place, or in all directions at once. Sometimes they blow so hard they blow the bark right off trees, and barrettes off the heads of little girls, and even the hides off puppies snuffling for chipmunks. They blow in clouds from a million miles away.

People look at those clouds, piling up, rolling every which way, and see elephants and hump-backed whales and eagles and lions, but not my Uncle Jake. He sees muskies. He sees muskies everywhere, even in his oatmeal and at suppertime when his gravy breaks a mashed potato dam.

Jake's right about the clouds. Whatever else they blow in, November's winds blow in big muskies. Say thirty-pounders. Say forty, if you want to. These fish are filling their bellies now to get them through the underwater droughts of winter. That's why after most people have tethered their boats in the back yard and kennelled their motors, Jake's out muskie fishing.

He necessarily dresses in his snowmobiling gear, goes to a particular lake that's deep and clear, and puts himself over a drop-off with a rocky, stumpy bottom. He hooks up a sucker minnow — maybe a twelve-inch-er — and freelines it with a sinker, thirty or forty feet down. Eventually, a muskie comes along, expecting to dine from the thick bowl of November's plenty, and takes the bait. Jake lets the fish have it until it stops with the full intention of eating it, which it does. When the muskie takes off a second time, Jake sets the hook, or I do. For from that side of the family, I inherited a soft spot between my ears and a madness for muskie fishing, which just goes to show you, though what I'm not quite sure.

in the eye of the beholder

NOVEMBER 4

When I get stuck between a full moon and a good night's sleep, I get to thinking about the weirdest things. I can't help it. Last night, though the moon wasn't altogether full, I got to thinking about these Christmas trees migrating from countryside to cityside, and what a shocker that must be, even for trees. Then, one thought led to another, and I got to thinking how when we're born, most of us carry on as if we're going to live forever. Then along comes Time and tricks us into a harness. We end up plowing through adolescence and marriage and motherhood or fatherhood and middle age, and then old age, and finally through the greatest practical joke of all, our final disappearing act. That got me to thinking about this elderly gentleman who used to come out to our deer shack every once in a while. He died a year or two ago, and out of sentimental consideration I paused at the thought of it.

One time a couple of the boys were arguing over what constitutes a trophy and what doesn't. Each had taken a deer right away that year, and they were maneuvering for bragging rights. The old gent quieted the conversation by telling them that such talk was ugly and inaccurate. He said there were no hard-and-fast rules that determine what is and is not a trophy. It's the person doing the shooting who does the deciding. A fourteen-year-old kid shoots a deer, be it a little doe or a spike buck, and that kid hangs that doe over the mantlepiece of his heart, now and forever. A spike buck holds as much glory for a little girl as a bull moose does for her daddy.

The old guy wasn't a regular member of our hunting gang, but he took his turn at supper dishes, and most of us thought he was okay. So when he died, we were surprised at how well his family took the news. That got me to thinking that I think too much.

magic circles

NOVEMBER 5

. . . thus the Birch Canoe was builded in the valley by the river, all the bosom of the forest; and the forest's life was in it, all the mystery and the magic …

After a child rides into their lives on unseen waves to claim their hearts, too many parents of very small children put the loon on hold. Too many set down the tent, put away the paddle and the camp stove, until the child develops wispy whiskers or the need of training bras. This is crazy. The world is a park today. Stars are taking up new positions now; the sun is sprouting new flames at this moment. Take your child as we speak and glide through walls and locked doors. It's the only way. Go like great gorillas shuffling through the jungle. Take the prizes of your life and rifle the flowers of their smell, or the sacred cause will slip away, and too late will you groan, "Ah me. I have waited one second too long, and now the kid wishes to be doing something else."

… draw a magic circle round them, so that neither blight nor mildew, neither burrowing worm nor insect, shall pass o'er the magic circle …

Formula heats beautifully on glowing embers. Diapers dry magnificently in the wind. Go. Take the wide-eyed little ones. Baptize them in the woodsmoke of quiet places. With an eye out to dodge disasters, edge along the outskirts of tomorrow. Stir up the glue of remembering and being remembered. Gently, go gently, but forge the bonds of a life-long love affair with purple evening mists.

… on the clear and luminous water launched his birch canoe for sailing, from the pebbles of the margin shoved it forth into the water; whispered to it, "Westward! Westward!" And with speed it darted forward …

Win their hearts and their souls, take them now and live your lives in great abundance.

… then the little Hiawatha learned of every bird its language, learned their names and all their secrets …

the genuine article

NOVEMBER 6

In a solitary confinement of my own construction, I am, this cold, cold day, in Mom's Cafe over on Main Street nursing a cup of coffee when a stranger comes in, sits down beside me and puts his hand on my shoulder. Before I can ask what the devil's going on, he clears his throat and says, "Are you or are you not a genuine student of the outdoor sporting life?" His eyes, though not unkind, are restless and uncompromising. "I am," says I.

"Then you should know," says he, "that you can search the world over and find nothing on cold, cold days that keeps you warmer than a bellyful of good food, though it occurs to me you may have already thought of that." "I have," says I.

"There is a place for calorie counting and weight watching," says he, "but duck blinds and deer stands are not the places. When they venture into the great, though cold, out-of-doors, the filling of their bellies is a responsibility men and women must take seriously."

"They simply must," says I.

"There are," says he, "pre-concocted belly-fillers, cellophaned and guaranteed, but they are not such all-around good times as this one is."

"You don't say," says I.

"Get yourself," says he, "quite a bit of bacon and sizzle it up crispy. In the grease grill a great big pancake. When it's done, spread a little peanut butter on it. The crunchy kind gives it character. If you've no need of character, skip it. Sprinkle it with brown sugar. Crumble the bacon into bits, scatter it on top, roll it tight and wrap it in waxed paper."

"Sounds a little coyote ugly to me," says I.

"So it does," says he, "but one, and two for sure, will get you through hell and half of Minnesota."

"Even if you live in Wisconsin?" says I.

"Especially if you live in Wisconsin," says he.

"Wow!" says I. "Teach a fellow to fish, and he eats a lifetime."

"I know," says he, patting me on the head and drifting out the door.

yes, no and maybe

NOVEMBER 7

You have no idea what a poor opinion our English teacher over at the high school had of himself last week, and how little he deserved it. He'd been bluegill fishing and hadn't caught any, so he was floating around here like a rudderless boat, like a keelless canoe, like a rusty galley without oars. It wasn't all his fault. Our English teacher fished along a row of cattails, a good-enough move that could have caught him fish. He used maggots, waxworms and night crawlers — good-enough November baits — correctly stuck to a number ten hook and a teeny bobber. No fish. Maybe the day before that or the day after, but not then.

We here at Lost Lake believe artists must dip their brushes into their souls and paint their own pictures, but we also believe in lending a hand in desperate situations, so when my Uncle Jake heard about his friend's puzzling plight, that's what he did.

In early November, bluegill fishermen have to hunt for their fish. As water temperatures drop, bluegills gather into nomadic clusters. They leave their deeper-water summer homes and cruise this way and that, in and out of food-a'plenty shallows.

Jake knows this, as you do now, so the two went out over a submerged, still-greenish weed bed, figuring the fish might be holding in the in-between. Using their ultralight gear, they added slip bobbers. Starting out at three feet from the surface, they kept adjusting the bobbers down in six-inch increments until they hit the jackpot and had a ball. And though it might seem a small matter to you, to one of them at least it was a wordless wonder of delight, and it gave him insight into the old saying, "When a person's education is finished, so is he."

sharps and flats

NOVEMBER 8

We're back here at the deer-hunting shack after dark to warm up and dry out. But it's not as simple as that. We almost commit a social blunder, which is nearly impossible at a deer-hunting shack.

Two of our boys, high school boys, good kids and fine hunters, have invited their girlfriends out for supper. Some of us look like we've been here for a week, which we have, and need airing out, which we do, so naturally the kids want to sit alone. They set up a card table in the corner with a tablecloth and the stub of a candle. It looks nice and brings a tear to the eye as we recall the mystery of youth and digest the memory. It's been a long time since we've washed the soup ladle, too, so they don't want to eat what we're eating.

The boys' mamas had come up with a meal they could basically make ahead of time and give the boys credit for. They cut four big green peppers in half lengthwise. In plastic containers, they put half a cup each of chopped onion and celery, a cup of seasoned instant rice, half a cup of milk, one egg, half a teaspoon of salt, one quarter of pepper, and a cup of tomato juice. They sent along a pound and a half of ground venison (what else?) and a can of Mexican style Manwich spread from the grocery store. They instructed their sons to brown the venison and add the other materials in no particular order, which they do beautifully, and fill the pepper halves heaping full, and put them in a covered baking dish, and bake for almost an hour at 325.

The girls would have loved it, but it gets to smelling so good, we crowd around and sample it until we eat it all. We feel like alarm clocks run down to nothing about it, but then we cut cards to see who drives the thirty miles into town for a couple of pizzas for the kids, which seems only fair. The ace I drew was the only one I'd seen in a week.

revved up and ready (more or less)

NOVEMBER 9

My life is a list, a long list of duties, a stack of yellow Post-it memos stuck to a refrigerator door. Do this! Do that! Imagine my surprise, then, to look up from all this doing and find myself smack-dab in the second week of November.

Everybody's deer hunting or getting ready for deer hunting or thinking about getting ready for deer hunting. Porcupines are shuffling through the woods with love in their hearts and lovemaking on their minds. So are moose on a much larger scale, and brown bats and weasels, though weasels are basically always that way. Porcupines at this time are very careless crossing roads.

Aquila, the Eagle constellation, is flying low on the western horizon. And empty nests are swinging in naked trees. And snowshoe hares are about all white but for the tips of their ears and the shadows of their tracks. They'll stay that way until sometime in March. If that's wishful thinking, make it April. Slugs and snails that haven't done so are burrowing into the yet unfrozen wet of swamps and marshes. Slowly, I suppose. Brook trout are laying eggs in gravelly nests. There are still a few woodcocks around, but not for long. We'll miss them.

Woodchucks are sleeping, nose to tail in bed-chamber burrows, breathing once every six minutes or so, living, if you can call it that, off fat they piled on days and weeks and months ago. And hungry November is taking big bites out of neatly stacked rows of firewood, paying us back with the smell and haze of smoke that drifts over resting fields and gardens and brushes the bald tops of trees. And finally and at last, cross country skiers are out and about. At least they are here at Lost Lake, and if you've been having the kind of weather we've been having, they are where you live, too.

a sour commentary

NOVEMBER 10

Quite unexpectedly, as I eked out a deer hunt from the fertile North Country woods, as my thoughts, like a child's thoughts, skittered to chickadees and cottontails and unnamed clouds, as I gnawed on a supper of squirrel stew and coaxed a lightly oiled rag through the barrel of my gun, as I readied for bed, quite unexpectedly, because that's all I did, the top blew off.

Quite unexpectedly, as I stopped along a stream dancing down a long, clean riffle, the sunlight turning it a shimmering silver, as I counted the stones on its bottom and knelt before it to drink its water, as sprinkles of wildflowers crowded around and nodded good day, as I cast to a beautiful bubble of a trout, because that's all I did, quite unexpectedly, the bottom fell out and the top blew off.

Quite unexpectedly, to me at least, as I sat upon a piece of prairie and ogled an antlered buck slipping along the tall grasses to its daytime hiding place and a dozen partridges picking at grasshoppers, as I watched two turkeys dine on acorns, a pheasant lunch on fallen corn, a moose wade into a cattailed sunset and a bear eat my peanut butter sandwich, and because that's all I did, quite unexpectedly, the sides caved in, the bottom fell out and the top blew off.

Quite unexpectedly, as I let someone else stand up and protect my constitutional responsibilities of keeping and bearing arms, as I let someone else work hard to maintain wildlife populations and habitats, as I wrote no letters and made no calls to editors and lawmakers, as I did nothing to combat the creeping scourge of sadly uninformed people working tirelessly to keep my hunting and fishing and trapping from me and my kids, because I did nothing, when I awoke one morning, the top had blown off and there was nothing for me anymore, nothing, nothing, nothing at all.

the bottom line

NOVEMBER 11

This happened awhile back, probably in August. My Uncle Jake was telling a counterful of customers at Mom's Cafe over on Main Street about a nice walleye he had caught. I took it as long as I could, then I said,

"Uncle, in reporting this nice fish you have landed, you vary the size of it with each telling."

"Yes, I do, nephew," he said, "because I never tell people more than I think they'll believe."

Then someone came in and tacked up a poster about a professional fishing tournament coming up in the next county. Besides the regular holidays, we don't get much excitement here at Lost Lake, so we took a vote to go to it and rub elbows with the fishing rich and famous.

The day came, we went, and we were sorry we did. The first thing the kids remarked on was that nobody was smiling with anything but their lips. Then we saw contestants carrying fish all day long in livewells and agreeing that it doesn't harm a fish to release it after the lengthy stay, nor does the handling of it. You don't believe that, and we didn't either. We saw our highly thought of tackle makers glamorizing the affair and paying money for it. We saw people attracted to fishing by the lure of profit. We saw the love of money displace the love of fishing — and all of it called sport. We saw ordinary anglers displaced by the pros and their keepers. We saw public accesses to the lake shut down to the public. We saw money making, profit taking. We saw good people doing bad things. We saw competition where none should be, and selfishness, and came home not feeling well.

What got me to thinking of that now is last night I was reading where Ralph Waldo Emerson wrote, "the louder they spoke of honor, the faster we counted the spoons," which may not be a direct quote, but it got me to wondering if they didn't have professional fishing tournaments back when he lived, too.

snowbound

NOVEMBER 12

It's crazy to be alive in such a strange world as this. It is snowing this morning, hard, very hard, tiny chipped-glass flakes, and the wind is blowing. Nobody is going anywhere outside, not hunting, not fishing, not to work or school. Consequently, I decide to ride my imagination over to a prairie stream and climb into an old canoe I keep hidden there. Before you know it, I am gone like a smiling hippopotamus, paddling through melodies I cannot hear because of the storm.

What a trip it is, too. I pass by three mongrel coyotes looking down from a little rise and wondering what kind of loony person rides his canoe in such a crazy world as this. I don't see any loons.

Catching the green light on the corner of Leisure Tension and Private Silence, I increase my speed and come up to three or four — it's hard to tell because of all that white against all that white — jackrabbits washing supper dishes at ten o'clock in the morning. Under a street lamp, two adolescent antelopes — one small and sleek, the other tall and curly — in leather jackets are trying to light cigarettes against the fearful wind. They offer one to me, but I don't have the time and I don't smoke, anyway.

I zoom right along and probably pass through St. Louis without even knowing it. I do note, however, when the wind lets up some, a buffalo with a television antenna growing out of his head. On his right ear is written Vert and on his left is Horiz. I am going to plug him in and watch a little TV — what else is there to do during a November blizzard? — when a dufus in a seventeen-footer honks his horn and passes me on a double yellow. It's crazy, I tell you, to be alive in such a world as this.

go to hell

NOVEMBER 13

I have always felt pot-bound like a petunia because nobody asks me questions. Everybody asks outdoor writers questions, but not me. Maybe it's because they've been hunting with me, or fishing. Maybe it's because they've seen me pitch a tent or paddle a canoe. Maybe they've eaten my campfire beans. I don't know, but you can imagine my astonishment then, one stormy night, when someone asked me a question.

I was trapped in the city and in need of air, so I left my hotel on foot. Snow was falling. The wind was blowing. Halfway across a long, high bridge that spanned a wide river, I was surprised to find that I was not alone. Standing upon the four-foot concrete railing, his arms upstretched, was a man. At first I didn't believe my eyes, then I didn't believe my ears. Above the wind, over the noise of the city, I heard his cry, "Why? Why?"

I appreciated it, too, so I reached up and tugged at the tattered hem of his overcoat. "Thank you," I said. "I can tell you why. It is because before deer-hunting season you washed your hunting clothes with scented laundry soap, which is not indigenous to the area in which you hunt. And you used scented softener in the rinse cycle, also not indigenous. Perhaps your cooler smells. You can eliminate the foul odors by sprinkling drops of artificial vanilla extract on paper toweling and wiping it out with that. Don't fret. Your luck will improve if you hunt your rabbits under cloud cover or after a storm like this one, when they are more active. Don't worry. You will never be cold in your sleeping bag if you wear a stocking cap snugly on your head. Sixty percent of your body heat escapes through the holes in your head."

"Now then," I said, "the storm is worsening. May I help you down from that slippery place up there?"

"No thanks," he said, and jumped.

the balance of power

NOVEMBER 14

The English teacher over at the high school missed the September meeting of the Lost Lake Fish, Game and Cribbage Club, so we elected him president. Right away he calls for a recount, but we threaten to hide his compass if he doesn't settle down and take the oath of office, which he does, what with deer season being right around the corner.

Then he uses the power of his position to tell us we've got to get our kids more involved in the great outdoors, because we'll all be dying off some day and who'll carry on the great American traditions of hunting and fishing and camping and things? We know that, but give him a round of applause anyway to keep his spirits up. So, being a teacher and not able to help himself, he assigns Katie, a sixth-grader, to give a report at the following meeting, which is tonight.

She chooses badgers, though we were hoping for something a little more exciting. "Badgers," she says, "begin life as blind, helpless little critters. Some people say they are born mean and spend their lives getting meaner. Badgers live alone. They can't even stand each other. Once they mate, the female kicks the male out. And though she's a good mother while it lasts, around the end of summer, she kicks the kids out, too. Badgers are cousins to weasels and can weigh up to twenty pounds. Hunting only at night, they prey on ground squirrels, moles, gophers, rabbits and even nesting birds. They don't go around looking for fights, but they don't turn any down either."

Katie has more to tell, like how they can dig a hole faster than a man with a shovel can, but her mother interrupts to say that tomorrow's a school day and the kid has to get home to bed. Something, she adds, arching an eyebrow at the president, her father ought to do, too. The meeting adjourned shortly thereafter.

how's that?

NOVEMBER 15

The Professor is getting married. This is kind of a shock to us, since his luck with the ladies has not been phenomenal. The two in town with whom he seemed particularly close always refer to him as a cross between an irritant and a social nuisance, though we don't. We do, however find his engagement, if not coincidence, then divine intervention, when he tells us she has a few dollars, which is of and by itself no reason not to marry someone. He met her through an ad in the Sunday paper.

The wedding is right after deer season, but the Professor got permission to join us out at the hunting shack, and just in time. One of the youngsters comes running in from his stand out of breath and tells us he's seen a nice buck acting goofy. Instead of its usual sneaky, deer-like moves, this one was coming on with his head up, his tail out and prancing more or less like a pony in a parade, and what the heck was going on?

Well, right away the Professor is glad he came out and fills the kid in. He says that as the rut commences, some bigger bucks, when there's another buck or two nearby, start to show off, act uppity, and if some nearby buck wants to start something, they'd be happy to oblige. Having the opportunity to show off his whitetail wisdom makes the Professor feel pretty good. But the idea of having two bucks or three close to him, ready to mix it up, and him coming in early, makes the kid feel terrible.

Then the Professor's beeper goes off, which kind of shocks us, too, because we don't even know he has one. He looks surprised himself, prompting one wiseacre with a literary background to comment, "Do not ask for whom the bell tolls, old boy. From now on, it tolls and tolls and tolls and tolls for thee."

a clean sweep

NOVEMBER 16

If you want to get out of Lost Lake, you have to go out the same way you came in. That puts us out a ways, but not so far out that we're not on the cutting edge of the intellectual revolution. We believe each of us is born facing a fork in the road, and which branch we take determines the kind of human being we are or will become. We believe one fork is that of the giver, the lover, the builder, the creator. The other is that of the taker, the hater, the wrecker. We don't believe there's a middle road.

We believe that if the universe is not ours alone, nor yours alone, to maintain, then the little corner of it that we call home is, and so is yours. We believe that each of us should clean and care for a stretch of roadside ditch, or little stream, or boat landing, or vacant lot scarred by the takers of the world. We believe we can do this as a family activity, reaping the by-products of teaching our kids by our good example to accept the responsibilities for the beauty and preservation of their tiny piece of heritage and domain. We believe that as we pick up the refuse left by the haters, we can also be a part of the unfolding seasons and interpret the mysteries of Mother Nature. We believe that as we mop up the rubbish of the wreckers, we are doing it on behalf of the birds and wildflowers and insects and fresh air and exercise. Sometimes we keep a journal or scrapbook of our observations, interpretations and accomplishments while we're at it.

While we're at it we also set out a bluebird house, put a feather in our caps and top it off with a picnic to remind ourselves what's at stake, because we believe if anything we do in this life matters, then everything we do matters. We believe we should speak not only with words but with our hearts as well.

old glory

NOVEMBER 17

The old man, like many old men, woke in the morning when he darn well felt like it, and when he did, he did it as snail-slowly as a rose unfolds. He unwound himself from sleep with a practiced precision, patiently waiting for the noisy cooperation of his old joints, before employing them in the act of rising. That is the velocity with which he also ate his breakfast and put himself into his deer-hunting duds. That is how he hunted, too, but when he saw the partial outline of a deer with considerable size and antlerage half-illuminated and intermingled with the stuff of dark forest trails, he fell to his hands and knees with the acceleration of a schoolboy.

Jeepers. Silently, he thrust his rifle through the tangled tag alders of his hiding place. Pressing and squeezing each second for more than its appraised value, he squinted for another look, though he tried not to look too long nor too hard, lest he prick the animal with his staring.

Of course, he had been in these circumstances before, but not in a long time. In fact, he had begun to adapt to the philosophy that it was not entirely necessary to actually see a deer to claim a successful hunt. Baloney.

He tried to ignore a cramp growing on his right leg. He tried to ignore sweat pooling in the sags and wrinkles of his skin. He merged, in the way of hunters, with the timeless rhythms of the forest as he raised his rifle. At the same time, the deer jerked his head up. And in the instant their eyes locked, the old guy felt again the enthusiasm and profound wonder of his youth.

evasive tactics

NOVEMBER 18

I am a dreamer. Especially day, especially here at work. I can't help it. Sometimes I dream about partridge. Sometimes it's pheasants or moose or elk or mallards or bobwhite quail. Today it's fish. You'd think with the opening of deer season only days away, I'd be dreaming of whitetails and mossy, many-sided antlers, but it's fish. I don't know why.

I get to thinking that to a fish, being a fish is at best a chancy business. For by far, most potential fish never get to be fish at all, or at least they don't for very long. Those that do, with every fin stroke and gill breath of their existence, face a never-ending struggle to keep on being fish. I get to thinking that for a little fish to become a big fish, it must first be a very lucky fish. Then it must be a very clever fish, clever enough to catch what it catches using up less energy than the meal supplies. If a fish goes tearing a quarter-mile after an itty-bitty minnow, or if it goes ripping helter-skelter after a measly fallen-in mosquito, it will quite obviously and eventually weaken and die of starvation or, all pooped out, it will itself become prey for a more conscientious fish. It follows, then, that fish, expert at being fish, must exert as little effort as possible in meal getting. It is therefore, for us who fish, important to understand the feeding behaviors of the fish we're fishing, to understand which are silent ambushers, which feed at night, which are lone feeders, which feed in packs and which in quick blasts of energy — and put our baits out when and where they'll do some good.

Then my boss, a real barracuda, comes by, sending shock waves down the rivers of my nervous system, and I get to thinking that it's time for a coffee break and dreams of blaze-orange coats and high-powered hunting rifles, which is the way it should be this time of year.

it's really very simple

NOVEMBER 19

Because it may be difficult for the non-hunter to understand why a person goes deer hunting, I will give an example from my own personal experience. This is what I did today.

I criss-crossed the upward and the downward slopes of hills. I was mauled by swamps, sucked up in muck and roasted by the sun. I froze to death. I forded wide-open fields a hundred miles across, scrambled up a thousand hills and clung to rocky cliffs. I fasted all day and almost went without a good night kiss. Do you believe that? I crawled on my hands and knees through briar patches of doubt and cobwebs, heart beating like a drum. I tramped back well after dark through heavily haunted woods. You should have been there. We'd have put together a little drive and got something going.

I wrestled wild birch trees that got in my way and fought off fits of loneliness. I got knocked down by clouds and found myself locked in mortal combat with melancholy. I was waylaid by fears ten sleek feet thick. I looked squarely in visual disbelief at things I saw out there. Some of it was dark and fierce and shrill, but that was okay. I was devoured by flights of fancy and suffered consequences enough to baffle the imagination.

I hope I'm not overdoing this, but here at the end of the day the clock is ticking down again — tick tick tick. After thirty-two thousand and four hundred more ticks, the sun will rise on another day, and I'll be up and out there once more. I'll be aloft like an eagle far out over the trees, lost to sight sometimes, but always coming back, high and swooping down, living life on the threshold with my new rifle, and I'm going to get me my deer. I hope I do.

Did you get all that, or did I lay it on too thick again?

inside the realm of possibilities

NOVEMBER 20

As Thanksgiving rolls around again to interrupt our routine, we should take a minute to check things out, to see what, if anything, we have to be thankful for besides Canada geese in the gray clouds of this departing November and the beautifully spreading white coat of snow sweeping in under winter skies. And besides the woods grown tall with cottonwoods, grown tall with maples and oaks and pines. And moons hanging motionless at the outer edge of the world. And the sad, slow murmurs of far and distant waves coming in thick with cold. And besides heavy-horned deer advancing along paths of morning stars. And clouds. And ice-fishing shacks and partridge drumming and pheasants crowing. And owls hooting and good dogs and music and friends.

And besides Christmas decorations on doors and lawns and good-smelling trees. And fresh air and clean, fishy waters. And tents and campfires and bushy-tailed squirrels. And cross-country skis and fireplaces and thick blankets. And rainbow trout and blue-winged teal. And woodsmoke and quiet places. And eagles. And moose. And frosty robins playing tag with the weather. And wood ducks. And loons and wolves.

And besides good neighbors and hunting partners and kids. And loving husbands and wives. And the magic of creation, no matter how it came about. And the good things people do for each other. And frogs and fireflies. And books, and hawks flying into the sun. And the Northern Lights. And hot coffee and oranges and smoked-oyster stuffing and the memories of childhood. And grandpas and grandmas. And uncles and aunts. And teachers and firefighters and doctors and cops and farmers and everybody else. I mean, besides that, what have we got to be thankful for?

dead to rights

NOVEMBER 21

Some of you know my Uncle Jake, my fishing Uncle Jake, and if you don't, you've probably got an uncle of your own just like him, in which case you know him perfectly well, which brings us more or less to the topic of bass fishing. It's after supper, and we're still out at the deer-hunting shack. You'd think we'd be talking about deer hunting. But we're tuckered out. Our defenses are down, and Jake catches us at a semicolon in the conversation and steers the talk toward bass.

"Bass," he is saying, "at one time or another will feed on nearly anything somewhat smaller than themselves, in the water or on top of it. So most folks who fish for bass figure they've got to carry a tackle box about the size and heft of the box on a half-ton pickup truck to hold all the baits necessary to catch them at one time or another. But not me," he says. "I do just fine on a mere handful of basic bass baits. All I need are some small surface lures resembling frogs, hellgrammites and insects for shallow areas and under overhangs. And some dark-colored bottom-bouncers that look like crayfish, tadpoles and minnows. And early in the season or after a rain, I like to use various plastic worms along shallow shorelines and the mouths of creeks. And my very favorites, which are spinners, to fish just under the surface. And lightweights for when the surface is smooth, and heavier ones for windy conditions. And a few designed for fast retrieves and some for slow. And weedless. And brightly colored ones for sunshiny days and dark for cloudy."

"All of which you squeeze," interrupts my aunt, who has come out to disinfect the pots and pans and supper dishes piled up around the sink, "into a tackle box about the size and heft of the box on your half-ton pickup truck."

flights of fancy

NOVEMBER 22

I am in love with camping, wilderness canoe-paddling camping. I don't use the word love here in some symbolic or colloquial way. I mean I am in love with it, the kind of love that twangs the guitar strings of your heart, if you'll excuse the expression.

I'm in love with the taste of morning air and the soft blowing wind, even in November, when I can take a good hold of myself and laugh. I'm in love with the smells of rivers and lakes held together by a lacework of pine trees. I'm in love with the high emotional balance this gives me. I'm in love with the possibilities so peculiar to getting somewhere in a canoe, how around every corner there is something curious and interesting, something I've never seen before or felt or done or known about. Though I'm no longer as optimistic as I once was, I know that with each paddle stroke I will never be quite the same again.

All the jukebox songs I've ever heard cannot match the sound of a smooth-running zipper opening my tent to the blessings of a new day. I'm in love with never having to feel poor on canoe-paddling camping trips, and how you can make promises to yourself and have all the time in the world to keep them, and how you can stay up all night if you want to, and make mistakes if you must. I love being a stranger in temporary exile. I love the romantic notion of it, of living a shining, perishable dream, of reducing the miraculous to a coffee pot bubbling alive on a campfire. I love being reminded of who I am, and why, and the sense of wonder at it. Every minute of it.

And, though I can't quite put my finger on it, I love it because when I'm camping, wilderness canoe-paddling camping, I'm twenty again and it's always springtime.

brief encounter

NOVEMBER 23

I'm an unpaid bill, a basket of clothes in need of sorting — the dark with the dark, the light with the light. I'm a vase of tulips without water, a burned-out light bulb, wet kindling. I am restless, in need of rearranging, airing out. You know how it is when the world crowds you. You want to put yourself in the bill drawer and come back to you later. That's how it is with me. Then I go hunting, because when I hunt where I hunt I am touched by the wonders that I find, and I find a part of me.

Today I get out quite a ways and eventually settle down next to a giant of a maple where the sun filters in to join me in a drink from my pack and a munch on my sandwich. I am wanting to be alone, but along comes this poorly dressed character, unkempt, bucktoothed, pigeon-toed, and bow-legged.

"How you doing?" I say, "and what brings you out this way?" He's stuck up and ignores me. I get an image of a loner who, like me, minds his own business. I'm on to him, though and read him like an encyclopedia. He's a loner, all right, except later on in January when he's looking for a girlfriend, and though neither of us can see that well, we both know I'm not it. When he finds her, they'll make love, and half a dozen hours later she'll kick him out because he eats the outdoor toilet seats of deer-hunting shacks and salt-sweaty ax handles and canoe paddles, so she's got a point there.

She's got several points, in fact, and between them they've got a thorny problem, a prickly situation, if you know what I mean, and I get to thinking maybe I don't have it so bad after all.

a pang of disappointment

NOVEMBER 24

One day last week, for just a minute there, everybody here at Lost Lake harbored fleeting thoughts of moving to Bay City, Mich. (AP)-. It was one of those ordinary mornings, teeming with life. We were having coffee at Mom's Cafe over on Main Street, each of us studying a section of the morning paper. All you could hear, if you were listening for it, was coffee sipping and page turning.

It was my Uncle Jake who broke the silence and got things going. "Holy cow!" he said, choking on a donut. "Listen to this!" And he read us word for word this article. "Bay City, Mich. (AP)-" he began, and everybody gathered around, including those who came over from the Post Office across the street to see what the commotion was all about.

"The northern pike is a voracious fresh water fish," he read, "weighing about *35 pounds* (the italics are Jake's) and reaching *46 inches in length*, whose lower jaw extends beyond the upper. New paragraph. Northern pike are extremely destructive to trout, carp and other freshwater fish. As well as frogs. They often lie like a log on the bottom, then make a sudden rush after their prey."

"Wow," whispered someone after a minute or two. We'd all caught northern pike, but not like that.

"Wow," whispered someone else.

"Where in hell is Bay City, Mich. (AP)-?" whispered the English teacher, in a state of shock at such a fish.

"I don't think you can get there from here," whispered the Professor, a tear rolling down his cheek.

And we all felt so bad. It was in the paper, so we know it's true, and if you can get to Bay City, Mich. (AP)- from where you live, and you hook onto one of those northern pike, please don't tell us. I don't think we could stand it.

fun and games

NOVEMBER 25

Accidents happen in the best-regulated families, so my brother's not the smartest dog around. But there is one thing he knows more about than the rest of us put together, and that's partridge hunting. The only problem is he's a little uppity about it. Like today. We're hunting with a couple of youngsters skipping school. And my brother is peeved because we have no birds, and he's taking it out on me during a baloney sandwich break. He's criticizing the kids, and though he's older than me and outweighs me, I tell him to knock it off. He forgets how it takes years to become a top hand partridge hunter, and then nobody ever gets it quite right. Yet, even I admit there are a few things these kids of ours, about age seventeen, could improve on.

For example, they hold their guns all wrong. My brother's kid holds his over his shoulder, mine in a cross-armed fashion. Both practically guarantee a loss of split seconds and produce hurried-up, poorly aimed shots. A serious partridge gun should be carried at something approaching port arms, ready for instant business. The right hand of right-handers should be on the grip, index finger or thumb near the safety. The left should cradle the fore end, ready to guide the piece. From the moment they reach the cover to the time they leave, they should grip those guns in both hands, ready to swing.

And another thing they should learn is how to walk. They're always off balance when a bird comes boiling up out of hiding. Good hunters are swivel-hipped and loose as ashes. When a bird lifts off, they stop, plant their feet and swing, all at once.

I don't know why I bother, though, because by the time I get this thought out, our kids are holding hands and giggling about something that has nothing to do with partridge hunting, and my brother whispers there's a rabbit in the bushes over to the left, so off he goes, and there's another day shot to hell.

twentieth century sublime

NOVEMBER 26

Outside our deer hunting shack, the great Dog Star Sirius is trailing its master, Orion the Hunter. Close behind is the puppy star Procyon, a pretty bright shiner itself. An owl is calling out a soft owl-clucking, who-cooks-for-you, and the popple trees are standing still and stiff as death. Inside, it's half-past eight and smelling softly of chili and onions and puffs of pine smoke from a pot-bellied stove. A couple of the boys are waiting for an overdue third who's still in the woods. They're keeping a low fire going under the chili and circling each other on a cribbage board. It's not like number three to miss supper, but they're not quite nervous about it yet.

Finally, number three shows up, and he's all smiles. He got his buck all right, at about sundown, and he's been taking his sweet old time gutting it out under an inspirational moon and dragging it in with the same delicious slowness that he smokes a good cigar. They hoist it up on the meat pole, and over chili he tells the other two how it came to be.

Confident in his whitetail savvy, he had scouted well and put himself where there was a generous chance of seeing deer. Then, that afternoon, he saturated a rag with buck scent, weighed it down and dragged it around, laying a heavy trail. After that, he climbed up to his stand and daubed a spot or two of porcupine scent behind each ear, in a manner of speaking. He pulled out a pair of rattling antlers and let go at them hard. He ground and clashed them ten seconds at a time between five-minute intervals. He got out his grunt call and blew short grunts, half a second in duration, six at a time every ten minutes. And, pretty soon, this big buck comes out, not fast but real steady, and that, as he said over and over again, was that.

don't ask

NOVEMBER 27

Well, on Monday morning the alarm clock went off like fingernails on a blackboard, so I got up, went to work and worked, came home and went to bed. Then it was Tuesday. The alarm clock went off like a cat with its tail in a sausage grinder, so I got up, drank a cup of coffee, went to work and worked, came home, hung my hunting clothes out on the clothesline, helped the kid with her spelling, ate supper and went to bed.

Then it was Wednesday. The alarm clock went off, brief and dismal, like a baby at a baptism, so I got up, had a piece of toast, kissed my wife, went to work and worked, came home, sighted in my deer rifle, ate supper and went to bed. Then it was Thursday. The alarm clock went off like an owl at an eagles convention, so I got up, ate a pancake, went to work and worked, came home, hauled wood, cleaned out the fireplace, played checkers with the kid, made a phone call, ate supper and went to bed. Then it was Friday. The alarm clock went off like two crows disputing a roadkill, so I got up, ate a doughnut, went to work and worked, got paid, stopped for a beer, went home, ate supper, said my prayers and went to bed.

Then it was Saturday. I got up before the clock did, fixed an omelet, made sandwiches, got dressed, packed my rifle, drove to my deer stand, climbed the ladder and fell asleep. When I woke up, there were deer tracks everywhere and a guy looking up my tree, so I went home, ate supper and went to bed. Then it was Sunday. The alarm went off like a mosquito doing Shakespeare, so I got up, went to the woods, walked a thousand miles in one-inch increments, saw lots of stuff but no deer, went home, read a story to the kid, ate supper and went to bed. How about you?

it's quite obvious

NOVEMBER 28

We go to this fish and game show in the gymnasium of the local college a couple of towns over, and they have this indoor trout pond there for kids. My eleven-year-old, who's up to her ankles in rehearsals for the upcoming Nutcracker ballet — she's in the party scene — naturally takes a night off to come along, though she'll probably have to do a hundred laps for it. Anyway, she lucks on to a nice little fish, all dog-food fed, and the guy in charge goes to wrap it up. She says to put it back.

"But you get to keep this," says the well-meaning gent.

"No," says my kid, "we release our trout." He is insistent, but she is adamant, and while you can argue with the ladies in my family, you don't ever win one, so he puts the fish in the bubbling pond to be caught again. It's enough to pop the buttons on an old man's shirt.

This kid of mine. She plays the piano and she paddles a canoe. She sings in the choir and she plinks arrows in a bullseye as often as it works out that way. She's a skier, a swimmer and a fisherman. She wishes eleven-year-olds could hunt deer with their dads, and she owes it all to me.

This kid of mine builds wood duck nests, follows deer trails, spots eagles from a couple of miles off, cooks beans on a campfire, reads the words of Pat McManus clean off a page. She's training a black Lab pup to fetch, and she knows everybody on the DU committee by their first names. In her hope chest, with all the other stuff, there's a jackknife, her first snowshoes and paddle, and I taught her all she knows. When her friends come for supper, and she says, "Dad, did we shoot this?" her friends say yuk, and she has no idea why.

I know a father shouldn't brag about his kid, so I'll stop here.

an out-of-body experience

NOVEMBER 29

Every year I want to get my deer so badly, but then I don't, and the sun goes down, and the fire goes out, and in the dark, with the truth right there in front of me like an antiquated cow, I kick myself for being so stupid. My disappointment is as big as a capsized tugboat and enough to bring about the collapse of my nervous system. But I am well insured with a wonder-welling heart, and my luck turned around this year, and all my troubles are behind me. Tonight we're having venison for supper.

We're going to brown two pounds of my deer's hamburger, half a diced onion, some cut-up celery, a cup of mushrooms and some salt and pepper. We're going to cook it until the vegetables are tender, and we're going to drain off all the fat. Then we're going to cook two cups of wild rice in two cups of water until it's tender. We're going to mix two cans (do you sense a trend here?) of cream of mushroom soup with two cans of milk and heat that up. Finally we're going to forcibly unite everything and dump it into a casserole dish and let it heat up, through and through and through.

If you're partial to onions, add as many as you like. If mushrooms are your cup of tea, don't stop where we do. And so on and so forth. And if your luck has continued its downward spiral, if you missed your buck this year, and you've gotten over it by now, go ahead and substitute a couple of pounds of beef hamburger for the deer meat. Then, while the radio is dancing some good old rock-and-roll or equally fine country tunes, while the homemade bread is getting done and a bottle of wine is cooling in a snowbank, set the table and, once again, float to the moon.

on thin ice

NOVEMBER 30

When you are committed, as we are committed, to living the gift of time to its utmost, there is no business like snow business. Consequently, a bunch of us regulars are hunkered down here at Mom's Cafe over on Main Street, waiting for the ice on Lost Lake to stiffen up enough to go fishing on. This is a long wait, an extravagant wait, one that passes with the slowness of an incoming tax refund. We measure the moments by counting the stars, one by one (an interesting way we have of passing the time between the end of deer season and ice-up), and hunkering down, in the way of outdoor sporting people everywhere.

The Professor, munching absentmindedly on a bagel, gives us a penetrating yawn and reminds us that the edge of a warm ice auger blade is more likely to chip than a cold one, so we should keep our augers outside awhile before putting them to use.

Gladys gracefully stretches and furthermores that we should also, each time we get home, wipe off the blade with a rag soaked in floor wax to keep it from rusting. Then Mom comes around like a pondering Buddha to pour refills. He puts in his two cents' worth by giving us a thorough and sober account of how to keep ice from forming in our fishing holes by filling a small cloth bag with salt and floating it thereon. "A Bull Durham bag used to be just right," he sighs.

I don't know what happens next because they send me out to the bay with a chisel to see how things are progressing. This worries me some, as you can imagine, because I figure civilization can't advance without me around, but I'll keep you posted as best I can.

MACIEJ

the ice age

DECEMBER 1

On the one hand, December is masterfully conceived and skillfully executed. On the other, it is an odorless, colorless compound that attacks the nervous system when inhaled or absorbed through the skin. It depends on how you look at it. From a purely bipartisan point of view, it is a month steeped in mystery, grace, meaning and finality, and we've had to scramble to get here.

In a year that's happened too fast for evaluation, December has come upon us by spontaneous combustion. Yet the cold flame of a December sunrise is only a guess at best. Even birds doubt a December sunrise. Resting on the brink of a bird feeder, they talk it over. Finally, one takes the plunge and says, "Yes, this is the dawn, all right." Others say, "Nope, not yet," and go back to bed.

No matter how you look at it, December lets the cold in, creating a tremble of excitement, a tremble of clouds rolling, a tremble of winds and jingling bells. Mars joins Jupiter in the evening sky. Serious icicles sprout like weeds. Sled-riding kids slide across and down the glittering specifics of a year grown suddenly old. No matter how you look at it, each of those snowflakes has taken roughly fifteen minutes to form and drops a couple of miles an hour, adding up. The last robin has officially dangled its last worm, and the unwashed threads of autumn are things of the past.

December's suns cast long shadows, and though at times we'd consider commingling with sleeping groundhogs, we'll basically pull out the long underwear, buckle up the snow boots, deck the halls, give a rebel yell, and make the most of this month of giving and sharing, this month of coming home, this month of The Cold Moon, The Moon of Popping Trees. At least that's what we here at Lost Lake do with December, and I suppose that's about what you do with it where you live, too.

another wise man

DECEMBER 2

Though it is early in the month, and most of us are firmly en route through the knotted tunnels of December, there's a fellow here at Lost Lake whose senses are reeling. He's feeling like a sinkful of dirty dishes, a house of dark smudges in need of cleaning. Christmas is around the corner and three weeks down the road, and he's the only person in the universe who hasn't yet bought presents for his kids. He would rather face the defensive line of the Minnesota Vikings all alone than go shopping. He would rather get into the ring with a sumo wrestler. He would. And what's he going to do? He's going to clean and order his tackle box, because when he cleans and orders his tackle box he cleans and orders himself.

Then it hits him. He'll give those kids a gift of adventure. He'll take them from a life of watching to a life of doing. He'll make presents of zoo-going and stone-skipping and eagle-watching. He'll prop them up with pine trees. Include gifts of beauty, like the splendor of wild roses, ripening blueberries and marshmallows roasting over open fires. He writes that down so he doesn't forget it.

He'll give them gifts of gratitude, teaching them that the Earth is sacred ground, and they must mind their manners when they're on it. He'll give them gifts of humor. Take them to where they can giggle at the work of long-tongued toads. Yes. He'll give them patience, too. Take them fishing and allow them the singular pleasure of waiting for fish to bite. He'll give them responsibility, put them in charge of moon-glowing campfires. He'll give them independence and the North Wind for when they're alone and the night holds its breath. He'll wrap it up with himself. He will. He will! He'll give them gifts of time. By Golly, Miss Molly, he will!

in the promised land

DECEMBER 3

It's been a long time coming, this good-time, top-water, hard-water ice-fishing time that the turning axle of the earth has finally rolled around to us again. And nobody's happier about that than my ice-fishing neighbor, good ol' Gladys, who's not that old nor quite that good, for all I know.

Gladys knows all about wishing and all about the mysteriousness of wishes coming true, and for her this is it. She is particularly excited about the possibility of hooking onto a couple of early-ice northern pike, the practice of which is an endless delight where she is concerned.

For some reason not entirely clear to Gladys, nor to me either, this first, conservative ice signals a lovely change in the behavior of northerns. Now they shed their laziness to become deliciously aggressive feeders. Believe me, with the decline of so much of the weed cover that previously concealed so many of their minnow dinners, they can afford to. Truly, according to Gladys, the big fish start behaving like hungry herds of sixth graders in a pizza parlor.

For this early kind of ice fishing, Gladys goes hunting for what weed beds still exist down there, because that's where little fish are hanging out, and so it follows that is where the northerns will be taking up their high-level positions on the food chain. She punches a hole along the edge of one of these weed beds or over an open pocket therein. To a tip-up she deftly sticks a good-sized golden shiner or an equally attractive frozen smelt. And there she sits, wrapped in an army-surplus parka, sitting on a five-gallon pickle pail, her nose as red as a poinsettia. And every once in a while she'll jiggle the minnow, or the smelt, into motion, and leave the rest to the angels.

snowbound

DECEMBER 4

I need to fill this page in a hurry. I'm waiting for someone, and I want to get right out and effectively test the theory that crappies are biting on the northwest corner of Whatchamacallit Bay, so let's suppose you are driving along in your jalopy. Without passing judgment on you, let us further suppose that, as usual, your foot is heavy. Your pedal is, in fact, to the metal. You are leaving November quickly, too quickly for conditions, and rounding the corner of December where the roads are snow-covered and icy. This catches you by surprise. Heaven knows why. Your jalopy does a little dipsy doodle and, kerplunk, you're stuck. You're good and stuck. Stuck in the snow and the wind and left out in the cold.

This is disappointing. And the disappointment of it, the heart-pumping, blood-rushing disappointment of this sticky stuck, brings wrinkles to your brow. You say gosh and gee whiz. In a worst-case scenario, you are defenseless and must halloo for help in the empty, early darkness of December. Bummer.

A fifty-pound sack of sand carried in the trunk of your car or in the back of your pickup truck is often very useful to people stuck on snow-covered and icy fields of bad dreams. But maybe your back is bad and you can't lift a fifty-pound sack of sand. Maybe you don't have room for one. Then substitute a couple of round boxes of regular table salt. Some of that sprinkled fore and aft of your tires can sometimes set you free. Or you may prefer to rinse out a large, plastic liquid washday detergent container and fill it with a combination of salt and sand. That will get you similar results when you round the corner of December in too big a hurry.

That about does it. We've filled our page, though that's as far as I was going with this anyway. The tow truck's here.

getting out while the getting's good

DECEMBER 5

I am at the Elkhorn Tavern and Wildlife Museum, working up the ambition to commence my Christmas shopping, when in comes Arnold and puts a damper on my day. He wants me to attend the Woodcutters Community Christmas Party at the Town Hall. I qualify because once I cut down a popple tree that fell on the REA lines, shutting off electric power to twenty square miles just as the ladies were making dinner. Uffda!

I remember the last Woodcutters party. There were thirty souls in attendance counting dogs, woodcutters arguing the merits and demerits of one thing or another, a gaggle of spouses and a herd of little kids in a search and destroy mode. The Town Hall was a whirlwind of cooking, cleaning, argumentation, conversation, meditation, celebration, rioting kids and bone-stealing dogs.

There were folks smoking in the non-smoking section, explaining that nicotine acid is really pure niacin, an important B-complex vitamin. Before the Christmas geese — three Canadas and two snows — were half done, three guys were slumped comatose out on the front porch. Santa Claus, who looked an awful lot like Arnold, sat staring into the fireplace, his eyes dancing like marbles in a blender. I'm pretty sure I saw two faint wisps of smoke coming from his ears. One fellow looked up, thought he was surrounded, and did a swan dive out the picture window.

"Bah! " I say to Arnold, buying him a shorty, "but I think I'll pass this year and celebrate where it's peaceful and a little more filled with the true spirit of the holidays. Then I plant a kiss on his grizzled cheek, effectively eliminating my name from future consideration and adding immeasurably to the intensity of the tic that danced periodically between his nose and earlobes.

rise and shine

DECEMBER 6

You say you're all in and tuckered out? You say you've put on a couple of pounds? You say what hair hasn't fallen out is turning gray, and the wrinkles in your face are deep enough to hide pennies? You say you're dreading snow? And ice? You say you've looked over your shoulder at the year that was and for every inch you've gained, you've lost two? You say you need a season to be jolly in, but the thought of Christmas sends shivers up your spine? You say the portages you travel are longer and uphill both ways? You say the ground beneath your sleeping bag is hard and lumpy and the real estate of your mind is full of vacant lots?

You say your casting arm is shot? The last time you went fishing you hooked a cottonwood tree, an oak and a couple of willows, and that's it? You say the cold is colder than it used to be, and the damp damper, and you just figured out there are ten thousand lakes in the world you're never going to fish in? You say the average goose hunter bagged 2.5 geese this year, and you'd like to know who in the hell got yours? You say the volume of your life can't fill the pages of a short short story, and if it did there wouldn't be a surprise in it anywhere? You say you missed your buck again this year, and the eye doctor upped the thickness of your glasses, and at the mall a little old lady helped you to your car? You say you're beat down? Your life's sailed out of reach?

Well, say no more. Spin your head around, Buckaroo. Put a smile on your kisser. Put a wiggle in your heart. There's an expedition of winter ahead. It can't go on without you. There's an adventure of winter on the horizon, and you're in the picture. There's a safari of winter just around the corner. So, don't anybody write anybody's epitaph just yet. It's nice out here. It is. Ride out the storm, tread water like a mosquito, buzz like a bumblebee and wake me when it's over.

a close call

DECEMBER 7

A hundred yards from my house, down past the sauna, down past the garden, is a pond. It's a small pond, a nice pond, and a bunch of neighboring kids, friends of my daughter, come to splash around in it in the summertime and to skate on it now in December. The ice is plenty thick.

Today my family is off to town, and I am home alone, except for a pondful of ice-skating kids. They don't bother me. After a while, though, they come trooping up to the house, interrupting the philosophical reflections I am having in front of the fireplace. They are understandably in need of hot chocolate, so I make some from the recipe on the box and dish it out. But this one little girl takes a sip and says with a predatory gleam in her eye, "Hey, this ain't nothing like the stuff my mom makes." And, simultaneously, I get a likewise noisy chorus of cheeky flak from the whole bunch of them who have tried and found me guilty of high crimes and chocolate misdemeanors.

"Okay, hotshot," I fire back at the kid to stem the undertow of discontent. "How's it supposed to go?" "Well," says the squirt from memory, "my mom mixes together an eight-quart box of instant, non-fat dry milk, a sixteen-ounce box of Nestle's Quik, a six-ounce jar of non-fat coffee lightener and a cup of powdered sugar and stores it in a covered container. And when the gang comes to my house or when we go camping, she puts half a cup in each cup and fills it with hot water. Yum-yum."

"Yum," they all say.

So I promise to follow suit henceforth and notice a relaxation of tension around the place. And with a little diligence and legwork, you, too, can avoid the disagreeable experience of rejection by making your hot chocolate the same way this kid's mother makes hers.

trifles

DECEMBER 8

It's starting to snow again here at Lost Lake, and since there's no basketball game tonight, the kids up at the high school are praying for a blizzard and a couple of days off. It's a war of prayers, since their mothers are sure enough working on the opposite. Actually, we've all got that snowy-day feeling, and a bunch of us regulars have come off the lake for coffee at Mom's Cafe over on Main Street.

One of the boys, being a bowhunter, is demonstrating how he avoids cutting his fingers and bleeding all over the place when he screws on new broadheads, or screws them off, by sticking them into a two-inch thickness of Styrofoam and spinning the shaft one way or the other, depending. We all think that is a fine idea and agree to do likewise from now on.

Harold, eager to participate in the conversation, tells us how to make our rusty, squeaky fishing pliers as good as new by putting them in the pocket of an old pair of pants headed for Monday's wash and oiling them a little when they come out. That brought an intermittent round of applause from most of us, since he described our pliers' plight perfectly and saved us the price of new ones.

"Shucks," says Uncle Jake after the raw hush of silence we observe when Mom is refilling our coffee cups. "If I'd known you was looking for helpful hints, I'd have told you how I use old eyeglass cases as nifty little first-aid kits."

"Humph," quibbles Gladys, my ice-fishing neighbor, playing out the theme and getting in her two cents' worth. "And I'd have told you how I use my old eyeglass cases as nifty little tackle boxes." To keep the peace, we agree we'll all use our old eyeglass cases as nifty little first-aid kits and as nifty little tackle boxes. Then we get back to the more serious business of watching the snow fall.

a personal philosophy

DECEMBER 9

Partaking in a celebration of outdoor adventure, we have ridden our snowmobiles over to Lost Lake's Elkhorn Tavern and Wildlife Museum. This is a nice establishment. The jukebox wails out country tunes like a family of coyotes lined up against the moon. The warm air smells of pleasure, and there's an ever-present layer of smoke that lends a green sheen to the place. The Professor, who led the caravan to this common stopover, racks up the balls on the old pool table.

Pete, the proprietor is getting a jump on the holiday season by putting up a Christmas tree on the little bandstand in the northeast corner. Naturally we help out but, this being somewhat on the early side, we express our concern that the tree will lose its needled niceness by the time our annual New Year's Eve combination Mardi Gras and Luau extravaganza rolls around.

The Professor, attempting to keep the fifteen ball from running off by itself into a side pocket, looks up and gives us a lesson on Christmas tree preservation. He says to take a gallon of water and to it add two cups of white Karo syrup, a cup of Listerine (who knows why?) and four ground up, iron-supplemented multi-vitamins. He goes on to say that we should also cut an inch or two off the bottom of the trunk, put the tree in a bucket of the stuff and don't let it run dry.

We don't doubt the old boy for a minute and scatter all over town for the ingredients. Upon our return, he reminds us while miscuing on an easy straightaway shot that Pete could keep his stinking cat off the tree, too, by posting bits of garlic cloves on it here and there. "Remember," he says, as he often does, "how you perform the simplest of your daily tasks speaks very loudly about what kind of person you are." We drink to that, though we're not quite sure what he means by it.

a sense of regret

DECEMBER 10

I strap on my snowshoes and hike from my end of the lake around to the town end, which leaves me feeling truly alive, except for my legs and bottom half, which are shot. I get to Mom's Cafe over on Main Street, and there's my Uncle Jake, reading the morning paper.

"You find a wooly mammoth," he moans to nobody in particular and everybody in general, "and nine times out of ten someone will make a big deal out of it. Put it in the paper. Set up a lemonade stand. Sell souvenirs. But you catch onto a northern pike, and you'll be ho-hummed to death in a matter of minutes, and it's not fair. Northerns have been around for twenty million years and maybe more, which is sixteen million longer than these debutante wooly mammoths."

With Jake it's hard to tell, but if he's making the point that the northern pike is a celebration of a fish, he has it right. They're solitary, lurking lunkers that feed mostly on other gamefish, but ambush frogs, too, and snakes and crayfish and small animals like muskrats and baby ducks. They grow to over three feet and twenty pounds plus, though I have not personally witnessed it. The record is forty-something.

Northerns, often low-rated and berated, are brawling, wonderful fish. No other fish has been the subject of as many myths, legends, fables, tall tales and downright lies. Indian tribes shunned certain bad-medicine lakes that were reported to hold northerns big enough to swallow whole canoes and anybody in them.

Then I get to thinking about how northerns have giant, yawning mouths, evil eyes and low, flat foreheads, when I glance over at my uncle, who's eating a donut, and I get this uncontrollable urge to cast a red and white Daredevil in his general direction.

maybe tomorrow

DECEMBER 11

It's a snowshoe walking day, so I walk. It's a day to leave work and worry and walk through the falling snow into the hills outside of town. I end up at the cemetery and wander through the front yards and around the stones that mark those souls whose journeys ended here. Resting, I take coffee and a sandwich from my pack and lean against a tall white marker. This is Jackson. Father. He has been here fifty-three years. Next to us is Jackson. Mother. She joined her husband here thirty years ago. Snow-covered sentries watch over us, rich and poor, young and old. Baby girl Hower. 1948. Grandmother Dzikonski. 1989. Families lie in final bond with perfect strangers. Some I know. George over there. And Bud. I miss Bud sometimes.

I wonder how it will happen to me, and when. Probably one day when I'm splitting wood or when I'm raking leaves on a Saturday, my heart in a duck blind. There will come a tap on my shoulder and a whisper, "Let's go." The inconvenience of it. "Wait a minute," I'll say. "Give me some time, a little more time. Let me sit in a tree once more to watch a doe and fawn feed, to hear a buck snort. Let me paddle again a canoe full of decoys.

Hold on! There must be time yet for a run to the river and a last cast. Let me smell bacon and eggs over a campfire, and throw one last stick to the dog to fetch and one last ball to my kid. They won't understand."

On the other hand, I've shot a couple of nice bucks in my day. I've paddled through glorious sunsets, walked through partridge woods and cornfields busting with pheasants. I've lain under the Northern Lights and slept with loons on moonlit lakes. "But it's not enough," I'll say, as tough as I can. "Somewhere there's a spring around the corner and robins and frogs and dandelions. I'll come right along," I'll tell the Tapper, "but I'll need a little time."

the inside scoop

DECEMBER 12

The day is an unblinking blue between the trees, and a cold wind is flattening the grass not already flattened by snow. It's an ice-fishing day, so I hike through the cemetery to Gladys'. For her and me, ice fishing is one of our stronger weaknesses. "C'mon, Gladys," I yell. "Let's go crappie fishing on this new ice." She scrapes a raffle of egg shells and orange peels off the dinette, says okey-dokey, and off we go.

Usually we fish together, but on our own terms. In a couple of weeks, however, a guy from the TV station in town is coming out to fish with me, and Gladys doesn't want me to blot the reputation of Lost Lake. She is, consequently, making a nuisance of herself, putzing here and there, hovering over my shoulder and scribbling misdirected postcards in my ear.

"Over this new ice," she tells me, "crappies will congregate near their springtime spawning beds — shallow bays and flats — and the best time to catch them is the first hour before sunup and an hour before sundown and a couple after it. Use this little rod and ultralight spinning reel with the drag set just right. Put on one-pound test, a half-inch sponge bobber, a little bitty split shot, and a number six short-shanked hook loaded with a two-inch shiner. Adjust the depth continually until you get a nibble. And when you do, don't jerk the hook to set it, but wait a second and sharply lift it up."

"For heaven's sake," I tell her, "I have caught a few crappies on new ice in my lifetime."

"Don't fret, deary," she says, "God and me, we take care of fools and fishermen." To tell you the honest truth, I'm not real sure which one of those she considers me.

up in arms

DECEMBER 13

Imagine, if you will, that an adult citizen — let us say, in this case, a woman — who has never before owned one, has decided she wants a shotgun. Perhaps she has wanted one since her father took her brothers hunting and left her home with dolls and dirty dishes. Perhaps her husband and children hunt and leave her home alone with the laundry and dirty dishes. Though honorable tasks, she's thinking enough is enough and to heck with that noise.

This citizen is a responsible citizen, so she carefully considers the grave responsibilities of gun ownership. Then, a woman of the modern era, she goes hence and thus and gets it. Let us say it is a sweet little .20-gauge. Maybe an over and under. Maybe a side-by-side.

Immediately she signs up for a hunter's safety course offered by the Department of Natural Resources. Let us say, to make a point, that these classes do not begin until two weeks from next Thursday. What does she do in the meantime?

Well, she cleans the gun. A gun that's cleaned often and well will last this citizen her lifetime. She can bequeath it to her daughter when the time comes. While she's doing this, she practices the most important of all safe firearm handling commandments, which is never to allow this gun to point at anything she doesn't intend to shoot. And she reminds herself that the safety on this sweet little .20-gauge is nothing but a mechanical device subject to failure, and she must never rely on it. As she does not store open gasoline cans next to the fireplace, she locks her gun up and caches the ammunition far away from it.

This citizen has no need to rely on Santa Claus for what she wants, yet right around Christmas time, all this stuff is nice to know.

on thin ice

DECEMBER 14

It was Otto in a mood. He paced. He drummed "Camptown Races" on the countertop with his fingers. He smoked incessantly, though he had never smoked before. It was obvious that things were not going well with him.

"What's up, Otto?" I asked, and this is what he said.

"Most of the time, on weekends, ice fishing for me is a leisured, laid-back affair. Once I get my hook down the hole, I am free to wander the ice and snozzle with others like myself. But sometimes there's too much space between weekends, and I lose control and play hooky from work. When I do that, there comes a sense of urgency to my fishing, perhaps to compensate for the time I have stolen.

"This hurry-up business is especially hard on bluegill fishermen, as I was that day. Bluegills hit at one depth one day and at a different one the next. One day they bite on a teardrop of one color, and on the next a teardrop of another color, or no teardrop at all, but an ice fly. By the time I have it figured, it's time to punch out.

"Then I overheard at the office one day how to pre-rig a line with one color lure at one depth and another of another color higher or lower. And on a second line to affix another combo, only differently. So I put a frog in my throat, called in ill and did just that. Before my teeth began to chatter and it was time for my first coffee break, I had the situation laid out. Except, when I was on my knees pulling up another beautiful bluegill, I found myself nose to nose with my boss doing likewise. What could I do but slide my catch over the ice to him and head for my truck?"

on a midnight clear …

DECEMBER 15

Strings of lights twitter like a ramshackle ride at the county fair. The air bulges and the world outside is full of the sounds of Christmas. Listen. You might hear a covey of six-year-olds, perched upon a snowbank, passionately practicing for the upcoming program:

Hark the herald angels sing,
Glory to the newborn king.
Peas on earth and mercy mild,
God and sitters reconciled.

If you listen, you might hear jingling bells and laughter as elegant as dragonflies, and now and then, like a glass of cold water, a sob, somewhere, of loneliness. You might hear, too, the crunch of a rickety grocery cart, piled with figs and sweet potatoes, roaming the frozen parking lot of some celestial supermarket. You might hear the racket of angels' wings deep in piney woods, and the hush of inner expectations (Dear Santa,) and tongue-tied fantasies (Hey, Santa Claus) and children's dreams taking flight (I've been good).

The world outside is equally full with the sights of Christmas. You don't have to look too hard to find glitzy, good-time trees, tinseled garlands, candles lit and old hands, cracked with labor, wrapping packages like a painting on the wall, benedictions and the fee-fi-fo-fums of expanding credit. If you look closer, you might spot a kid reaching up to grab a handful of stars. (In the northwest, Cygnus the swan is stretching its wings along the lower reaches of the horizon. You might call it the Northern Cross.)

If you peer closer yet, you might see shoes shined for midnight Mass, breathless promises you could nail to a two-by-four, looks you could pour on pancakes, and without so much as a magnifying glass, you might spot the star of Bethlehem where it's been all along — in the tough-cookie corners of your heart.

a bum deal

DECEMBER 16

I wish I had a better understanding, a more special knowledge, of birds and bird life. Of mergansers and chickadees and eagles. Of bluebirds and falcons and pheasants and quail. Of partridges and loons and mallards. Of wild turkeys and grosbeaks and wrens and warblers. I wish I could walk through the woods or work in the garden and to a cheep or chirp or tweet, say, "By golly, that's a … whachamacallit," and hit the nail on the head.

I wish I knew more of animals and had a better notion of their ways. Of white-tailed deer and moose and elk and bears. Of wolves and bobcats and coyotes and otters and skunks. Of buffalo. Of jackrabbits. I wish I could hear a grunt or a groan or a screech, or see some sign in the snow or mud, and think to myself, "Son of a gun, if that isn't a so-and-so." I do. And I wish I had a keener grasp of fish and what they do outside a frying pan. Of trout and walleyes and northern pike. Of bass, bluegills and bullheads. I wish I knew the names of wildflowers and mushrooms and grasses and bees and butterflies. And frogs. And bugs.

I wish I could track the stars across the oceans of the skies and chart the courses of the constellations. Of Orion and the Great Bear and Casseopeia. I wish I could read the clouds with some perception. Billowy stratus. Cumulus. Cirrus. Nimbus. I wish I could look up and say with accuracy and confidence, "It'll rain in a week and a half." I wish I could read the wind and interpret the tides.

I wish there was more time, more time than a mere lifetime, to learn and understand and do. We open the book of our lives, the Book of Wonders, and never get past the first chapter. Before you know it, it's the first day of winter, and we're old and gray and full of sleep, or the woodpile runs low, and we're done for.

the great escape

DECEMBER 17

Without ice fishing, my neighbor Gladys' life would be as hollow as a jack-o-lantern's. I stop over to her house the other day with eggs from my wife's chickens. She's making her annual Christmas call to her sister Alyse, who lives in Florida and hasn't seen ice in years. It sounds as if it's going to be a long, one-sided conversation, so I pour myself a cup of coffee and sit down.

She's telling her sister that she'll be spending the holidays ice fishing and that she's going out late this afternoon for walleyes, because now's when she catches the biggest and the mostest fish. She's going to this shallow, weedy, cabin-ringed lake that hardens up early. Weed pockets provide the most critical element in a walleye's life, namely minnows. And, she adds, walleyes bite the best at dawn or dusk and on overcast days, when the sky is low, gray and uneasy.

I pour myself another cup as Gladys tells Alyse that she puts twenty-pound braided line on her tip-up with an eight-pound, three-foot monofilament leader. Then she hooks a shiner in front of the dorsal fin on a #8 hook. She says that when a walleye takes the bait, she lets it run until it stops and starts to run again, and then she gently sets the hook with a quick snap of the wrist.

Just then, the sun goes under a cloud, and all this talk about fishing starts a stampede of adrenalin coursing through my body, so I head for the door. "Where ya goin', ya bum!" Gladys yells. It's refreshing to find such downright honesty in this day and age.

"Nowhere," I say, and hot-foot through the cemetery to my place, and then to this shallow, weedy, cabin-ringed lake that hardens up early.

the promised land

DECEMBER 18

Carpe Diem reads the sweatshirt on a body loaded down with Christmas presents strolling down a hall at the mall. *Seize the day.* Seize the day indeed, so I do. I get the kids and head for The River.

Every time I look at those waves and wrinkles there, I feel a small uneasiness. I get to wondering why so many of us are satisfied to live out our lives without getting involved in the hands-on and philosophical aspect of things. Like floating, shifting, faceless clouds, we don't get tangled up in things we ought to, and mostly, we get away with it, even when the stakes are high. We, your everyday outdoorsmen and women, I'm talking about.

The nitty, no-nonsense gritty situation is this. If we truly wish to preserve the wild places, we have to take our kids camping in them. If we are sincere in our efforts to make our lakes and rivers clean forever, we have to take our kids paddling on and fishing in them. If we want to keep wild animals in the wild and birds bountiful, we have to take our sons and daughters hunting for them. If we want the memories to roll on, the traditions to continue, we can't rely on the fickle nature of politics and politicians. We can't lay the responsibilities of conservation at the feet of anonymous someone elses.

In the American tradition of rugged individualism, the duty to preserve the natural state of things is yours alone. It is mine alone. The hope, the salvation of our children — all children, those of inner cities and single-parent families, too — and the great out-of-doors (for of what value is life without the out-of-doors?) lies with you and me. We have to teach our kids today. We have to lead them today. The future of their trees, of their fishing waters, of their sky-blue skies, of their hunting fields, lies with them through us. We must not fail them. We must not fail the universe.

sweet talk

DECEMBER 19

It is the bottom of the ninth, and everywhere in the world the bases are loaded.

We're having coffee here at Mom's Cafe over on Main Street when the Professor puts a poser before us. He tosses it like a knuckle ball, and it hangs there like the muddy question you laid on your dad when you hit him up for five bucks and the keys to the pickup on Saturday night.

"What's the most important piece of outdoor sporting equipment each of you owns?" he inquires of us, a particle of powdered doughnut dangling from his moustache. That's a good one. We squirm and wiggle and scratch and pull on our earlobes thinking it over. We don't look right at him, so he won't call on us.

Finally, my Uncle Jake takes the plunge. "It's your fishin' pole," he says with some satisfaction.

"Nope," insists Gladys. "Now that the ice is broken, it's your tip-ups."

"No," claims Ramona, the dark-haired lady. "It's your knife." Then we all join in, and the debate accelerates to bows and arrows and axes and tackle boxes and compasses and matches and so on and so on.

"Not at all," corrects the Professor, who always knows the answers to his questions. "It's your ballpoint pen." This leaves us blinking in confusion, but he explains that as active, participating sporting men and women, each of us should realize how much hammer-handle clout we have in the managing of our natural resources, in setting guidelines for hunting, fishing and trapping.

"Lawmakers listen," he tells us. "If the majority of the people voice opposition to hunting and fishing, if enough polluters plead their causes, then that's the way it'll be. The opposite is also true, of course."

"So speak up," he says, "speak out and speak often. Make sense and make a difference. Make yourself heard where it will do some good."

Isn't he amazing?

a piece of the action

DECEMBER 20

The sun and the moon and Sagittarius, the celebrated bow and arrow shooter of the night skies, have lined themselves up like ducks in a row to signal the first day of winter, and we don't mind it a bit. Winter is not a heartless beast that locks us up like wickless candles in dresser drawers, but a lamp burning on a foggy night.

Darkness is now a consistent thing, and days are as short as gratitude, but get out anyhow and make a snowball. Throw it. Make a snowman. Though hungry shadows gnaw at each end of the sun's rotation, haul out holly and deck the halls. Cover perfectly poetical trees with ropes of popcorn and cranberries and lights the color of peach blossoms. These are days and nights of the first magnitude. Put your imagination to work, your ingenuity, your will power, your strength and speed. Hang a red-ribboned wreath from the front door.

Winter's here. Take a walk. Let your tracks criss-cross squirrel tracks that criss-cross rabbit tracks. Strap on the snowshoes. Bring out the skis. Skate. Chip holes in the ice, drop your doubts down there and watch them scatter. You are no ordinary hero, so light a yule log and share its warmth and its hope with those you love. Dust the dust off the toboggan. Build a fort, gas up a snowmobile. Lie down on the snow and make an angel.

Winter's here. It's the only star in our sky, so make a wish on it. Hang your hopes on it and dangle your dreams from it. Make it happen, for busyness is the solution to the riddles of life. It sustains the body in its continuing efforts to catch up with the soul, and how far can you go, anyway, when you don't put your heart into something?

a goosebumps affair

21 DECEMBER

We have rounded, as you know, the corner of winter, and here at Lost Lake, it's cold. It's so cold it's the topic at every meal. This is the home of cold. Other towns in need of cold import it from here, put it in a warehouse and let it out as needed. It's so cold we can't let the children out to play. No matter how we dress them, in a matter of minutes they're kidsickles.

It's so cold cusswords freeze in their tracks and drop in piles all over the place. The ladies over at the church are dreading the January thaw. It's so cold we've had to install tank heaters on the dogsleds to get them started in the morning. Even then, it's iffy. We had to bake the candles on my wife's birthday cake three hours each at 350 degrees before they'd burn. That took a long time. It's so cold some folks are heading to Siberia for suntans. It's so cold here the sun quit altogether. It moved to a crummy motel in Florida. It's colder than a money lender's heart.

It's so cold havoc doesn't run wild. It can't. It creeps in like an old man, wraps an afghan around its shoulders and sips hot soup. If you spit against the wind, it'll freeze, come back at you and knock a tooth out. It's so cold polar bears are moving in. They're selling frozen daiquiris on street corners in a state of ecstasy. It's that cold.

It's cold wide and it's cold deep. To get closer to hell, water in the well 180 feet down sank clear out of sight. There's nothing on TV but snow. Fax machines are pumping out frantic calls for hot water bottles. Foxes take turns being each other's fur coats. In suicidal attempts to get warm, snowmen are sneaking into saunas. We put up the flag and it flew south, so if you're coming for coffee, dress warm and drive careful.

cosmic forces

22 DECEMBER

On this side of the mountain it's the season, and what's happening out there, anyway, besides the decking of halls? Well, for one thing, we've got a little more than nine hours of daylight and about fifteen of the other stuff. And wintry stars, delicious as Christmas cookies, seem so close sometimes we can climb up a snowbank, gather a basketful and string them on our apple trees as temporary substitutes for the far-away blooming blossoms of spring.

To the delight of ice-fishing folks everywhere, northern pike are active. Not so active, maybe, as they were last fall, but on the go nonetheless. And golden-eyed walleyes are nibbling, quite carefully, at minnow-tipped jigs and filling, once in a while, country kitchens with the fine smells of their frying.

And Procyon in the little dipper and Sirius in the big dipper and Betelgeuse on Orion's shoulder are making up the world famous Winter Triangle. And bobcats and coyotes are hunting for nearly invisible snowshoe rabbits, fairly famous themselves. And at busy bird feeders, nuthatches are clowning around upside down. Gray squirrels are feeder-raiding. Some people mind that. We don't. Kids, of course, are closet-peeking and present-rattling and being ever so good. To the delight of tired teachers and proud parents, they've just about wrapped up the last school programs and final Christmas concerts of the season.

And in case you haven't noticed, this year's earliest sunsets are almost sunsets of the past, when every little bit helps. The sun is creeping southward no more, but edging, with each sunset, a tiny bit to the north. We here at Lost Lake take some comfort in that, and I suppose you do where you live, too.

skunked

DECEMBER 23

I have come to Lost Lake crappie fishing through the ice, and if you had any feel for history and the role of the underdog, you'd be rooting for me. I'm crappie fishing, all right, but I'm not catching any crappies, and by the looks of things, I'm not going to be. I've got four-pound-test monofilament line tied to a number six bronze hook tipped with a world-class shiner minnow with a bronco-like enthusiasm. No crappies. I've got just enough split shot on, so the business end of the rig gets down to where it's going at a steady pace. No crappies. I've got a small, but big enough, bobber on to perfectly balance the shot. The slightest shadow of a crappie bite will bounce that bobber.

As I say, I'm peeved, and I have a right to be. I'm fishing by the book — a foot and a half off the bottom. No crappies. It was strange, but these are strange times we live in, so I'm packing it up and in, when along comes Ol' Gladys. With the to-do of a setting hen, she settles down atop a five-gallon pickle pail over the hole I've just vacated, rigs up the same way I did, but — what the heck! — without the bobber. Poor Ol' Gladys.

And instead of dropping her line freely to the bottom, she lets it out very, very slowly, keeping in full control of it all the time. Sure enough, about twenty feet down, she feels a tap-tap, and she flies into action. Quickly, she marks the depth with a bobber, gently but firmly sets the hook, and ices a beautiful fish. And then another. And another. "They're not a foot and a half off the bottom, don't you know," she hoots. "They're suspended." Well, naturally I want my hole back, but she won't budge. It leaves me with a lingering pain in the heart.

silent night …

DECEMBER 24

I have laid the last package under the Christmas tree. I have drunk the cold hot-chocolate milk left out for Santa Claus and half-eaten the gingerbread cookie. In the dim light of Christmas tree lights and a burning-down fire, I sit and I think. My kid will be twelve years old in a couple of weeks or so. My goodness. For this story, however, you might have to add ten or fifteen or twenty or even forty years for yours, or you might have to subtract.

However long ago it was (or will be), when you first laid your eyes on that wet, bug-eyed little button of a being that was your child, your heart filled with such a love you thought surely it could hold no more. And then came the kid's first Christmas. (You can substitute your choice of holidays here, if you wish.) And as you placed one-year-old gifts — tiny snowshoes, maybe, a wee backpack, a little-kid fishing book — under the tree, you were surprised to find that a love so great it could not grow had doubled. Later came a second Christmas and gifts of little skis and little poles and a sled and camouflage PJs, and sure enough, your love had multiplied even more.

With another Christmas, that love had jumped immeasurably. Under the tree went a Snoopy fishing pole and a pair of the world's smallest Sorels. There came another Christmas and ice skates. Another and a canoe paddle. Another and a BB gun. There were dolls and puzzles and stuff like that, too, of course, and always a love that grew and grew even more.

And here we are again, another year of days and nights gone by. A pair of bigger-kid skis is under the tree, and a classy fly rod and reel and love to the ninth power. My goodness! You know how it is, riding the wind, flying with eagles.

If you're still up, and even if you're not, from me and my family to you and yours, Merry Christmas. Happy Hanukkah. Happy anything and everything.

technical shortcomings

DECEMBER 25

Merry Christmas. Merry Christmas to you who hunted deer this year and must answer, "Nope," to the inevitable question. Merry Christmas to you who got neckties instead of fishing tackle. And to you whose pups ate the gift intended for your good-luck spouse, and to you who got the flu. Merry Christmas to you who didn't set the drag and lost a big one. And to you whose tent blew off with you in it. And whose snowmobile ran out of gas way out there. And to you whose paddle slipped from your grip and left you and led you fifteen miles downstream. And to you who lead partridge too little and ducks too much.

Merry Christmas to you whose boats leak, whose dogs have gone lame, whose shotguns have pockmarks and whose tackle boxes have tumbled down cliffs. Merry Christmas for your frozen fingers and toes, for every fire that didn't go, for every fish that didn't bite and for every pheasant that didn't flush.

Merry Christmas for everything you've ever been skunked at. Merry Christmas for every turkey that's seen you, every deer that's smelled you and every squirrel that's heard you step on a stick and snap it. And for stews you've burned and oatmeals you've boiled black over campfires. Merry Christmas for the inside straights you've drawn to, and every checker and crazy eights game you've lost. Merry Christmas for the kids who dropped your stuff overboard, who tipped your canoe, who lost your decoys and caught your waders on barbed wire. Merry Christmas for weddings during hunting season, for the ones that got away, for backlashes, for soggy sandwiches, for mud up to here and blowing sand and blizzards and dull knives and lost mittens and missed steelhead runs and broken rods. And picker bushes.

Merry Christmas.

pass the butter

DECEMBER 26

There is no one in all of Lost Lake we admire more than Mom of Mom's Cafe over on Main Street. Not even the members of our volunteer fire department, nor the congregation of scattered clergymen, all fine fishermen and women, are so admired.

To demonstrate, some of us regulars are bunched for breakfast over at Mom's on a very cold morning. We're having coffee and one-upping each other with our Christmas presents, while Mom prepares breakfast. As I say, it's cold outside, but the older duffers are going ice fishing anyway, and the younger ones skiing. Uncle Jake is heading out to flush an old rooster pheasant that's been teasing the dickens out of him all season, and a local tourist is going to take a Christmas beagle on a maiden voyage into the realms of rabbitdom. To a person, we understand that no matter how many new scarves and mittens and high-tech long underwears we've got on, there's no way we're going to stay warm out there if we don't stoke the furnaces in our bellies first. Fortunately, none of us are style-impaired, so we've come to feast on Mom's guaranteed-to-keep-you-warm omelet with the works and side orders of hash browns, bacon, sausage and toast.

"Your bodies produce heat as a by-product of the metabolic processes that release calories contained in the fine food you are about to eat. Amen," says Mom, with a flair for customer relations, coming out of the kitchen, his arms loaded with steaming plates. "The more you eat, the more heat you produce, and the more heat you produce, the more of it reaches to the surface of your skin and on out to the tips of your toes," he says, sounding an awful lot like our mothers, minus the tattoos, of course.

food for thought

DECEMBER 27

There is a flurry of snowfall this morning, a sudden swelling of off-white charm. Standing before the patio-door window, I watch it fall to the sidewalk and driveway that I scooped free of the stuff yesterday. I spot Gladys, too, taking the shortcut through the cemetery to my house. Every community, I think, has someone like Gladys, an older woman with a more or less mysterious manner that conveys the idea she knows or suspects a great deal more than she lets on.

Today she wants to go ice fishing for walleyes, and we go, though we're not doing so hot. Finally, my toes get cold and, speaking the obvious, I say to Gladys, "It seems as if the walleyes have left town, and we should do likewise." But no. She won't budge without supper in her pickle pail, so she does some adjusting.

She hooks up a bait, like the baits we've been using, only scaled way down, basically a very small bait. She drops it to the bottom and lets it lie there. By now she's got my interest in high gear. She gently lifts the rod tip about six inches, maybe not quite that much, and lets it hang there, except every few seconds she gives it a very weak twitch. Then she lays it back down and repeats the process, always in slow motion.

And, sure enough, on the second or third go-round, she hauls up a very nice (not a walleye but a) perch! Then another, and another, until we're both doing it and catching enough for her supper, supper for my family and supper even (though we naturally don't overdo it) for the neighbor kid who's chopping my firewood, so I can go walleye fishing with good ol' Gladys.

a reasonable miracle

DECEMBER 28

Specifically, it's an otter, at ease in the stream of its creation. It's not much to look at, though who am I to talk? At first glance, it appears to be a cross between a long-tailed dachshund and a giant weasel. Its coat is nice, a rich glistening brown broken by an irregular patch of lighter fur at its throat. But its face is as flat as a pancake, and its muzzle is bulldog stubby. Its upper lip is puffy with muscles and studded with thick, stiff whiskers. Its ears are bat-like small, and its eyes are dark and beady like lava on the run. But fate has put its finger on the otter, and it is a most remarkable critter.

With a slap on the water, it drops below the surface to forage along the streambed. Its long whiskers, controlled by that bunch of marvelous upper-lip muscles, move delicately, like tentacles, over and around stumps and stones in search of snacks like crayfish and frogs and turtles and snails. Snake-like, it pokes its head in and out of snake-holding holes.

Its quick, dark eyes catch sight of a movement, a mere shadow of a movement. The otter whirls and dives. The deadly cat-and-mouse game, the outcome of which has long been determined, is begun, for the current has delivered a Christmas dinner, a brook trout, to the otter. The trout is faster than the bigger otter and makes a run for it. But in its panic, the befuddled fish loses its chicken-little wits and corners itself in a box canyon of a trap, from which there is no escape. And it's down the hatch for the trout.

Some prefer one thing, some prefer the otter, and some are of the opinion that there's a niche for all of us somewhere in the universe. I'm with those.

a tendency to wander

DECEMBER 29

I am buried in pheasant thoughts. This is nonsense, I know. It's twenty-five below zero outside, and I'm snuggly behind my patio door. And I don't live in pheasant country, anyway. Nevertheless, I'm shot through my heart with thoughts of pheasants.

When I hunt pheasants like this behind my patio door, it's easy. I slog through rain and fog; it doesn't bother me at all. I don't mind getting wet. I'm gutsy. I hunt chunks of broken terrain with pretty good prospects. I hop from one small cover to another in a pattern that so often works for me. I find much satisfaction in poking into nooks and crannies less flexible hunters overlook. Farther south, where the country is not so big, I sneak through long strips of swamps and woodland edges, which sometimes give up exciting moments and an occasional partridge.

I lean, of course, to long-rowed cornfields, but settle gladly for briars, weed patches and islands of brush. When hunting behind patio doors, the more inaccessible the cover, the better I like it. I creep through a three-acre patch of thick willows surrounded by rolling fields of alfalfa and soybeans. I'm the guy on the outside who takes the bird topping out of the tangle. I'm the man in the middle looking for the explosive rise of a bird cornered or pushed too hard. One … two … three. My gun comes up. It's easy to hunt pheasants like this.

Hunkered in my bathrobe before a pokey coffee pot gurgling on the stove, I hear pheasants calling to an equally pokey sunrise. At the sound of it, I am moved to check the bathroom for birds, to poke behind the sofa, to sneak a peek in the pantry. But there are whiskers to shave, a shower to take, breakfast to make, a car to start, a job to do. I am quiet, so as not to wake the family, or spook the pheasants of my dreams.

betrayed!

DECEMBER 30

We had completed the monthly meeting of the Lost Lake Fish, Game and Darts Club in the back room of the Elkhorn Tavern and Wildlife Museum. A blizzard was raging outside, so we bellied up to the bar to talk about that. Suddenly, the door swung open and in staggered Ewald. He was deathly pale and visibly shaken. He stared with the protruding, vacant eyes of a madman. We sprang to our feet and looked in amazement at this ponderous piece of wreckage.

"What is it, Ewald?" we asked, putting a glass of blackberry to his lips.

His puckered eyeballs quivered. He worked his nutcracker jaws and spilled his guts. "It seems," he gasped, pointing, "a certain Mr. X has traded away our secret venison and rosemary ragout recipe to Pederson two counties over for the fishing rights on a mile and a half stretch of a world-famous trout stream. He has treacherously revealed how we roast a three to four pound venison roast for 45 minutes until it can be cut into lean chunks, how we reserve two tablespoons of the fat, how we lightly flour the chunks, sprinkle them with salt, add half a bottle of dry red wine and the fat and simmer it in a big skillet for 45 minutes more, how we put in a teaspoon and a half of dried rosemary, a pound can of plum tomatoes, four minced garlic cloves and a dozen small potatoes, how we simmer it uncovered for half an hour until the sauce runs low and thickens, how we add a 14-ounce can of black olives and simmer again for ten minutes, how we add eight sprigs of parsley, chopped, adjust the seasoning and remove the fat, and how we eat it with crusty French bread."

For the second time that night, we jumped to our feet and turned to look with loathing and horror upon the face of the dirty double-crosser, who quickly bought a round of drinks to stay our fury.

all's well that ends well

DECEMBER 31

Outside, the snow is falling into the past. In the fireplace, a section of birch bark sparks like it's dancing and caves into ash. What do you remember best about it, the old year? Was it the rose-garden days of July when the sun tuned its rays to the chords of summer? Was it paddling spring-high rivers in the shallows of early April mornings, dimly glowing?

Is it even now, as you observe the daily amputation of time, since it is your intention to seize winter between your teeth and bite a chunk off it? Was it the swaddling days of March and the boom-booming of March prairie chickens and the putt-puttting of proud partridges? Could it have been the Solomon days of October's elk bugling and the dashing in and darting out of bandit days and nights and tides? Was it September and the crazy congregation of birds thick enough to tote your soul, when you ran off to hunt for squirrels and empty ends of kite strings? Was it the fragrant days of January? Was it tiptoeing carefully over ice, lest you disturb its natural order, past fishermen in search of vineyards?

Was it when you dived through burning hoops of August afternoon walks? Where you later found yourself the winner in a look-alike contest with movie star whip-poor-wills? Was it February, a double-chinned dowager that set fire to the blades of your skates and made your skis go lickety-split over smoking lips of snow? I don't know. Was it the bumpy kisses in the back seat of November speeding over country roads? Or was it the whole shootin' match, day in and day out, wrapped up in camouflaged clowns' suits, playing tag and laughing that the last one in a sentence, and this book, is a period? Period.

However it was for you, thanks for taking me along. Let's do it again sometime.

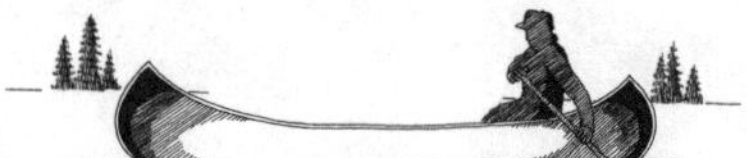

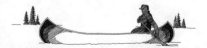